If you are thinking of moving to Hawai'i do it with your eyes open! Read this honest and informative book.

> \- Jean Auerbach
> Spokane, Washington

In today's growing "virtual world" many people can choose to live and work anywhere... But for many the question regarding a move to the islands is not "could I do it" but "should I do it." Toni Polancy's insightful guidebook and well-balanced portrayal of life in the islands would be absolutely indispensable to those considering a move here.

> \- Jim Powell
> Los Angeles, California
> www.logisticstraining.com

After 25 years on the mainland, I moved back home to rejuvenate my soul with Aloha Spirit. **So You Want to Live in Hawai'i** *peels away romantic blinders and enables a more realistic view of* **kama'äina** *life.*

> \- Jolyne Rego
> Makawao, Maui, Hawai'i

... I have always felt a deep down desire to move and try life in these very special islands. However, it is a very long way from England and a much closer scrutiny of life in Hawai'i is required than just my previous visits as a travel photographer. This book has the answers to just about everything I really need to know...

> \- James Davis
> Hampshire, England

[We] had a lot of questions about moving to Hawai'i. **So You Want to Live in Hawai'i** *answered them all.*

> \- Larry & Maria Lospinuso
> Brick, New Jersey

So You Want to
Live in Hawai'i

A guide to settling and succeeding in the islands

by Toni Polancy

Barefoot Publishing: *Practical Books About Paradise*
Kihei, Hawai'i

4   Disclaimer

This book is designed to provide suggestions and resources regarding the decision to move to and live in Hawai'i. This book is sold with the understanding that the publisher and author are not engaged in rendering legal or professional advice or services. This book should be used only as a general guide. In no way is it to be regarded as the ultimate source of information regarding your move to the islands or your success there. You are urged to read all available material before making such decisions. Every effort has been made to make sure this information is as accurate and timely as possible, however there may be mistakes both in typography and in content. Facts and figures may have changed, and probably will have changed, from the time of writing and time of purchasing and reading this book. Figures quoted are used only as examples of prices and amounts and neither the author, the publisher nor the sources of such information should be held responsible for changes. The author and Barefoot Publishing shall have neither liability nor responsibility to any person or entity with respect to loss or damage caused or alleged to be caused, directly or indirectly, by the information in this book.

So You Want to Live in Hawai'i
A guide to settling and succeeding in the islands

Library of Congress Catalog Card Number: 98-073548

Printed in the United States of America
10 9 8 7 6 5 4 3 2 1

Polancy, Antoinette
  So You Want to Live in Hawai'i: A guide to settling and succeeding in the islands
  Includes index
  ISBN 0-9666253-0-7

Cover painting ©1998 by Karen Lei Noland
Maps ©1998 by Toni Polancy

http://www.bookshawaii.com

Photos by

G. Brad Lewis

and

Matt Thayer

Additional Photos:

Steve Brinkman

Steve Strand

Bob Fijal

*This book is dedicated
to my mother,
Josephine Jaskiewicz Falk,
whom life has made strong.*

Table of Contents

Chapter 1: The People
page 15
- Our real lives • Wealthy, poor, and the rest of us • Economy
- Prejudice & *aloha* • Ethnic groups • Hate crimes
- The gay community • Tips • A little plastic bag

Chapter 2: Politics & Issues
page 37
- Kaleiolani's first *haole* • Hawai'i's past • Monarchy & missionaries
- The Democratic years • Politics today • Future issues • Is *aloha* real?
- Sovereignty • Largest landowners • The *ahupua'a*
- Development vs. conservation • Tips • Resources

Chapter 3: General Information
page 51
- The $5 lunch • Arts & Culture • Holiday • Establishing residency
- Movies • Dining • Sports • Religion • Health • Resources • Tips

Chapter 4: Necessities
page 79
- A kama'aina shops • Food • Housing • Transportation • Clothing
- Furniture • Insurance • Travel & communications • Taxes • Tips

Chapter 5: Work
page 113
- A successful bellhop • The job market • Working *ukupau*
- Wages • Employee turnover • 15 jobs in search of workers
- BYOB (Bring Your Own Business) • Tips • Job phone lines • Resources

Chapter 6: The Military
page 139
- Assignment Paradise • Perks & problems • Advice from Family Services
- Cost of living • Tips

Chapter 7: Retirement
page 147
- Starting over at 66 • Retiring to Hawai'i
- Looking to the future • Bringing elderly parents • Residential complexes
- 8 good reasons to retire here • 8 good reasons not to
- Great sources for more information • Tips

Chapter 8: The Children
page 161
- Breanna turns one • Hawai'i's kids • Child care • Schools: Public or Private?
- Racial and ethnic differences • Home schooling • Drugs & alcohol
- What students say • Adjusting at your new school • The University of Hawai'i
- Resources • Tips

Chapter 9: Romance   181
• Emily and Rufino wed • Dating *kama'āina* • *Menage a trois*, Maui style
• Great free dates • Tropical dreams • Tropical realities • Escaping to paradise
• Seeking wealth • Finding a mate • It's the law • Tips • Resources

Chapter 10: Trouble   193
• Tsunami • Hurricanes • Ocean dangers • Crime • Alcohol, bars & brothels
• DUI laws • Rules you should know • Gangs • Creatures & insects
• Do tourists cause accidents? • Tips

Chapter 11: Which island?   215
• Important choices • O'ahu • Kaua'i • Maui • Moloka'i • Lana'i
• The Big Island of Hawai'i • That cheap Hawai'i land
• *Kapu* (forbidden) islands: Kaho'olawe & Ni'ihau
• The Decision: Tips from a psychologist • The 7-Day Trial • Resources

Chapter 12: Moving   265
• A family who did it right • Packing • Shipping
• Should you bring your plants? Your pets? • Your Budget • Tips
• You know you're kama'aina when...

More resources   281

Additional reading   285

Useful Internet sites   286

Chambers of Commerce   287

Footnotes   288

Index   291

Mahalo   302

About the author   303

Matt Thayer

Introduction

A fax full of questions arrives one afternoon in my office. It is from a Texas woman. Her questions are simple; the answers are not.

If my family decided to move to one of the Hawaiian Islands, what can we expect to find there besides the ocean, beach, tropical vegetation and the lovely resort areas?

Aside from the breathtaking beauty, the romance of paradise...

Can you give any information for family living?

Beyond the beachfront estates and the golf villas...

Are there any hospitals or medical centers?

Are there any schools?

Are there any churches for Sunday services?

What conveniences are available for shopping for daily needs?

Thank you for your information!

Sincerely, Sandra[1]

Aloha, Sandra,

Yes. All of the six habitable islands offer all of the amenities and necessities you mention. But you have asked the wrong questions; living here is not that simple.

What will your life in Hawai'i, paradise, really be like?

Most likely, buried deep in your subconscious is a special image of the islands that we all share. You live in a solitary shack on a secluded beach. Wearing a sarong, you step out and sniff the flower-scented air. You pluck a banana from a bunch hanging conveniently near the door, gather a coconut off the ground, and stretch out on the sand to enjoy dinner. The setting sun tinges ocean waves with gold while, in the distance, Elvis Presley sings "Blue Hawai'i."

Our visions of Paradise are similar because neither you nor I created them. Hollywood and our school books did.

This is reality: bananas are picked green; if they are allowed to ripen on the stock, hundreds of ants invade them. Palms need trimming; their fronds can weigh as much as 30 pounds, and a falling frond or coconut could give you a concussion. Elvis Presley is dead — although if he ever *does* come back it's a wise bet he'll visit Hawai'i.

Day-to-day, *real* life here is probably very different from life as you live it now; it is certainly different from a vacation at a posh resort, and it is a far cry from the picture painted by movies. This book is about living here as a longtime resident, as *kama'āina*. It is about real life in Hawai'i, about surviving and succeeding in this incredibly beautiful paradise.

In a kind of giant swap-meet of lives, thousands of people move to Hawai'i each year, and thousands leave. Some stay only a few weeks or a few months before packing up knapsacks, cardboard boxes, or *Louis Vuitton* luggage and traveling back to where they came from.

"So many people move here and then go back. After a while, you find yourself being a little careful," says one longtime Hawai'i resident. "You don't make close friends as fast with newcomers. You kind of wait a year or two to see if they will stay."

"Hawai'i is beautiful, but it is not for everyone," declares a prominent realtor. "Sometimes I spend the first half hour with a client helping them decide if they belong here at all."

Much has been written in recent years about Hawai'i's struggling economy, about its high prices. Still, 1,184,000 people do live here, most of us happily and many of us successfully. For optimistic newcomers eager to work and daring *malihini* willing to take a chance, Hawai'i offers opportunities for success beyond what you can imagine.

Will you "make it" in Hawai'i? If you decide to join the more than 40,000 people who move here each year, will you be among the many who leave? Or those who stay? Can you find satisfying work? Will your children, if you have them, be content? Do you have the flexibility and perseverance to succeed here? This book should help you answer those important questions.

Four little words

Come to Hawai'i and you will learn some new words. Hawaiian words, like *malihini* (mal-a-HEE-nee), *kama'āina* (ka-ma-EYE-na) and *haole* (HOW-lee) are spoken nowhere else in the world. Familiar words, like "local" take on new meaning. You will begin using these words yourself, in everyday conversation, barely thinking. You will forget that these words, uttered a certain way, with a curl of the lips, with a soft smirk, become tiny daggers of discrimination.

Kama'āina is a positive term. It literally translates as "land child" and, according to a Hawaiian dictionary, means "Native born, host... acquainted, familiar." *Kama'āina* refers to someone who has lived on the islands for a long time and is *akamai* (smart) about life here. *Kama'āina*, like most Hawaiian words, also carries more subtle meanings: acceptance and belonging in the islands.

Malihini, usually a neutral term, means newcomer. "They are *malihini*," simply states a fact.

The other two words, "local" and *haole*, are used often in everyday conversation. "Local" indicates a person who was born and raised on these islands. "Local" usually refers to anyone except Caucasians, and sometimes connotes a darker-skinned person of any race. "Local" can also be derisive: "A truck full of locals sped by."

Haole once meant foreigner; today it means a white person. Like "local", *haole* can be derisive. A *haole* may say about himself: "No thanks! This *haole* doesn't like fish!" But a local hollering at a light-skinned tourist, "Go home, *haole*" is hostile.

We use the words *kama'āina, malihini*, "local" and *haole* often in this book because they are specific. Here, they are meant in their most positive connotations.

The islands are its people: here's what we say about us

"For me, moving to Hawaii was a matter of surrendering to forces. It's spiritual. It was a leap of faith."
- businessman, Maui

"I worked many years for the success I've had. I pushed my children to get a lot of education, to be somebody and have good jobs. And then I retired and I moved here. And I say, what's that all about? All that Mainland bullshit about getting ahead in life?"
- retiree, O'ahu

"There's more intellectual freedom here, more openness and acceptance of ideas. In my hometown, I was a crazy guy with wild ideas. Here, everyone has hopes and dreams and schemes and it's okay. We're allowed to dream here. If we fail that's okay too. But we can dream."
- entrepreneur, Kauai

"The culture, the traditions are very different here. It's America, but it's not the Mainland. You need to know that."
- social worker, O'ahu

"You're at a restaurant and you look up and the guy waiting tables by night is your attorney by day."
- realtor, Kaua'i

"If you are a man in your 20s or 30s there's a pecking order here and you should know it."
- violin maker, Maui

"We in Hawaii live in a classless society, which is beautiful. When you go to the beach in your swimsuit it doesn't matter if you got there in a Rolls Royce or if you rode a rusty bicycle...nobody cares."
- bellhop, entrepreneur, Maui

ka poʻe
the people

"I came for the

scenery and weather;

I stay for the

beautiful people"

- writer, Maui

Deborah Booker / The Honolulu Advertiser

At the Hawai'i Tomorrow Conference in Honolulu, hundreds of citizens of various races and ages explored ideas on improving life in the islands.

Real lives in paradise

It is 5:30 p.m., a Monday in December. Tourists and *kama'āina* gather on beaches. The setting sun slashes the sky with bronze and vermilion and spills color across the ocean. The sound of conch shells echoes across the islands, signaling the end of day.

• At the corner of King and Kalākaua Streets in busy Honolulu, 86-year-old Josephine Falk is returning from a swim at Waikīkī's Kuhiō Beach. She carefully exits TheBus, glances up at the sun and sighs with relief. She has plenty of time to get to her apartment, tucked into one of hundreds of Honolulu's tall buildings, and keep a promise to her family back on the mainland not to be out after dark.

• At a table on the *lāna'i* of her home on the bank of Mount Haleakalā in Maui, Marty-Jean Bender, a single mom employed as a middle school registrar, is planning the busy week to come: school; two sales parties (her second job); dance lessons for her 11-year-old daughter; a trip to the meat market across the island in Makawao; and practice for the Christmas pageant at her church. Marty-Jean bought her home, paid more than she could afford because it has ocean views. Now she glances out at the sunset and reminds herself to enjoy it.

• At the Kamakou Preserve atop a mountain on the rural island of Moloka'i, Scott Hemenway, 31, high school teacher and volunteer guide, is leading a group of Japanese tourists and walks just a little faster to finish the hike before dark.

PEOPLE

> "The islands take care of their own. You'll either make it here or you won't, and it has more to do with what kind of person you are than how much money you have."
>
> –A longtime resident

• In Kurtistown on the Big Island, Jane Sutton, 45, goes into the living room to call her husband and daughter Sarah in to supper, finds them fast asleep and covers them gently with a throw quilt. Len is juggling two fledgling businesses — a fruit farm and a bed and breakfast he is constructing next to a waterfall on 20 acres of land — and, although he clearly enjoys it, Jane often worries that he works too hard.

• At Wailua Homesteads, a pristine valley behind Sleeping Giant Mountain on Kaua'i, Holly Lang, 32, a graphic artist, looks up from her computer and notes that the rain has stopped. The setting sun glistens golden on puddles in the front yard, and in the field across the street, a rainbow forms. It's time for supper, which she'll eat in front of her only companion, the television, watching the news.

• At Renaissance Wailea Beach Resort on Maui, Daryl Davis helps a honeymooning German couple into their rental car, stacks the luggage into the trunk and repeats directions to the airport. As the car pulls away the reflection of the setting sun reminds him that his shift is over. Daryl glances at his watch; he'll have time to stop at the Kīhei Canoe Club on his way home, to help to clean the beach and grounds.

Life here goes on much the same as it does anywhere. Learning, working, playing. Celebrating, surviving. But here, it is eternal summer. Breathtakingly beautiful. And very expensive.

"We are so busy trying to survive financially," says one ten-year resident, "that it doesn't matter that we live in Hawai'i. We are in our own little houses, our own little cubicles, working, working. Then a visitor comes from the mainland and we look up and say, 'Oh that's right! We live in paradise. Let's go enjoy it.'"

We work long hours, yes, but despite the rush of everyday life, despite the stress of making ends meet, the beauty of this land influences our lives in many ways. We work at resorts or on tour boats, sell art or activities, clean condos or paint pictures, sit at computers creating vacation brochures — all because Hawai'i's natural beauty lures tourists and provides about 40 percent of us with our daily *poi* (food).

Still, we live on six small islands thousands of miles from the nearest continent, and no matter how busy we are, most of us acknowledge the ocean that surrounds us. Several times a day we feel compelled to check its condition, simply because it is an ever-present part of our lives.

Each morning most of us awaken to the scent of plumeria or *pīkake,* to the cries of exotic birds, or, occasionally, to the smell of cane smoke. We end each day watching sunsets or at least noting the sun's glow tingeing our computer screens or glinting off the chrome on the cars in our office parking lot.

Some people spend their first year here drunk on an overload of beauty. Flowers, fragrances, rainbows. Double rainbows. Triple rainbows. Here, you may sometimes see a moonbow, ghostly brushes of color against a dark sky.

• A 34-year-old computer specialist quit consulting positions that paid six-digits, left his mom and dad and siblings back in New York City, and moved to the Hawaiian Islands where he expects to start his own business.

"I tell friends back there: You will work until you are 60 or 65 and then retire so you can spend five or six years doing what I am doing now, living in warmth and sunshine. Paradise. Even if I can only enjoy this on weekends," he says.

• Sisters Meg Skellenger and Sarah Jones have lived on Maui for several years. One is a graphic artist, the other a high school teacher and neither has had an easy time making ends meet. They occasionally lie on a beach near Maui's main airport, watching planes soar into the sky. "We look up," Meg says, "and raise our arms up high and laugh, 'Ha-ha, ha-ha...we live here! We don't have to go home! We are home!'"

The best things about Hawai'i — warmth and beauty — are free, delivered democratically to bank presidents and condo cleaners alike. Beyond that, the day-to-day structure of your life will depend here, as it does everywhere, on your circumstances and your priorities: How much do you want? How much do you *need?*

Being rich and/or famous in paradise

Both newcomers and *kama'āina* express a common fear: that Hawai'i is becoming a land of the poor and the very rich, those who serve and those who are served. Our nation's ever-widening income gap has long worried mainland sociologists too, but the division between haves and have-nots is more visible where sleek limousines with darkened windows glide past battered Hawai'i cruisers, where homeless people spread towels on beaches in front of million-dollar homes.

There is so *much* wealth here.

G. Brad Lewis

A modern palace: the Mauna Lani Resort on the Big Island.

• A South African family, worried about violence in their hometown, buys mom a practical birthday present: a one million dollar home and luxury car so she can move to safer Hawai'i.

• A young Maui woman lives on a luxury estate, free. "I house-sit for a gentleman," she says. "He comes from Japan just two or three times a year for a couple of weeks, but he likes to entertain and everything has to be just right. All I have to do is make sure everybody does his job: the pool man, the gardener, the cleaning lady."

All of the islands have posh neighborhoods where seclusion, a backyard beach or an ocean view are status symbols. On O'ahu, cruise **Kāhala Avenue**, **Pacific Heights** or **Portlock**; on Kaua'i, **'Anini** and **Po'ipu** beaches; on the Big Island, **Wailea** and **Keauhou Estate**s; on Maui, **Makena** or **Napili**. Ornate gates shield entrances to modern marble and *koa* wood palaces.

Our transplanted rich include successful writers, entertainers, sports figures, and entrepreneurs. Usually, the famous are allowed their privacy. Residents barely react when they encounter actor Richard Chamberlain answering phones at the public television station telethon; singer Jim Nabors pushing a paddle on his Diamond Head neighborhood rowing team; entertainer Kris Kristofferson jogging along a Maui roadway; or singer Randy Travis at a favorite Kahana restaurant.

Also among Hawai'i's privileged are "trust babies" — heirs and heiresses whose biggest worry is whether the trust check is deposited to their bank accounts on time.

Being poor in paradise

A family — mom, dad, two teenagers — helps prepare dinner at a Hawai'i homeless shelter and tells their story. They sold their Iowa home and moved to the islands several months ago. Dad, a highly qualified handy man, was sure he could easily find work here. He did and life was fine until he was installing a window and severely cut the ligaments in his arm. The family has no health insurance, dad cannot work for several months, the funds they brought dwindled and the bills mounted, landing the family at the shelter. Still radiating the awed glow of island newcomers, the family is overwhelmed, mom says, by Hawai'i's kindness and generosity.

Matt Thayer

Many *malihini*, like this family, have no health insurance or job benefits when they first arrive and are just an accident away from poverty. Fortunately, gentle Hawai'i is about the best place in the nation to be broke. There is no residency requirement or waiting period to qualify for state aid. And a family of four can collect tax-free income, including cash grants, housing, food stamps and medical benefits, to a total of $15,482 a year.

Should you come to the islands expecting to live on the public dole? Absolutely not. While $15,000 sounds like a lot, consider that living here can cost as much as 40 percent more than in some states and that figure barely covers a year's rent for most homes.

About half of all shelter residents are families and 8,000 families at any one time seek permanent public housing. They will wait approximately four years, according to Amalia Bueno, public information officer for Hawai'i Public Housing.

Facing federal funding cuts, the state is moving people off welfare rolls. A program called PONO, the Pursuit of New Opportunities, trains able-bodied poor for new jobs and has had some success in cutting welfare rolls, social workers say.

The rest of us

And what about the rest of us, that 70 or so percent of us who comprise the middle class and working class, we who foot the bill for government and life in general? Most likely, when you first move here you will live in an apartment. If you are single, you might consider sharing expenses with a roommate. In Honolulu, you can wait to purchase a car, since bus service is efficient. On the neighbor islands you will need a car as soon as you arrive. These everyday aspects of life are discussed in other chapters of this book.

What will your life be like once you have settled in? Once the thrill of life in this new, incredibly beautiful place, has worn off? *Will* it wear off?

You may work longer or harder than you do now or you may be forced to work in a position other than that for which you trained; but if you do survive paradise — and remember why you came: to *enjoy* it — your life here may be simpler and more easy-going. Your co-worker is apt to tell you he cannot work tomorrow because the surf is up. He loves to surf. He lives in Hawai'i to surf, not work. He hopes you understand.

Your priorities change

Maybe it's the warm soothing weather. Maybe it's the serene atmosphere. Maybe it's the gentle spirit of the people here. But after you've lived on the islands a while, your priorities change. The sprawling house with koa wood floors is nice, but the trade winds blow in dust that coats those floors. The long white Cadillac has a lot of surface to polish, metal to rust in the ocean air. Oak antiques can be invaded by termites. Silver tarnishes in the humidity. And all those material possessions are not what you came to the islands for anyway. What you are coming for is there, right outside your window, whether that window is in a condo, a tract home or a marble mansion. Sunshine. Fresh air. An ocean to swim in. A beach on which to jog.

The economy

It's not easy to live an easy life here. The old pineapple and sugar industries that supplied the bulk of jobs and money for so long are being phased out, moving to parts of the world where labor is less costly. Ideally tourism is supposed to pick up the slack, but competition for the world's visitors is tough. And relying on tourism for our income puts us at the mercy of events around the world. In 1991, the Gulf War and economic troubles in Asia and the U.S. set off a drop in tourism and the real estate market from which Hawai'i is just beginning to recover.

A popular saying here is that the islands are about five years behind the mainland economically. The current U.S. prosperity is slowly drifting across the Pacific and buoying hopes here. Meanwhile, each island competes for visitors and looks for other ways to bolster its economy, some with more success than others. Computers, high tech devel-

Slow down. Speak softly. Relax. Talk story. Do nothing at all. Or play a quiet game of chess at Waikīkī Beach.

opment, movie making and exotic produce and coffee production are the enterprises most often mentioned. (See chapter 4: Working)

Unwritten rules

More than 140 people were interviewed for this book, and many of them voiced the same concern: that giving back to the community is very important here. Newcomers on these small, isolated islands, we must be each other's caretakers, each other's *'ohana*, or family. To succeed here, to be considered *'ohana*, you must contribute in some way to the overall welfare of island residents or to the preservation of the islands, whether by performing a song, cleaning a roadway, serving on a town development committee, or dishing out food at a homeless shelter.

Many people here are also spiritual; they feel drawn to the ocean and mountains, which exert a mystical pull. And there is an almost religious fervor here, as though nature is a being in its own right. *Kama'āina* tend to speak of God and the Hawaiian goddess *Pele* in the same sentence, giving due respect to each.

Mable Haas, wife of a retired veterinarian, has lived on Kaua'i for 40 years and raised four sons there. Sipping coffee at a Kapa'a music store one rainy Sunday morning, I told her my story — that I gave up a good, steady, safe job, came to Hawai'i to start a business and made little money for the first two years; how scared I sometimes was. She gazed over the rim of her steamy cup, a gentle smile on her creased face. "But after you were here a while," she murmured, "you realized that you were accepted, that you'd be taken care of."

"The islands take care of their own," said another longtime resident. "You'll either make it here or you won't, and it has more to do with who you are — what kind of person you are — than how much money you have."

➤ TIP: **Good advice for** *malihini* (newcomers): Slow down, speak softly, relax. The islands are changing in many ways, but among long-time residents some customs remain and one of them is "talking story," an old term for relaxing and chatting about nothing in particular. Long sessions of "talk story" are apt to precede business deals, especially on the neighbor islands, and newcomers who want to fit in should respect that tradition.

➤ TIP: **Don't try to speak pidgin**, the patois of the islands. "Newcomers don't know how to speak pidgin and it is almost insulting when they try," says a local Maui man.

➤ TIP: **Avoid honking your car horn**. Nothing is absolute, but overall people here are courteous and patient when they drive. It is considered very rude to honk your car horn.

➤ TIP: **Smile**. It is the custom in most parts of the islands to make eye contact and smile at people you pass on a street, on the beach or in a mall. That's part of the aloha spirit, but it's also smart. A frown can be mistaken for "stink eye," an antagonistic or challenging expression.

Prejudice and aloha

The fact that prejudice exists in Hawai'i comes as a surprise to many newcomers. Tourist brochures never mention it; nor do Chamber of Commerce or visitor bureau materials. Tour guide books offer only a half-hearted warning suggesting visitors stay off some beaches at night.

Yet :
• A Big Island family with a twenty-year history on the islands leaves after the father is involved in an altercation at a sovereignty protest. It is one of several reasons the family left, but the mother warns, "The sovereignty issue is heating up and it added to our decision."
• A young homosexual man tells of threats and beatings.
• A 44-year-old Pennsylvania attorney, tall and blond and very *haole*, visits the islands annually. At least once every year someone yells "*Haole*!" or "Go home, *haole*!"
• At a beachfront wedding celebration, a group of local bodyboarders advances threateningly toward the Caucasian bride and groom, murmuring "*Haoles* go home." When the groom's local friends show up, the hecklers apologize. The groom, who has lived here for several years, warns, "If you are in your 20s or 30s, there's a pecking order here and you should know it."

Hawai'i's nearly 1,200,000 people are an eclectic mix. Recruited as labor in the sugar and pineapple plantations, a potpourri of races came from around the world: Chinese, Filipino, Japanese, Portuguese, Russian, Polish and others. Plantation owners encouraged ethnic groups to live apart, each in its own company-owned "camp," small neighborhoods isolated deep in the tall cane fields. Labor unions, voted in during the 1940s, advocated brotherhood, the bringing together of races, and camp families began to mingle more.

Today, everyone in Hawai'i is a minority. Caucasians make up the largest single group, but no one ethnic group is a majority unless it is the 37 percent of the residents who are *hapa* or mixed race.

Today, as the islands grow more crowded, few residents ask who belongs in Hawai'i and who does not, but the topic — accompanied by a shrug of the shoulders, a shake of the head — surfaces occasionally. Does a person whose ancestors sailed here in a *wa'a* (canoe) hundreds of years ago have more claim than one whose grandfather shipped over as a plantation worker several decades ago? Does either have more claim than someone newly arrived on a jet plane?

Several of the people interviewed for this book echoed this statement: "This is America, but it is not the United States. You have to respect that." What they mean is that living in Hawai'i is living with people of many cultures, all of which must be acknowledged.

"Here, you are no longer American, top dog," commented another person. "Here, you are one of at least thirty cultures that make up the islands and many of those cultures have prior and more valid claims to power than we do."

"It's misleading," says a transplanted New Englander. "We use American currency and have American laws; English is the primary language. But other than that, you are living in a foreign country."

An unlikely U.S.

Hawai'i will never be the United States as mainlanders know it, with one primary culture that dictates beliefs and customs. The European and Asian immigrants who came to mainland America in the late 1890s and early 1900s aspired to become part of the American culture, to meld into it. Today, the nation's newest immigrants — Mexicans, Cubans, Koreans and Eastern Europeans — have that same goal.

But in Hawai'i, perhaps because of our geographic isolation, ethnic groups struggle to retain heritage, cling to old customs and promote them. They have no desire to be "Americanized"; instead they see the islands as a place where various cultures can flourish, not diminish. Hawai'i businesses boast of the state as being "like a giant cultural stew." In truth, it is more of a traditional Hawaiian plate lunch, each food item sitting separately on the same plate, yet contributing to the overall meal.

The disdain some locals have for Caucasians has roots in recent history. During the 1800s and early 1900s, most of the powerful plantation bosses were Caucasian. These days, displays of prejudice against Caucasians or Japanese are apt to be spurred by the huge influx of both ethnic groups during

Ethnic Stock	State total	City and County of Honolulu	Hawaii County	Kauai County	Maui County
All Groups	1,138,870	844,729	130,195	54,092	109,854
Unmixed	717,409	549,402	74,224	30,793	62,990
Caucasian	265,211	189,859	34,379	11,183	29,790
Japanese	224,801	178,123	22,930	8,534	15,214
Chinese	52,612	50,229	1,248	502	633
Filipino	119,256	82,786	12,773	9,014	14,683
Hawaiian	9,118	5,420	1,476	729	1,493
Korean	16,051	14,834	409	335	473
Black	19,998	19,415	363	91	129
Puerto Rican	4,823	3,347	646	377	453
Samoan	5,539	5,389	N/A	28	122
Mixed	421,461	295,327	55,971	23,299	46,864
Part Hawaiian	211,629	139,363	35,066	12,697	24,503
Non-Hawaiian	209,832	155,964	20,905	10,602	22,361

Table excludes persons in institutions or military barracks, on Niihau, or in Kalawao.
Based on a sample survey of 13,943 persons.
Source: Hawaii State Department of Health, Hawaii Health Surveillance Program, special tabulation. 1992 figures. Island populations have increased. See Chapter 11 : Which Island, for most recent population figures.

For updated statistics see http://www.hawaii.gov/dbedt/index.html

the past 30 years, buying up property and driving up land prices, claiming higher paying jobs and, in some cases, desecrating the land.

Resentment against Asian residents is apt to be tinged with respect, and perhaps, envy. Their grandparents were imported to work in the plantations, but today's Hawaiian Asians are often highly educated and have prospered. For many years after World War II, Asians dominated business and politics.

In *Honolulu* magazine (July, 1995), the Rev. Al Miles, an African-American, argues there is relatively little racial bigotry here compared to the mainland. He says Caucasians feel prejudice because they are so accustomed to special treatment by virtue of being white. Nevertheless, some sociologists predict ill will and ethnic unrest will escalate as the islands become more crowded. And in the second volume of *The Price of Paradise*, Franklin Ode, director of Ethnic Studies at the University of Hawaii, and Susan Yim, a freelance journalist, conclude, "The truth of the matter is that ethnic tension in Hawai'i is growing and a tradition of tolerance tends to mask this."

Ethnic crimes

Hawai'i's diversity leads to thousands of cases involving minority victims, but there are few examples of a victim being singled out specifically for their ethnicity, culture, sexual orientation or other differences, officials say.

Unlike most other states, Hawai'i does not track ethnic or "hate" crimes.

"Given the uniqueness of Hawai'i, where nobody's a minority because everyone is, it's very difficult to tell whether someone was targeted because of their ethnicity or they became a victim for some other reason," Paul Perrone, chief of research for the state attorney general, said in a Honolulu *Advertiser* article.[3]

"There's the ongoing problem of locals and military mixing it up in bars, but attacks against the Asian community or other communities are rare," said Honolulu police Capt. Doug Miller in the same article.

Budget restrictions have prevented setting up a hate crime reporting program. "It's not that nobody cares about these crimes, or that anyone's naîve enough to believe it doesn't happen here," Miller said.

African Americans are a true minority on the islands, less than two percent of the population. And, in a state so proud of its ethnic mix, this race suffers the most prejudice.

"Hawai'i can be brutally racist in its treatment of this particular minority," Ode and Yim comment,[2] and a longtime Hawai'i school teacher concurs.

"There is much discrimination against blacks and you see it particularly in the schools," says the Caucasian middle school instructor. "Here, African Americans are called *pōpolo* (PO'polo), which is very derogatory. It's ironic. We have so many dark-skinned people, but somehow if they find out there is just a little bit black, there is this extreme prejudice."

Gilbert Githere, an award-winning Kenyan filmmaker who has lived on O'ahu for eight years, says smiles and *aloha* are an easy way out, a method of covering racial prejudice.

"Segregation, although not part of the law, although not admitted, is prevalent in Hawai'i. Segregation means 'cutting away from livelihood.' Prejudice becomes economics," Githere says. "They [other races] are polite, but they are waiting for you to go away. They make it very difficult for you to stay. [They say] 'Why are you giving this man a job? Why is he living in Hawai'i?"

'Basically gay friendly'

Hawai'i is very gay-friendly, says David Morehouse, director of the gay and lesbian community center on O'ahu. "Well, basically gay friendly," Morehouse corrects himself. "Hawai'i does share *aloha* (love or friendship) and *'ohana* (family). Hawai'i is a state of nondiscrimination because it has always been a melting pot of culture from all over the world. Hawai'i does not discriminate against race, religion or sexual orientation."

Morehouse is speaking of the law. Housing laws, employment laws, federal laws are enforced and appreciated here, Morehouse says. Officially.

A young, slight, blond, homosexual man tells another story. Walking along highways, he has twice been accosted by "locals" and beaten, he says. A third time he was followed into a men's room at a local bar and warned "We don't need more fags here."

"Those times on the road, well, I couldn't help that," he says thoughtfully. "But, I should have known better than to go to a local bar."

"You have to be careful," Morehouse says, "to judge wisely. It's not just a gay thing. You don't, as a single woman, walk out the door of a cocktail bar and walk down an alley late at night. You don't walk around wearing Versace clothes and carrying a gold bag and be surprised when you are mugged."

Hawai'i has a long tradition of being tolerant of gays, recognizing homosexuality not as an aberration, but as an accepted part of nature. The Hawaiian word *mahu* refers to men who take on the role of women, cross-dressing and helping to raise children. There is no stigma to it, Morehouse says. "Unfortunately, you may see cross-dressing guys working the street as prostitutes and they are called *mahu*, but that is not the real meaning. It's a much gentler meaning."

An effort to legalize homosexual marriages in Hawai'i failed in 1996, but not before it provoked anti-gay feelings. "With the gay marriage suit, some people who were not as prejudiced [became] more so...afraid we are going to take over the world and start with Hawai'i," Morehouse says. The fears do not seem to come from any particular ethnic or age group. Some argue that homosexuals will flock here, somehow changing the ambiance of the islands; others say recognizing homosexual marriages will be a burden on taxpayers.

"I get along with everybody, but I've learned to get along," Morehouse offers. "Newcomers to the islands have to establish what a comfortable territory for them is and respect the local's territory. The culture, the traditions are very different here. It's America, but it's not the mainland. You need to respect that. You have an obligation to understand the environment."

➤ **TIP: Gay and lesbian job hunters should "do their homework"** before they disclose their status during a job interview, says David Morehouse. That is, try to ascertain the feelings of people with whom they interview or the reputation of the company with which they are considering a job. It's illegal to discriminate against homosexual work-ers, but some places can be more understanding and more pleasant to work in than others. "Whether or not you disclose that you are gay depends on the attitude of the business, of who you are interviewing with," he says.

➤ **TIP: Know the territory.** Some parks and beaches are local territory at night and they can be the same areas that are filled with tourists during the day. Stay off the beaches at night until you learn which are safe. And avoid anyone who has been drinking excessively or appears argumentative.

Steve Brinkman

Descendants of *ali'i* (chiefs) and leaders of high-ranking families gather in an *'awa* ceremony. People who have lived in a town or area for a long time are welcomed into the community as official members with this ritual.

If you are going to live in Hawai'i, it is important to know that prejudice exists. But prejudice, its anticipation and its effects, are sometimes hard to gauge. What is real? What is imagined?

A little plastic bag...

A few years before I moved to the islands I was visiting my mother on O'ahu. We sat on a bench reading the Sunday newspaper, patiently waiting for a bus. It began to rain, but before we were really wet, the bus appeared.

We gathered up our papers clumsily, boarded the bus in noisy confusion, fumbled for our fares. We turned to find seats and looked into a silent sea of Asian faces — eyes staring at us resentfully, mouths pursed in disapproval. The rain pelted the darkened bus and I shuddered as we sat down in front of a middle-aged woman who seemed to be scowling.

My mother, who has been in love with Hawai'i for the 20 years she's lived here, chatted happily and seemed oblivious to all this. *How can my mother live in this place?* I wondered. *So far from friends and family, so full of angry strangers.*

The words of a Big Island missionary ran through my mind. "They love tourists, but they distrust *malihini*, people who move to the islands. Caucasians, after all, have taken the land that is theirs."

Just then, I felt a tapping on my shoulder.

I turned and the woman behind me, still scowling, was reaching into her purse. "Here," she said, pulling out a neatly folded plastic bag. "You take."

"What? I don't understand," I frowned, shaking my head.

"Give me," she said, taking my damp newspaper. She carefully refolded it and neatly put it into the bag. "Now stay dry. More better to read."

She gave the parcel back to me and said some words I could not translate. Finally she smiled slightly and nodded in a kind of short bow.

My mother nodded to the woman and smiled. Then she explained. "She says you must always carry a plastic bag in Hawai'i because you never know when it will rain. And she is giving you hers."

O'ahu

"The Gathering Place" has gathered three-quarters of Hawai'i's population. Honolulu, the state capital, often gets a bad rap for crowding and traffic. Yet it's one of the most livable and lovely cities in the world.

G. Brad Lewis

And on the windward side of O'ahu, too far for most commuters, the Ko'olau Mountains shelter a more rural lifestyle.

G. Brad Lewis

Kaua'i

Lihu'e

O'ahu

Honolulu

← **Asia**
3,800 miles

New Zealand
4,400 miles
↙

The Hawaiian Islands

Nighttime: Honolulu

The city lights up like a giant fireworks display. Silver-painted mime Johnny Ginbeny, an English transplant, awes onlookers in Waikīkī every night.

Toni Polancy

Matt Thayer

nā kālai
'āina

politics and issues

To understand modern life

in these islands you must know

at least a little of our history

Kaleiolani's story

Ten year old Kaleiolani was excited as the airplane landed at the San Francisco airport. It was August, 1956, and his family was moving from rural Niu Valley on O'ahu to Portland, Oregon, where Kaleiolani's father would attend college. As the family began a long Greyhound bus ride, the boy stared out the window: such tall buildings, so many people, so many cars on wide highways.

The child Kaleiolani

The bus moved slowly through the traffic and Kaleiolani's eyes rested on some men digging a ditch along the highway. He blinked and looked again, amazed. The men were *haoles*, white. It was the first time Kaleiolani had ever seen white men working as laborers. Until then he had pictured Caucasians only as bosses, as people in charge. "All the mid-level managers at the plantations were always *haoles*," he remembers.

Today, Kaleiolani is Allen K. Hoe, 50, an O'ahu attorney in private practice, a Vietnam combat veteran, and a member of the Hawai'i Sovereign Election Council. The council seeks a meeting of Hawaiian minds on a major issue: sovereignty. Over the past 140 years, land and the power to govern themselves have been taken from native Hawaiians. Now they seek restitution and self government.

"For everyone who has come to Hawai'i, Hawai'i has represented a dream and an opportunity," Hoe says. "And everyone has come and used Hawai'i as a means to an end. The Hawaiians have always welcomed them and Hawaiians have paid the price."

Allen K. Hoe today

The past

First, the ali'i [1]

For about 800 years, between the time the first Tahitians sailed to the islands until Western missionaries arrived in 1820, Hawai'i was governed by kings, *ali'i* (chiefs) and *kupuna* (teachers). Commoners lived under strict *kapus* or taboos — the penalty for walking on the same ground as *ali'i*, eating the same food as a chief or crossing his shadow could be death. Hawaiians were unfamiliar with the concept of land ownership, but they believed *ali'i* were caretakers of the land for the gods. Commoners planted, harvested and fished, and tithed to the *ali'i* a portion of their take, similar to the way we support our religious leaders today.

Then, Captain Cook

English explorer Capt. James Cook was on his way to the Arctic to find a northwest passage between the Atlantic and Pacific Oceans when he sailed into Kaua'i's Waimea Bay in 1778. He arrived during the harvest celebration of *Makahiki* and Hawaiians believed he was Lono, the god of harvest. They welcomed Cook and his men who brought both tools of construction — nails — and tools of destruction — guns — and traded them for yams and pork, as well as sexual favors from eager *wahine*, women. Aware that his men carried venereal disease and other illnesses to which Hawaiians had no immunity, Cook tried to limit contact. He failed.

Hawai'i's feudal past dictated its development, influences today's government, and overshadows our future.

The nails, much valued by natives, eventually led to Cook's downfall. On a later visit, a group of Hawaiians seeking more nails burned one of Cook's ships. A fight ensued and Cook was injured. Seeing his blood, a sign of mortality, the Hawaiians were enraged that he had let them believe he was a god, and they killed him.

40 Kamehameha I unites the islands

Cook initiated change in the islands and, a few years later, in 1795, so did the Hawaiian warrior King Kamehameha I. Using weapons he had seen Cook use when he was a young man and waging relentless war on rulers of the other islands, one by one Kamehameha gained control of all the islands, gathering them for the first time under a centralized government. As he matured, Kamehameha I, from all historical accounts a warring and lusty king, grew to be a kind and wise monarch whose laws benefited his people, especially children and the elderly.

After Cook's visits, Hawaiians, including the *kupuna* and *ali'i*, had begun to question the restrictive *kapu* system. Among other things, the *kapu* forbade men and women dining together. Kamehameha II, known as Liholiho, succeeded his father. He shared power with the dowager queen, Ka'ahumanu. One day Ka'ahumanu and Liholiho's mother, Keopuolani, persuaded Liholiho to dine with them. The gods did not retaliate and the *kapu* system was broken, leaving Hawaiians divided over the issue. A civil war broke out but was quickly put down.

Author Robert Lewis Stevenson, left, dines with Lili'uokalani, fourth from left, and King Kalākaua.

Missionaries arrive

The first missionaries — nearly all idealistic young men under the age of 30 — were affiliated with the United Church of Christ. Since the American Board of Commissioners for Foreign Missions stipulated all must be married, several of them quickly found wives. They left Boston on Oct. 23, 1819, and after a long and grueling journey eventually arrived at the Puna side of the Big Island in 1820. It was a fortuitous time for them: *kapu* had been broken and Hawaiians were adrift in a rapidly changing world.

The missionaries were literally greeted with open arms by powerful *ali'i* and *kupuna*. Hawaiians saw the work of missionaries as being twofold: *pule* (worship) and *palapala* (learning).[2]

The ahupua'a

In early Hawaiian times the islands were divided into *ahupua'a*, pie-shaped slices of land running from the top of a mountain to the sea. Ideally, an *ahupua'a* could produce everything needed to sustain life. It included an ocean to fish, valleys in which to gather plants and food, and mountains from which waterfalls and streams ran.

HISTORY

Hawaiians dug coral and hewed wood to build churches and homes for the first missionaries, who were soon followed by missionaries from other sects, including Roman Catholic priests from France in 1827.

Whalers and traders had also begun to ply the islands. They too were welcomed by the natives; *kane* (men) shared food and knowledge; *wahine* (women) eagerly shared their bodies, much to the missionaries' horror. Missionaries discouraged Hawaiians from wasting time in games, *mele* (song) and dance and eventually the hula, which they considered lascivious, was banned. They also urged *wahine* to cover their bodies, introducing the loose, modest *mu'umu'u*.

The missionaries were strict and puritanical, but they were also hard-working and, by most accounts, devoted to their converts. They eventually taught Hawaiians — a race without a written language — to speak, read and write in English. Meanwhile, they taught that salvation came through reading the Bible and so they developed a written version of the Hawaiian language and translated the Bible. Many Hawaiians wanted to learn to study. The missionaries labored long and hard, fulfilling the role of minister, teacher, doctor and building contractor. Eventually, urged to do so by royalty, a few missionaries and many foreigners also became active in island government.

The missionaries also started numerous schools, some of them still among the best private schools in Hawai'i. To educate their own children in English, they founded Punahou School on O'ahu in 1841. So great was the desire for education that when the last of the Kamehameha dynasty, Bernice Pauahi Bishop, died she bequeathed her wealth — an inheritance of all the royal lands — to the establishment of the Kamehameha Schools. The holdings of Bishop Estate are estimated to be worth $10 billion in today's market, making it the largest charitable trust in the United States.

Business takes over

By the 1850s, benefiting from a modern concept — being in the right place at the right time — descendants of missionaries (as well as other Caucasians) began to take advantage of the opportunities the islands afforded. They went into business, establishing first sugar, and later pineapple plantations. They controlled the commerce that followed: banking, shipping, retailing. Some of them married the offspring of *ali'i*.

Challenged by foreign sailors and growers who felt they were exempt from island law and who were attempting to claim the island chain for foreign powers, Kamehameha III in 1840 proclaimed the first constitution of the Kingdom of Hawai'i. In 1848, his Great *Mahele* or land division allowed first Hawaiians, then foreigners, to own land. But the concept of land ownership was unknown to Hawaiians, who had no money to buy anyway. So Westerners — including *haole* businessmen — bought up about 80 percent of the land, many in large estates. Disenfranchised Hawaiians worked virtually as serfs on land they had for hundreds of years considered on loan from the gods. Some Hawaiians left the rural areas of the islands and went to work in towns, hoping to earn enough to buy their lands. Others gave up and left the islands to live elsewhere.

But the greatest threat to the Hawaiian people was disease. Foreigners brought new illnesses — venereal disease, small pox, measles and others — for which the isolated Hawaiians had no immunity. By 1870, the Hawaiian population, about 300,000 when Cook arrived, had dwindled to 60,000. Some historians say it was more than disease. Some say the communal Hawaiians, separated from their *mana* (land and spirit) and their *'ohana* (family) died of broken hearts.

There were too few Hawaiians to work the burgeoning plantations, so beginning in the mid-1800s and for more than 70 years, thousands of plantation workers were imported, first from China, then from Japan and Portugal, and finally from the Philippines and other places around the world. They would forever change the face of the islands, making them the most multi-cultural place in the modern world.

The Hawaiian Islands grew more valuable as huge plantations prospered. For over a hundred years, a few companies — known as the Big Five — dominated commerce: Castle & Cooke, Alexander & Baldwin, American Factors (Amfac), Theo H. Davies, and C. Brewer Co. Most of these companies are still powerful today.

In 1852, a new Constitution reduced the king's power and increased the power of an elected Legislature. The United States took control of the Hawaiian islands in 1887, when King David Kalākaua was forced by a *hui* (group) of American businessmen and plantation owners to accept the "Bayonet Constitution." It limited his power, as well as the voting power of Hawaiians and Asians.[3]

A queen imprisoned

After Kalākaua's death in 1891, plantation owners formed a provisional government and in 1884 declared the "Republic of Hawai'i" with sugarcane baron Sanford Dole as president. Kalākaua's sister, Queen Lili'uokalani, tried to regain political power for native Hawaiians in 1895, but she was arrested and confined to her bedroom at Honolulu's 'Iolani Palace for nine months. As her subjects kept vigil outside, Lili'uokalani sewed quilts, wrote beautiful songs (including the moving lament "Aloha O'e") and waited for United States President Grover

Queen Lili'uokalani

Hawai'i State Archives

Hawai'i's Largest Landowners

In acres, unless otherwise specified

Landowner	1964-65	1995
7 large landowners	1,203,487	995,574
(Percent of total land)	29.3	24.2
Bernice P. Bishop estate	369,700	367,509
Richard S. Smart		
(Parker Ranch, Big Island)	185,610	140,000
Dole Food Company, Inc.	154,759	121,982
Includes:		
Dole Food (88,792 acres), Castle & Cooke, (45,422 acres), and Kohala Sugar Co. (20,546)		
Samuel M. Damon estate	143,842	121,608
Alexander and Baldwin, Inc.	122,788	90,800
Brewer and Company, Ltd	145,147	81,997
Excludes 4,126 acres transferred to C. Brewer Homes, Inc.		
James Campbell estate	81,641	71,678

Source: The Hawaii State Data Book, 1996, from Robert H. Horwitz and Judith B. Finn, Public Land Policy in Hawaii: Major Landowners; Legislative Reference Bureau, Report No. 3, 1967; Department of Business, Economic Development & Tourism annual survey of major landowners.

For updated statistics see http://www.hawaii.gov/dbedt/index.html

Cleveland to send help. Cleveland expressed his support for the queen in a message to the U.S. Congress, but Congress did nothing. The annexationists simply waited until William McKinley was in office before successfully seeking annexation again in 1898. Two years later Congress adopted the Organic Act, creating the Territory of Hawai'i with Dole as governor. By 1902, Republicans (primarily wealthy and powerful businessmen and landowners) had taken control of the state Legislature.

The Democratic years

After World War II, returning veterans, especially young Japanese Americans, as well as sons and daughters of other plantation workers, began to unite, largely through the Democratic Party and the unions which had begun to organize plantation workers in the 1930s. In 1954 the Democrats gained control of the territory's Legislature in "The Democratic Revolution." No longer were large landowners in control of government; the new liberal government aimed at democracy and equality for all, breaking the control of the Republicans, big business and the Caucasian-owned sugar and trading companies.

In 1959, Hawai'i became the 50th American state and a 30-year period of unparalleled prosperity began. With the advent of modern jet travel, tourists from around the world flocked to the islands. Land prices swirled upward in a climb that would peak in the late 1980s. Tax money rolled in.

The Democrats made great strides in fulfilling their goals: Hawai'i moved from a rural plantation society to an urban service society. Today, the state's biggest industry is tourism, not agriculture. Small business, not big, provides most jobs.

Politics today

First Hawai'i was ruled by *ali'i*, then in effect by plantation owners and businessmen. And despite the Democratic Revolution, vestiges of that paternalistic background remain. Hawai'i's government, strongly centralized, is the most powerful state government in the country.

The state collects the bulk of tax moneys and decides how it will be allotted and spent, including funding for public education. It has almost total control of all the state's schools; it issues all business and professional licenses. Some allotment of power seems blurred — while the individual island counties can issue traffic citations, the money collected goes to the state.

As we enter the next millennium, Hawai'i remains one of the most liberal, most generous, most spending, and most taxing states. And, perhaps thanks to its indentured past, one of the most docile. Longtime residents seem reluctant to rock the boat. Here, speaking ill of someone, creating bad *mana*, is still frowned upon, is still taboo. But, attitudes are changing — slowly.

When the economy flourished, as it did during the '70s and '80s, money

Is aloha real? Ask a newcomer

Longtime residents sometimes ask if *aloha*, the loving spirit for which Hawai'i is famous, still exists, if it ever existed, or was just the figment of the tourist industry's imagination. But newcomers from less gentle parts of the world know the answer is yes, *aloha* is alive and well.

Shortly after Serge and Gloria King moved to Kaua'i, they went shopping in Līhu'e, about 40 miles from Princeville Resort. They bought several chairs and were trying to figure out how to get them into their car when a local man — dark-skinned and of mixed race — asked where they lived and offered to follow them home, carrying the chairs in his truck. When the caravan arrived in Princeville, the man helped unload the chairs and Serge offered him money for the delivery. The man declined, accepting only a beverage to quench his thirst, and said he had to be on his way back home.

"Where's that?" Serge asked. He assumed the man lived in his own neighborhood.

"Waimea," the man said, motioning back the way they had come. "Long way."

Serge was stunned. Waimea was across the island. "I thought he helped us because he lived on this end of the island... and here he had gone all that distance, altogether about 100 miles out of his way, to help, to make a newcomer, a *haole*, feel welcome!"

The unsolicited good deed put a happy tone to the Kings' transition to Kaua'i. They settled in easily. "Within two weeks on Kaua'i," says King, "we made more friends than in all our years in Malibu (California)."

poured into the state coffers. It was easy to pay for the good life, liberal perks for state residents and government (federal and state) workers, who make up 10 percent of the workforce. The Gulf War and world economic difficulties brought a halt to that prosperity during the 1990s. When times get rough — and in Hawai'i they are rougher than they have been for most of the last 50 years — disgruntled constituents seek change and look to state government to solve problems.

The future

Hawai'i, facing economic problems, is seeking solutions. Late in 1997, a Task Force on Economic Revitalization recommended a cut in personal income and corporate taxes, an easing of the restrictions on small business, and — controversially — a 35 percent increase in the regressive state excise tax. Although the state legislature adopted none of the recommendations, the seeds of change were sown. The task force at least brought focus to Hawai'i's economic problems.

Meanwhile, Republicans are grooming strong candidates with an eye to regaining power. The 2000s should be interesting years for Hawai'i.

Sovereignty

Although President Cleveland sent no help to Lili'uokalani in 1885, he called her imprisonment and the overthrow of the monarchy "not merely wrong, but a disgrace." More than a hundred years later, the United States agreed the coup was illegal and President Clinton signed a formal Apology Bill. The bill did little *but* apologize; it specified no course of action to make amends. But Hawaiian activists hope the President's apology will serve as an acknowledgment of U.S. guilt and lead to an eventual rectification.

Over the years, the government has agreed to set aside some areas as Hawaiian Homelands, to give to those of native lineage a small part of the lands that were taken from them. But due to the high value of Hawai'i land and its scarcity, relatively little has been made available. Many

Matt Thayer

A sit-in at the State Capitol building includes hula, ancient chants and an all-night vigil.

Hawaiians have been waiting years for land of their own; some grow old and die waiting. Meanwhile, Hawaiians continue to be displaced from land they consider their own, some of it having been in their families for generations.

Especially in the past twenty years, a quiet anger has smoldered among native Hawaiians. Bolstered by the renewed interest and concern for true Hawaiian history, but often hampered by in-fighting, the sovereignty movement — a demand for self government — has taken shape.

48   Three possible resolutions

Hawaiians are divided on the sovereignty issue, but three resolutions are possible.

The first, considered very unlikely, is a totally independent Hawaiian nation. The Hawaiians would take back the islands, making the state of Hawai'i a separate nation.

The second, more likely, is "nation within a nation" status, setting aside certain land as the Hawaiians' own, similar to American Indian reservations on the mainland. In that case, homes and businesses outside such areas would hardly be affected.

The third, expected by many people, even as they read the headlines and watch television, is that nothing at all will change.

U.S. Sen. Dan Inouye[4] of Hawai'i has said Congress would most likely grant Hawaiians only the nation-within-a-nation status, similar to that of Native Americans on tribal lands. An independent Hawaiian nation free to negotiate alliances with foreign governments, as some sovereignty activists propose, would never be supported in Washington.

"I cannot envision any Congress approving an act that would propose the seceding of, say, a segment of the state of Hawai'i or the entire state of Hawai'i from the union," Inouye said. "We had a civil war over that. I think that was very clearly articulated with blood."

Some Hawaiian activists say the issue should be taken internationally. They advocate letting the world, not the U.S. government, decide.

"No one honestly believes that the state or the federal governments are going to, of their own good will, give back to the Hawaiian people what was illegally taken. But I think once the Hawaiian community rises up and expresses its will," said Allen K. Hoe, Hawaiian affairs activist, "there will be a powerful alliance of governments within the international community that will compel that justice be done for Hawaiians."[5]

Those of us who have come late to Hawai'i tend to be split on the issue. Many of us sympathize and agree that some form of restitution is in order. But an O'ahu man sums up the feelings of those opposed to any form of resolution. He says that throughout history countries have been conquered, most with war and loss of many lives, and insists Hawai'i's people have fared no worse.

The point could be made, however, that Hawaiians continue to suffer. Gilbert Githere, a Kenyan immigrant who lives in O'ahu and is active in

African American concerns, makes a strong assessment of the Hawaiian **49** rights issue.

"[The Hawaiians are] facing a power, the biggest in the world. Even Colonialism in Africa never was as bad as it was here. Colonialism never killed a language," Githere says. "We are talking about the extinction of a people; their lives have become extinct."

Development vs. conservation

In Hawai'i, development, conservation and economy form a peculiar *ménage à trois*. Construction has dwindled from the busy 1980s. Pineapple and sugar are slowly moving to other parts of the world where labor is cheaper. Development provides sorely needed jobs and lures tourists, who have become the lifeblood of these islands. But over-population and over-development on some islands are already detracting from the natural beauty that draws visitors.

On O'ahu and Maui, natural resources like water are becoming scarce as housing developments are built. Aquifers in the O'ahu mountains pour water to a new community and restrict its flow to an old one. Desalination of ocean waters is considered.

The H-3 freeway through O'ahu's Ko'olau Mountains comes under fire from Hawaiians because it disturbs a *heiau*, or burial ground. At Honolulu Hale, the state building, Hawaiians march for gathering rights — legal permission to enter properties to collect traditional food and flowers for *leis*. Their protests, as befits these gentle islands, include *mele* (song) and hula.

Meanwhile, a developer's plan to uproot a banyan tree for a two-tower O'ahu housing complex is protested by an environmental group that includes mostly *haoles*. On Kamehameha Highway in O'ahu, conservationists protest the installation of tall aluminum lighting poles that detract from nature's beauty and the state spends thousands to remove them, halfway through the project.

A Big Island protester wears the image of Queen Lili'uokalani.

G. Brad Lewis

50   In South Maui's desert-like environment, developers plan a "rain forest" shopping center, and an aquarium blurs ocean views. Conservationists fight to keep beachfront vistas open.

On Moloka'i, development faces stiff opposition from Hawaiians who want to retain the remnants of an old lifestyle — living off the land that belonged to their ancestors. On the Big Island, protesters halt the lease of former sugar lands for eucalyptus forests by a Japanese paper company, and environmentalists oppose construction of a radiation facility to disinfect produce so that it can be sent to world markets.

The problem, a conservationist says, is that these islands are a democracy and anyone who wants to move here may. If people would just visit and go back home instead of moving here, we'd have fewer problems, she asserts.

It is, in effect, the islands' beauty that feeds us by luring tourists — and is destroying us by attracting new residents.

➤ **TIP**: **Immerse yourself** in real Hawaiian culture through books, classes such as language, dance and song, or in local sports such as canoe paddling. Become acquainted with the Hawaiian community and its traditions and beliefs. Newcomers may feel they are intruding by joining in such activities, but Hawaiians interviewed for this book, including activist Allan K. Hoe, welcomed newcomers' interest. Another suggestion from Hoe: "The first place they go after getting off the airplane should be Bishop Museum [in Honolulu]."

➤ **TIP: Become involved.** On small islands, it is very easy to have a voice, to make a difference. Become active in the issues you feel strongest about. Or help govern these islands by becoming involved in politics. In addition to the traditional ways — calling party headquarters and volunteering or attending fund-raising functions — you can call the mayors' offices directly. Volunteer to serve on boards and commissions for which you have expertise.

RESOURCES

• Voter information
(800) 422-VOTE (8683)
• The Green Party, Honolulu
(800) 288-3377
• The Democratic Party
(808) 596-2980
• The Republican Party
(808) 526-1755

Your elected representatives
U.S. SENATORS
(6-year term)
Daniel K. Inouye
300 Ala Moana
Boulevard #7325
Honolulu, HI 96850-4975
(808) 541-2542
Daniel K. Akaka
PO. Box 50144
Honolulu, HI 96850
(808) 522-8970

'iki kumu

general information

A guide to health,

religion, culture

and entertainment

Bali Hai, Bloody Mary and the $5 lunch

We are sitting at the restaurant at the **Princeville Spa**, a health/workout center built of glass and stone with marble staircases and brass railings. Its windows look out at ribbons of waterfalls streaming into glistening Hanalei Bay. Bali Hai, the seductive "island"¹ Bloody Mary sang about in the movie *South Pacific*, floats in and out of a mist in the background.

"Where else," asks Serge King spreading his arms, "can you enjoy all this for a $5 lunch?"

Serge writes and lectures all over the world on the Hawaiian philosophy of *huna*, which he describes as teaching people how to think positively in regard to mind, body and relationships. Ten years ago he and Gloria, his wife, were sitting on an ocean bluff, watching the sunset, and lamenting the end of one of their frequent vacations to Kaua'i. Suddenly they realized that their two sons were grown and Serge's occupation (and avocation) allows them to live anywhere they choose. They moved to Kaua'i a few months later.

One of the benefits of living in Hawai'i, Serge says, is that *kama'āina* can enjoy, on a regular basis and sometimes at reduced rates, those amenities for which tourists travel thousands of miles: lush island scenery, top-notch restaurants, posh hotels and outdoor activities. This lunch is a good example. It's April — "off season" — when fewer tourists visit the island and the $5 lunch is designed to generate business.

Middle-class residents do a lot of the same things tourists do — enjoy facials and massages, dine, dance, shop, snorkel, tour, visit hotels — often at discounted *kama'āina* rates, anywhere from 10 to 50 percent below what tourists pay. Many businesses, restaurants, tours and activities — and even food markets — offer discounts for people who can show a Hawai'i driver's license or other proof of Hawai'i residency.

Arts and culture

Hawai'i's rich ethnic mix means there is an occasion to party almost every weekend on most islands. Some celebrations propagate traditions: Hawaiian hula competitions; Filipino *barrios* (parties); Mexican *Cinco de Mayo* celebrations and *fiestas*; Chinese *bon* and dragon dances.

The International Festival of the Pacific on the Big Island in July includes costumes and dances of Japan, China, Korea, Portugal, Tahiti, New Zealand and the Philippines. In March the **Honolulu Festival** features a traditional ancient Japanese custom. Warriors on horseback thunder down a sand track on a Honolulu street, shooting arrows.

Carefully stacked rocks and pieces of lava appear mysteriously on lava fields and deserts, to the awe of tourists. Is it the mischievous menehune, Hawai'i's industrious nocturnal elves, up to their age-old tricks? Or just someone practicing balancing skills?

Flowers play a major part in Asian culture. The **Narcissus Festival** in Honolulu welcomes the Chinese New Year with a Chinatown open house, lion dances, firecrackers, food booths and art and crafts. The **Cherry Blossom Festival** honors Japanese culture with crafts, drummers and dancers, games, tea ceremonies and *mochi* (a rice flour used to make candy and pudding) pounding in Waikīkī's Kapi'olani Park. The **Okinawan Festival** is held in the same park in September and also includes dances, arts and crafts.

On Kaua'i, the Garden Island Arts Council stages **E Kanikapila Kakou,** during which the audience participates in Hawaiian music and dance. **The Mokihana Festival** in late September is a week-long celebration of Kaua'i composers, *lei* making, slack key guitar playing, men and women's hula, and other Hawaiian arts.

➤ TIP: **You'll have abundant opportunities** to learn from Hawai'i's mix of cultures. One issue of *Honolulu Weekly*, a popular alternative newspaper, offers Tai Chi lectures, Western square dance classes and Scandinavian folk dance exhibits, as well as classes in Israeli language and American jazz. The *Honolulu Weekly* is free and available at locations throughout Waikīkī and downtown Honolulu.

The Hawaiian renaissance

Since the mid-1970s, Hawai'i has enjoyed a renaissance in Hawaiian and Polynesian culture: no longer the glittery plastic-grass-skirted Hollywood version, but authentic chants, dances, *mele* (songs) and stories. Libraries, schools, resorts and cultural centers host *hula halau* (schools) that perform to traditional chants and *mele*, as well as *kūpuna* (grandparents or elderly people) telling stories of Polynesian history.

Hawai'i has its own modern music too, created and performed by musicians and writers like **Keali'i Reichel**, the late **Israel Kamakawiwo'ole** and others who have promoted interest in the native language and culture around the world. Reichel, a *kumu hula* (teacher), chanter, songwriter and singer, has performed in New York's Carnegie Hall. Songwriter and singer Kamakawiwo'ole, a gentle giant at over 700 pounds when he died in 1997, had come to represent the downtrodden Hawaiian who succeeds.

A melee of concerts and gatherings — like the **Gabby Pahinui/Atta Isaacs Slack Key Guitar Festiva**l at Honolulu's Waterfront Park in August and the **Ukulele Festival** at the Kapiolani Park bandstand in July — allow music and musicians to shine. And events like the **Brown Bag to Stardom** at Kaua'i War Memorial Convention Center in January give amateurs their time in the spotlight.

The Big Island reigns when it comes to *halau* competitions, hosting the famous week-long **Merry Monarch Festival** in the spring time and the **World Invitational Hula Festival** for three days in November.

Makahiki

In ancient Hawai'i, four months each year were set aside for the observance of *Makahiki*, a time of thanksgiving and peace, from late October to February. *Makahiki* commenced on the day when the star group Pleiades, the

constellation the ancients followed to Hawai'i, appeared on the eastern
horizon at sunset. This was the time of freedom from labor and war, when no
large projects could be undertaken. Taxes of food were collected, displayed
before the gods, and then distributed among *ali'i* (chiefs).

In modern times, *Makahiki* begins with the eerily beautiful full moon
in November and ends with closing ceremonies during the full moon in
March. Only in very recent years have others than Hawaiians been invited to
participate in a few traditional observances, but the sharing spirit of *Makahiki*
is quietly honored by everyone in Hawai'i, the same as Thanksgiving Day.

Holidays

Every American holiday is celebrated here, as well as every Hawaiian holiday,
like **Prince Kuhio Day** in March; **Lei Day**, May 1; **Kamehameha Day** in June;
and **Admission Day** in August.

Add days of celebration from other ethnic groups — for example, Japan's
"**Girl's Day**" in March and "**Boy's Day**" in May — and you have a very full
calendar. Until recently, businesses and banks — but not the U.S. post office
— celebrated the Hawaiian holidays as well as American ones. Recently,
banks announced they will no longer close on Hawaiian holidays. Still, it is
common for newcomers to find a business unexpectedly shut in honor of
some ethnic holiday. In fact, one transplanted businessman was surprised
when his local staff did not show up for work. They simply assumed the
business would be closed on Kamehameha Day.

Art and entertainment

It has been said that the historic whaling village of **Lahaina, Maui,** is the third
largest art sales center in the world, behind only Paris and New York. Three
or four galleries per block line eight-block-long Front Street. On Fridays,
world-famous painters and sculptors visit "Art Night in Lahaina" where they
share opinions and glasses of wine with visitors.

Commercial art galleries dot all the islands; some of them staffed with
high-powered salespeople. More interesting are the quiet co-op galleries
where artists take turns at floor duty and converse pleasantly with browsers.
The Big Island has two such galleries: at the **Keahou Hotel** near Kailua-Kona
and at the restored **Waimea Fire Station**. Maui's most interesting galleries

are co-ops in upcountry **Makawao** and the crafts guild located in a rustic old store in the hippy town of **Paia**.

On Kauai, several interesting shops and galleries offering local arts and crafts are located at Hanalei, south at Hanapepe, and centrally at **Kilohana Plantation**, an estate near Līhuʻe. The **Kauaʻi Society of Artists** presents three exhibitions a year, including a six-week event at the State Building each spring and a juried show in the fall.

Little Lānaʻi has a nameless downtown shop where artisans work and sell. On Molokaʻi, artists and craftsmen gather at the Molokaʻi Ranch town of **Maunaloa** on the far western part of the island.

On Oʻahu, numerous shops and galleries feature local artists and craftspeople. Among the many: the **Contemporary Museum** in Makiki Heights, the **Honolulu Academy of Arts** on Beretania Street and **Native Books & Beautiful Things** at Bishop Museum and on Merchant Street, Honolulu.

The islands are small; but there is no shortage of top-notch entertainment — from rock groups like the Rolling Stones to Broadway shows to world-renowned musicians and dancers. Honolulu's **Neal Blaisdell Concert Hall** and the **Honolulu Theater** glow with special events several times a month. Some of the most famous performers jet over to the **Maui Arts and Cultural Center.** The center also holds outdoor concerts and Friday night *pau hana* (done working) parties in its outdoor courtyard.

The Lodge at Kōele on Lānaʻi hosts creative people from around the world, like humor columnist Dave Barry, Pulitzer prize winner Jane Smiley, and Chef Emeril Lagasse. Their appearances are open to all Lānaʻi residents and visitors without charge.

Internationally acclaimed artists from all over the world assemble to perform chamber music at the **Kapalua Bay Hotel**, Maui, during the **Kapalua Music Festival** in June. And the **Kauaʻi Concert Association** hosts internationally acclaimed performers.

Museums

Hawaiʻi's most famous museum is the **Bishop Museum**, off H-1 near the Pali Highway in Honolulu. Endowed through the will of Bernice Pauahi Bishop, a descendant of Hawaiian royalty, the museum is devoted to Hawaiian history and contains many artifacts from the days when kings and *aliʻi* ruled.

One of the neat things about Hawai'i: slippers

Opt for loafers, sandals or zories, those little rubber soles with just one toe strap. You'll be removing your shoes often to comply with one of Hawai'i's unwritten laws of courtesy: *Remove your shoes before you enter a home.* Don't disregard the custom. Many people here take it very seriously and failing to remove your shoes can be a major breach of etiquette, showing disrespect for your host. The custom comes from Japan, but it makes great sense in Hawai'i, which can be very dusty or muddy. Going shoeless also provides a treat for tired feet: cool tile floors feel soothing.

The Bishop Museum is so revered it seems sacrilegious to say that despite its beautiful mansion-like buildings, display space is small and disappointing. However, the museum is well known for research and is a good starting point for learning about island history. A mile or so up Pali Highway sits a cozy museum that is a true gem: **Queen Emma's Summer Palace**. This modest home exhibits the very personal side of Hawaiian royal life, humble by mainland standards, and quaint.

'Iolani Palace in downtown Honolulu is a grander look at imperial life. It is said that Hawai'i's last king, Kalākaua, had 'Iolani Palace built to prove to the world that Hawaiians were not savages. In a bedroom of this palace Queen Lili'uokalani was imprisoned when American businessmen took over the government.

Across a driveway from the 'Iolani Palace sits the **National Archives** and the **Honolulu Library**, both gold mines for researchers. **Washington Place**, the governor's mansion, and historic **Saint Andrew's Church** are two blocks away. This area of Honolulu, with its parks and historic government buildings, is well worth an afternoon's stroll for anyone who lives on the islands or plans to. Fridays at noon the Royal Hawaiian Band presents a concert on the 'Iolani Palace grounds. (Good luck parking in this area; bring lots of quarters to feed parking meters — or take TheBus.)

Kaua'i Museum in Līhu'e has a permanent display of artifacts as well as changing exhibits highlighting the history and crafts of both Kaua'i and

Establish residency

Establish residency as soon as you can to take advantage of *kama'āina* discounts, to make check cashing easier, and just to feel more at home in the islands. The most accepted proof of residency is a Hawai'i driver's license or a state identification card.

•   **Driver's license:** If you are new to the islands, you must pass both a written and manual driving test but both are relatively easy. Buy a copy of the *Hawai'i Drivers' Manual*[1] at a book store, drug store or convenience store (less than $5) and study for the test. Satellite offices of the state Motor Vehicle & Licensing Division are conveniently scattered throughout the islands. See the front of the manual or the county government section of your phone book for the closest office. No appointment is necessary, but expect to wait an hour or longer.

•   **A state ID card:** This card is primarily a convenience for those who don't have a driver's license. To obtain this official state card, you'll need a certified copy of your birth certificate, your social security card, and, if you are married, a certified copy of your marriage certificate. On O'ahu, call **(808) 587-3112** for information; Maui, Lāna'i and Moloka'i, **(808) 243-5398**; Kaua'i, **(808) 274-3100**; Hilo, Big Island **(808) 974-6265**; Kona, Big Island, **(808) 329-9066**

Ni'ihau. **Kōke'e Museum** details the history of Kōke'e State Park as well as the future of eco-tourism, interpreting the environment for visitors.

Many missionary homes have become small museums. **The Baldwin House** in Lahaina, Maui, and the **Lyman House** in Kona, on the Big Island, are excellent examples of how missionary families lived *after* they had been on the islands for several years. They do not depict the hardship many missionaries endured. Maui's **Alexander and Baldwin Sugar Museum** at Pu'unēnē is an interesting peek at plantation life; some of the museum attendants lived on the plantation as children and share interesting stories with visitors. And the **Parker Ranch** at Waimea on the Big Island provides an intimate look at both rich and poor ranch life.

Theater

The word "amateur" is less than appropriate in regard to the islands' many theater groups. Former actors and would-be actors, many with professional

experience, live in these islands. The quality of musical and dramatic presen-
tations can be very high. If you are a would-be actor and not intimidated by
the talent, you'll no doubt revel in the environment.

Plays are presented weekly on O'ahu and Maui. Auditions are usually
open to the public and are announced in the weekly entertainment sections of
most island newspapers. Theater groups are nearly as popular in Hawai'i as
they are in England and the following is only a partial list of what is available.

On O'ahu, the **Diamond Head Theater** offers both musical and dramatic
productions October through August. **The Hawai'i Performing Arts
Company** is situated in the Mānoa Valley Theater (performances September
to June) and the University of Hawai'i at Mānoa has various drama
groups at **The Kennedy Theater**. Cultivating budding talent is
The Honolulu Theater for Youth, ranked the second best youth theater
organization in the United States. **Kumukahua Theater** presents locally
written plays as well as productions about the Hawai'i/Pacific region and
experience.

The Maui Community Theater performs at the historic 'Iao Theater in
Wailuku and the **Baldwin Theater Guild** presents plays and workshops at
Baldwin High School Auditorium. Both adults and children perform with
The Maui Academy of Performing Arts.

On Kaua'i, the **Kaua'i Community Players** and **Kaua'i Kids at Play** offer
musicals, comedies and dramatic plays throughout the year. And **Hawai'i
Children's Theater** in Kapa'a provides fun and formal education in the arts.

The Big Island has several groups. The **Hilo Community Players** present
Broadway and off-Broadway productions. The **Kahilu Theater Foundation** in
Waimea has its own western-style building across from the Parker Ranch
Visitor Center.

Radio and Television

In addition to Hawaiian music, classical, popular, jazz, country and
rock music are also played on various radio stations on most islands.
Some stations feature ethnic "hours," with Filipino or Japanese music
and news.

Cable transmission brings television to most parts of the islands, but
Honolulu has the only studios broadcasting network television. Some remote

areas of the islands have no cable service, so if you are a TV-aholic check before you commit to a living space. Most cable stations broadcast on mainland time; shows on national networks — ABC, CBS, NBC and Fox — are usually broadcast an hour earlier than eastern standard time. (For example, prime time starts here at 7 p.m. and winds up at 10 p.m.) All four major islands have community television — non-profit stations that broadcast local information. Cost of cable television is about the same as on the mainland, from $24 per month for basic service.

Movies

Popular movies are presented on all islands, except Moloka'i and Lāna'i, at about the same time they open at mainland theaters, but if you want to see an art film or anything that diverges from the popular, you'll have to be quick. Chances are it will play on these islands only one or two nights, if at all.

Honolulu's **Movie Museum** shows classic, art and foreign films five nights a week, Thursday through Monday. The theater has just 18 seats (naugahyde recliners), and you can bring your own food. Price is $5, $4 for those who belong to the museum's video rental club. **The Honolulu Academy of Arts Theater** also shows *avant garde* films and so do community colleges throughout the islands. **The Maui Arts and Cultural Center** offers a schedule of foreign films.

➤ TIP: **The Annual Hawai'i International Film Festival** is one of the cultural advantages of living on these islands. The state-subsidized festival brings two weeks worth of new and art films from around the world to all islands in October. Watch for schedules in weekly entertainment guides or pick up a free catalog (limited quantity available) at bookstores in late September.

➤ TIP: **The Kaua'i Alliance** offers a brochure highlighting all culture, humanities and arts organizations and events on that island. Write **P.O. Box 3344, Līhu'e, HI 96766**.

Dining

The islands serve up an appetizing variety of local foods and ethnic cuisine. You'll spend your first few months here sampling *manapua* (steamed dumplings filled with pork or vegetables); *musubi* (rice and Spam wrapped in seaweed); cone *sushi* (rice in an egg batter cone); plate lunches (any popular meat plus two scoops of rice and macaroni/potato salad); *malasadas* (fried hole-less donuts); *saimin* (broth with noodles and fish cakes plus any number of ingredients; so popular that even local McDonald's restaurants offer a version). All are inexpensive local favorites that can be eaten on the run.

Here, as on the mainland, families are eating more meals outside the home. The same golden arches and red-roofed pizza places that flourish on the continent dot the roadways on Oʻahu, Maui, Kauaʻi, and the Big Island. Lānaʻi and Molokaʻi remain franchise-free at this time. Some fast-food franchises offer meals at mainland prices; but most tack the cost of shipping to your bill. You may find, for example, that a $2.99 special advertised on national television costs $3.49 here.

Several national restaurant chains like **International House of Pancakes**, **Sizzler**, **Tony Roma** and **Denny's** offer meals in the $10 to $15 range, considered low here. Fancier restaurants cater to tourists and, especially on the neighbor islands, are expensive. Expect to pay a minimum of $40 for a meal in an upscale restaurant. Residents here are more apt to celebrate special events at *lūʻau* or potlucks at the islands' numerous parks and beaches.

➤ **TIP: It is usually assumed that you will bring a dish to share** when you are invited to dine at someone's home, at a picnic or *lūʻau*. If asked whether you should bring some thing to the gathering, the polite hostess will say no when she means yes, and you'll arrive to find that everyone but you has contributed. If you want to discuss food with the hostess in advance, ask *what* she would like you to bring, not *if* you should bring any thing.

➤ **TIP: Traveling to another island for a cultural or sports event?** Check out the *kamaʻāina* packages at Pleasant Island Tours, Roberts Hawaiʻi or similar island tour agencies. They often feature "overnighters" — airfare, room and rental car — at reduced rates. Book early; rental cars can be scarce during holidays or when a big event is scheduled.

62 ➤ TIP: **It's wise to keep abreast of holidays** and customs; you could "lose face" by not knowing how to respond. Chinese celebrate the new year at the end of January with dragon dances. Costumed dancers parade from door-to-door or store-to-store. Chinese custom calls for monetary gifts, preferably in little red envelopes that bring good luck. The money usually goes to charity.

➤ TIP: **Get a local calendar** marking Hawaiian holidays as well as American ones. A few banks give them away at the beginning of the year and bookstores usually carry them year-round. (American Savings Bank produces an exceptionally nice calendar, featuring the work of local artists.) Talk to people and businesses you deal with to see how they are celebrating. When you register your children for school, ask for a calendar of days off.

RESOURCES

All of the following are on O'ahu

• Honolulu Academy of Arts
  (808) 538-1006
• Hawai'i Academy of Recording Arts
  (808) 534-4272
• Hawai'i Youth Symphony Association
  (808) 941-9706
• Honolulu Boys Choir
  (808) 395-8888
• Honolulu Children's Opera Chorus
  (808) 521-6537
• Hawai'i Opera Theater
  (808) 521-6537
• Manoa Valley Theater
  (808) 988-6131
• University of Hawai'i at Manoa Kennedy Theater
  (808) 956-7655

G. Brad Lewis

Our varied culture is most often liberal and tolerant of various beliefs. At Pāhoa, on the Big Island, a hemp store hangs a sign encouraging "plant freedom."

Religion: a litany of faiths

It's Sunday in Hawai'i. More than 100,000 people kneel in prayer, stand to sing, or sit harkening to sermons in 758 churches and temples, worshipping in traditional rituals as well as some unique to these islands.

On the Big Island, the **Honpa Hongwanji Shin Buddhist** temples host a convention.

On O'ahu, **Calvary By The Sea Lutheran Church** members celebrate annual Clown Sunday with Bible stories and personal testimony in mime, song and dance. Participants include the Outrageous Calvary Clown Choir and the Crazy Keiki (Children's) Choir.

In Kīhei, Maui, members of **St. Theresa's Roman Catholic Church** sell fresh *leis* in the church vestibule gift shop. A hula dancer will perform during the offertory.

Programs bow to all ages, genders and interests. Later in the month, the **Spiritual Life Center** will lead a three-day pilgrimage to Kalaupapa, Moloka'i's former leper colony. Members of the **O'ahu Jewish Young Adult Group** can attend an End of Summer Beach Party — in November — and children from several churches are invited to "A Youth Lock-In" at O'ahu's **St. John's by the Sea**, billed as an overnight adventure. The **Assemblies of God Church** plans a family skating party. **Nu'uanu Congregational Church** will host a program on "Caring for the Caregiver" and **The Central Union Church** seniors group will study "Creative Memories," a program on preserving family history.

O'ahu women may attend a discussion on the "The Feminine Soul" in the **Mystical Rose Chapel** on the Chaminade University campus, or the **Kailua Christian Women's Club** luncheon, "Home is Where the Heart Is."

And for those re-thinking their religious allegiance, a support group for former **Mormons** is meeting in a private O'ahu home.

There are many paths to worship in these islands. Hawai'i is host to 43 recognized religious groups and at least a dozen new or less-organized faiths. Led by Rev. Hiram Bingham, the first missionaries, **Congregationalists**, arrived in 1820. They were followed by a variety of priests and missionaries who built schools and churches. Plantation workers, imported from around the world, added other faiths, including Roman Catholic. (See chart on page 65.)

The Mormon Church — with 7,000 members and owning 6,000 acres on windward Oʻahu — has a long, well-rooted history in the islands. Purchased in 1865 as a place for Mormons from around the world to settle, the "reserve" at Lāʻie includes Brigham Young University; the Hawaiʻi Temple of the Church of Jesus Christ of the Latter-day Saints; and the Polynesian Cultural Center, one of Hawaiʻi's most popular attractions; plus a hotel, a shopping center and many homes.

And the variety of religions continues to grow. New denominations, such as Hope Chapel and the Assemblies of God, have ever-blossoming congregations attracted to lively family-oriented programs. Various New Age religions and services are also available on most islands.

➤ **TIP: Participating in church activities** is one of the best ways to become part of a new community. Most Hawaiʻi churches, both traditional and non-traditional, are organized to accommodate our transient population — welcoming newcomers, winter residents, military families, and tourists. To locate the church or denomination of your choice, use the local telephone yellow pages or watch the weekly religion sections of newspapers.

Toni Polancy

ʻĀina, *the land, has a special, spiritual meaning for Hawaiians. A gift from the gods, the ʻāina provides trees for shelter and food to sustain life, most importantly taro from which poi is made. A taro patch in Hanalei Valley, Kauaʻi, where the gods provide abundant rain.*

Church Membership

County or Denomination	No. of churches	Membership (confirmed, full members)	Number of adherents (expressed believers)
State total	758	87,579	390,827
By counties:[1]			
Hawai'i	156	10,760	48,900
Maui	107	6,677	36,279
Honolulu	434	65,839	288,507
Kaua'i	59	4,278	17,051
By denomination:			
Assembly of God	69	8,475	13,005
Roman Catholic	102	[2]	232,780
Latter-Day Saints	109	[2]	38,303
Episcopal	40	6,990	10,396
Southern Baptist	56	16,245	20,331
United Church of Christ	110	18,202	22,852
United Methodist	31	6,677	8,348
Jewish	6	[2]	7,000[3]
All others[4]	235	30,990	44,812

[1] Not included is Kalawao (Kaluapapa, Molokai) with 2 churches, 25 members and 90 adherents
[2] Not applicable
[3] The American Jewish Committee estimated a 1992 Jewish population of 7,000 in Hawai'i.
[4] (35 denominations, each with fewer than 6,500 adherents.)
Source: 1996 Hawai'i Data Book quoting Martin B. Bradley et al., Churches and Church Membership in the United States 1990.

For updated statistics see http://www.hawaii.gov/dbedt/index.html

People of various religious beliefs and ethnic backgrounds join hands during a canoe blessing on the Big Island.

G. Brad Lewis

Sports*

With its abundance of clear, sunny days, warm weather, blue ocean and clean air, this island state has lured many outdoor sport enthusiasts to pack belongings in boxes and crates stamped "Hawai'i."[1]

This sports-minded influx continues a long and storied tradition dating back to the first Hawaiians. Hawai'i's initial settlers ruled the seas as master sailors, oarsmen and fishers. They invented surfing and many other games to test their skill, accuracy, strength and courage. One competition involved skimming down the sides of steep cinder cones in wooden sleds that resembled the modern-day luge.

European contact in the early 1800s brought new sports to Hawai'i's shores, as did the influx of plantation workers. Ranchers brought horses to the islands and locals soon embraced events such as **rodeo** and **polo**. **Baseball, football, basketball, track, bowling** and dozens of other sports all found their niche in island life. This athletic base seems to pervade an overall island lifestyle that is healthy, energetic and supportive of most sports, especially those for Hawai'i's youth.

Spectator sports

With no major professional sports teams to claim as their own, Hawai'i fans are big supporters of local college and high school action. The University of Hawai'i is the biggest draw and many of its football, basketball, baseball and volleyball games are televised live throughout the state.

There are opportunities to see the top competitors live when they play in all-star events such as the **Pro Bowl** and **Hula Bowl** football games, the **Maui Invitational** and **Rainbow Classic** college basketball tournaments. All three professional golf tours have at least one stop in Hawai'i. Golf events include the **Hawaiian Open**, **Kaanapali Classic**, **Senior Skins** and **Mercedes Championships**. Islanders also have an opportunity to rub elbows with the pros when they play in various celebrity and charity events during their off-seasons.

The biggest challenge for mainland sports fans who want to keep up with

---

* Matt Thayer, a photo journalist at the Maui News, contributed to this section.

Matt Thayer

A fan wears his enthusiasm well at Maui's Hula Bowl.

major league baseball or the NFL are not simply things like finding box scores or being able to dig up in-depth information about favorite teams. Not at all. The hardest part is getting accustomed to football games starting at 7 a.m. And convincing mainland friends to stop calling every Monday night and ruining the game by giving away the scores of the tape-delayed contests. The five or six-hour time difference means games are broadcast hours earlier here. However, there's a good side to the early morning broadcasts — you'll have time to take the family swimming or on a picnic Sunday afternoons.

Among the big spectator sport heroes here are some *really* big ones: sumo wrestlers. In this intriguing Japanese sport, men who weigh 400 pounds or more wrestle each other in bouts that usually last less than a minute. The sport carries much tradition, from the way wrestlers' long hair is dressed to their humble bows when they've lost a bout. To newcomers, the sport may seem absurd; but to locals and most *kama'āina* it is mesmerizing. Hawaiian sumo wrestle in Japan and highlights are broadcast in Hawai'i nightly. Wrestlers are considered national heroes here, as they are in Japan.

Participation sports

Pick a sport that is popular somewhere in the world and there's a good chance it has a league or group of enthusiasts here. Hawai'i's giant waves, strong winds, triathlon circuits and golf courses may be reason enough for some fans to adopt an 808 area code, but for the rest of us, it's just nice to know that after the move it won't be too hard to hook up with a softball league or bowling tournament or bridge club.

Most islands feature a healthy number of public parks and recreation facilities. Through the years locals have petitioned for public pools, athletic fields, skateboard parks, basketball courts, youth centers, tennis courts and even in-line skating rinks. The result has been a gradual upgrading of the sports infrastructure that hustles to meet the needs of a growing population.

Hiking, camping

Most of Hawai'i's volcanic mountains are too steep for amateur mountain climbing, but others are perfect for less strenuous hiking to near summits with spectacular views and unusual flora. For safety reasons, you should never go hiking alone. Group hikes — including weekend or overnight trips — are a favorite with *kama'āina*. A camp-out under the star-filled sky on a secluded beach like Wai'anapanapa State Park near Hana, Maui, is an unforgettable experience and some families make it a weekly ritual.

Fishing

Hawaiians don't kill just for sport. Hunting and fishing are ways to provide food or income, especially on rural islands. Most of the fishing is of the deep sea variety and catches include marlin (*a'u*), yellowfin tuna (*ahi*) and *mahimahi*. You'll also see local fishermen casting nets from shore.

Rock lobsters, crabs and shrimp are netted or simply plucked from rocks and underwater caverns. Night-diving for eels and lobsters is popular too. If you walk the beach at night, you may spot the eerie glow of hunters' search lights under water. Catch is taken home, sold to markets or restaurants, or peddled from homes or out of cars at roadsides. Fishing tournaments are a western concept, but a few are held on the islands. The most famous is the five-day invitational **Hawaiian International Billfish Tournament** off Kona (Big Island) shores every August.

Every day is a celebration

Steve Strand

Only gifts in tiny red envelopes can satisfy the hungry dragon who dances during the Chinese New Year.

Matt Thayer

Modern Hawaiian royalty take part in an historic celebration.

Matt Thayer

Sport and culture mix: the Hula Bowl half time on Maui.

G. Brad Lewis

Plumeria leis amid blond curls on the Big Island.

We're healthier

We're outdoors, we're active
and usually the weather's fine

A montage of windsurf sails at Ho'okipa Beach, Maui

After-school surfers run for a wave at Wailua, Kaua'i.

Abundant rain keeps the grass green at Hanalei, Kaua'i, and perfect for playing Frisbee.

Swimmers at 'Ohe'o Gulch in Hana, Maui, commonly known as Seven Pools.

and more active

A hiker nears the summit of Haleakalā on Maui.

A religious experience: walking to Sacred Falls, O'ahu.

Canoe teams take their sport seriously. Near Kona, The Big Island.

A few boys, a basketball and the West Maui Mountains.

A runner ascends from Maui's central valley.

Hunting

Most islands also have hunks of state land where hunting is permitted with licenses. Among the bounty: **feral pigs, goats, pheasant** and **francolin,** a small pheasant-like bird.

Boar hunting is a particularly exciting local sport. Trained dogs scour the mountains for the huge horned beasts, wild ancestors of hogs imported decades ago as food. Boars are vicious when cornered and aren't particularly friendly when they're free. Smart dogs go for the boar's jugular; smart boars go for another very tender part of the dog. It's not unusual for a dog to be severely injured in the encounter. However, the big pig provides a great *lu'au* and is a popular source of food.

➤ **TIP: Let your hobby be your occupation.** This is one of the few places on earth where your avocation can become your vocation. Like to swim? Snorkel? Fish? Consider a job on one of the excursion boats that traverse the ocean daily. Hankering to hike? Consider a career taking tourists up into those pristine mountains peaks.

➤ **TIP: Organized campouts and hikes** are a great way to get to know your island and meet new people. Watch the newspapers entertainment sections for announcements or ask at sports equipment stores.

➤ **TIP: If you like a particular tourist activity** — bike riding, scuba diving, fishing, hunting — and would like to participate often, tell the owners or managers that you live here and are available to fill in on tours. Some will let you participate at a low *kama'āina* rate just to cover expenses, rather than have the tour or activity go partly empty.

➤ **TIP: Fishing and hunting are regulated** and checks by law enforcement are frequent. Call the Department of Parks and Recreation permit office in any county to get more information.

➤ **TIP: If you bring guns or firearms into the state**, you must register them with local police within 24 hours of your arrival. Guns rented or purchased here must also be registered with police. For information, call the Hunting Seasons Hotline **(808) 587-0171**.

SPORTS

Andrea's farewell

It was fourteen months from the time Andrea Heath-Blundell, 46, learned she had lung cancer until the time she died. They were important months. Andrea rejected her husband Brian's offer of a trip to anywhere in the world, telling a friend, as they lay on a beach looking out at the ocean, "Everything that matters is right here."

She had come to the islands as a young woman 18 years before, met Brian and given birth to their daughter Kim, now 14. She was active in her adopted community, the historic town of Lahaina on Maui's west side. Over the years she had taken part in PTA, Girl Scouts, and a community advocacy group.

Andrea's last months were spent absorbing sights and scents, as though she hoped to preserve memories of the beauty she loved, and in quiet times with friends and family. She found comfort planning her own funeral. She died at home, peacefully, and her body was cremated.

About 300 friends gathered at a memorial service at an old prison in the residential section of Lahaina. In bright-colored dresses, mu'umu'us and aloha shirts, mourners carried leis and flowers. Friends and relatives shared memories. Among them was a young woman Andrea had met at a support group for cancer victims. "I'm a new friend," the woman said, "and knowing Andrea has given me strength."

After the ceremony, guests boarded a boat at the Lahaina harbor and traveled silently, watching the sun dip into a glossy sea. A moon rose over the West Maui Mountains and multiplied itself on the ocean. Four flower-laden canoes appeared, a tribute from the people of Lahaina. Kim and Brian scattered Andrea's ashes into the ocean. Flowers, leis and hundreds of petals floated over the water. A friend sang a Scottish song as the flowers drifted out to sea. On the way back to shore, guests shared food and socialized, all as Andrea had planned.

As people here live for the beauty of nature, of sun and sea, so do many people here say their final farewells. Funerals and memorials tend to be intimate and less structured than the funeral parlor wakes common on the mainland. And they are often held at a beach or a garden. In Hawai'i, about 57 percent of those who die are cremated, a larger percentage than any other state.[1] There are two reasons: the high number of Asians who traditionally cremate their dead and the scarcity of land here.

The memorial service of a transplanted resident is apt to be attended by many people from the community, casual acquaintances as well as longtime friends. Explains one *malihini*, "Many of us live far away from our hometowns and relatives so everyone must be your *'ohana* (family)."

Health

Hawai'i has, for the past 30 years, enjoyed an excellent reputation as the "health state." In a recent year, an independent research and publishing company named Hawai'i the healthiest state[1] in the nation, and a national children's advocacy group rated Honolulu one of the best cities in the nation to raise a healthy child.

This state leads the nation in the percentage of citizens who have health insurance. Just 7.5 percent of residents are without health insurance compared to a national average of 16 percent. By state law, employers must provide health insurance for employees who work more than 20 hours a week. They can ask the employee to pay one-half of the premium or 1.5 percent of their wages, whichever is less — but many employers choose to pay the entire cost of health care for their workers. They usually ask the worker to pay the additional costs for family coverage.

We live long, we live well, we have fun

Two major non-profit health care giants, Kaiser Permanente and Hawai'i Medical Service Association (Blue Cross/Blue Shield) provide most of the health insurance in Hawai'i. Because they are big and powerful, they are able to negotiate with providers and keep health care costs down. In recent years, numerous smaller health insurers have also come on the scene.

Both HMSA and Kaiser offer a variety of plans. Under HMSA's most popular group plan, clients can choose a participating doctor and HMSA picks up 90 percent of the cost of the office visit. Clients also have access to a wide-range of testing services and other health care providers.

Kaiser Permanente clients can choose from staff doctors at convenient Kaiser clinics around the state for a $7 per visit fee and have on-site access to routine procedures such as blood tests, mammograms and heart monitoring, as well as pharmacy services. For advanced care, they are flown — usually at Kaiser's expense — to Kaiser hospitals and centers on O'ahu or referred to other facilities as necessary. Participants of both plans seem satisfied and loyal — ready to defend their choice of health care provider.

HEALTH

A family affair: *ho'oponopono*

Ho'oponopono, an ancient Hawaiian "cure" for illnesses, physical as well as emotional, is still practiced today by some families. In *ho'oponopono*, members of the family gather to resolve a problem or cure a lingering illness. The family chooses a leader, often the oldest family member or a minister or healer. After prayers or a Bible reading, the leader asks each person to admit any grudges he may have or transgressions he may have committed. The ritual can go on for hours or even days, as problems are discussed by family members. Then forgiveness is asked between the individuals involved. The *ho'oponopono* is effective, some doctors surmise, because it uses a very modern psychological "cure": openly discussing problems and getting to their root, instead of letting them fester and multiply.

Thinner and older

Statistics show Hawai'i residents live four years longer than U.S. mainlanders. Men here typically live to age 76, women 82.[2]

And Hawai'i has the fewest overweight people in the nation.[3] About 19.7 percent of Hawai'i residents are overweight compared to about 30 percent on the mainland. Our average body mass (fat) index is 24.1; the nation's is 31.6.

We may be thinner and live longer because we are more physically active. The good weather means we aren't as likely to be holed up watching television and nibbling potato chips. Even the oldest among us can be outdoors throughout the year, swimming, walking and paddling. Hawai'i also has many Asians who tend to maintain healthy diets high in fish and vegetables and low in fats.

We smoke less

Another healthy statistic: Hawai'i residents are less likely to smoke cigarettes and may be less likely to inhale someone else's smoke. Compared with the national average of 22 percent, only 18 percent of Hawai'i residents are smokers.[4] That figure, however, does not allow for tourists who make up 15 percent of the population. Tourists from some parts of the world smoke a great deal and so you may be exposed to second-hand cigarette smoke in tourist areas.

Health problems

Our nearly perfect climate seems to alleviate such ailments as arthritis and bronchitis, but it doesn't mean you'll never have another cold or totally avoid the flu. Healthcare officials say these minor illnesses are difficult to track since most people simply treat themselves with over-the-counter drugs or "take two aspirins and go to bed" but it is almost as common for people to complain of flus and colds here as on the mainland.

Overall, Hawai'i is healthful, but it is not without health problems.

- **Hawai'i does not fluoridate** its drinking water and a nationwide study showed Kaua'i children have the worst teeth in the country. About twice the national average of elementary school-age children have untreated cavities. The state health department has sought the few thousand dollars it would cost to install fluoride injectors into the state's water system, but efforts to fluoridate the water have failed in the past, partly because people want their water source to be natural and untainted by chemicals.

- **Hawai'i has the fastest growing teen suicide rate** in the nation, up 126 percent since 1980. The general level of mental health support is considered poor, particularly on neighbor islands and rural O'ahu, says one health care spokesman. Even if you can reach it, the state mental health system is so heavily used it cannot always respond effectively.

- **Teen pregnancy is very high**, increasing 26 percent from 1989 to 1997; on the Big Island it doubled. Traditionally there is little stigma to being an unwed mother in Hawai'i, where family helps raise children; but the teen birth rate is particularly high in economically depressed rural areas.

- **Health care in O'ahu's major hospitals is adequate**, judged by the amount of expensive, sophisticated equipment that seems to be a measuring stick throughout the U.S. for health care. Queen's Hospital, for example, has advanced scanning machines used for biomedical research as well as treating patients. Residents usually must travel to Honolulu for sophisticated tests such as brain and body scans and critical operations, including heart surgery. Neighbor island hospitals vary greatly in quality, say a neighbor island doctor and nurse interviewed separately.

- **The number of organ donations in Hawai'i is the among the lowest** in the nation. Hawai'i recipients must wait very long for vital operations and some die waiting. Two factors contribute to the low donor rate.

HEALTH

78

Organ removal goes against some ethnic and religious beliefs. And our population is highly transient — many people just don't stay long enough to fill out donor cards.

➤ TIP: **How far is help?** If you have a serious health problem that may require emergency trips to a hospital, consider carefully which island you will live on. Hospital care can vary greatly from island to island. You should also consider how long it may take you to get to a hospital in an emergency during busy traffic times. For example, Kaua'i's Wilcox General Hospital is able to handle most emergencies and is generally considered a fine hospital. But if you were to live in Princeville or Kīlauea, it could take an hour in rush-hour traffic to reach the hospital.

➤ TIP: **Be prepared to travel elsewhere** for some treatments and procedures. Several health care providers recommended bypassing Hawai'i hospitals and traveling to the mainland for serious elective surgery. For example, because of the larger population, hospitals near major cities perform more valve and joint replacements and heart surgery, therefore have more experience, and may have more success.

➤ TIP: **Avoid cane fields.** Air quality on these islands is among the best in the world because of the trade winds and our isolated location in the Pacific. But if you have sinus or breathing problems, avoid living near cane fields. Part of the harvesting process involves burning the cane, which creates smoke and black ashy debris that can blow across several miles.

RESOURCES

- Crisis numbers: Call **911** on any island or **ASK-2000** from anywhere in Hawai'i 24 hours a day
- O'ahu Suicide and Crisis Center **(808) 521-4555**
- Military help line **(808) 622-HELP** Hawai'i **(808) 329-9111** Kaua'i **(808) 245-3411** Maui, Moloka'i, Lāna'i **(808) 244-7407**
- United Self-Help, all islands **(808) 926-0466** (call collect)
- Alcoholics Anonymous O'ahu **(808) 946-1438**
- Narcotics Anonymous O'ahu **(808) 737-6949**
- Catholic Services to Families O'ahu **(808) 536-1794**

ke kumu kū'ai

necessities

Can you

afford

paradise?

A kama'āina shops

"When I lived in California," says school registrar Marty-Jean Bender, a long-time Hawai'i resident, "I would sit down, decide what to have for dinner for the upcoming week, make out a grocery list, and go shopping.

"Here, I see what's on sale, and that's what we'll have to eat. I'll buy whatever vegetable or fruit is in season, for example. If something's really a bargain — say ground round at $1.59 a pound — we'll have it maybe three or four times in a week. You have to shop like that here. It's the only way to feed a family."

Marty-Jean is the sole support of herself and her 11-year-old daughter. To supplement her public school salary, she sells candles and gifts at home parties. And to meet the mortgage payments on her $340,000 home, she rents an apartment on the first level and occasionally takes a boarder in an extra bedroom of her home.

For "serious grocery shopping — stocking up" she shops at Price Costco, a shopping club with warehouses in Salt Lake and Hawai'i Kai on O'ahu; Kona, the Big Island; and Kahului, Maui. At Costco, food is sold in large amounts, but with a growing daughter to feed and numerous friends to share with, Marty-Jean finds that no problem.

Toni Polancy

Marty-Jean Bender and daughter, Makana

She shops carefully for everything, occasionally visiting weekend garage and moving sales, and perusing thrift stores for clothing. Among her favorites is Savers, a chain operated by the charity Big Brothers, Big Sisters. From stores in Kailua and Kalihi, O'ahu, and Kahului, Maui, Savers sells used clothing and household goods, including donations from retail stores like Sears and Ross.

Busy as she is, Marty-Jean exudes energy. Her social life is active, but relatively inexpensive: board games and frequent buffet suppers with friends, church-sponsored boat trips, camp-outs and whale watches. She splurges occasionally to attend a concert of her favorite Hawaiian musicians and catches their acts when they promote new releases.

Surviving Hawai'i prices

Hawai'i has long had a reputation for being costly. What most newcomers — and even some residents — don't realize is just how expensive island life is. Tally up the prices of rent, food, and taxes, and the cost of living in Hawai'i can be well over the 35 percent figure usually quoted.

Depending on which part of the world or the mainland you come from, the additional costs can range from as little as 10 percent (California) to about 65 percent (rural Southern U.S.).

"You can tell people about the high costs here, but they just don't believe it, " says a Honolulu businessman. "People moving here are caught up in a kind of excitement. It's like being in love. The hormones are kicking in. They hear about Hawai'i's high costs and they tell themselves, 'That's okay. I'll live in [a smaller] house; I won't eat as much' or 'I'll work hard; I'll make myself succeed.' And some of them do, but it's much, much harder than anyone can imagine while they are caught up in the throes of love."

> **"You can tell people about the high costs, but they just don't believe it."**
>
> — Honolulu businessman

Food

"Guess what I had to give up when I moved here?" one *kama'āina* laughs. "Cucumbers! They just cost so much and I never get over that when I go to the market. My boyfriend offered to gift wrap one and give it to me for my birthday. I told him I'd rather have a diamond, although pound for pound I bet the cucumber costs more here."

Most major Hawai'i food markets say their profit margins are about 1.3 percent, the same as mainland markets. Yet, food costs are typically 35 percent higher here. Markets maintain that the extra cost is due to freight charges incurred shipping the food to the islands. Food prices are usually greater on neighbor islands, reflecting additional shipping charges.

Unfortunately, family necessities like bread, milk and cereal seem to bear the brunt of high food costs. Although bargains can be found, milk costs as much as $5 a gallon in convenience stores and the price fluctuates

Food costs 35% more – plus tax

in Hawai'i:

Shoppers in four Hawaiian islands and six cities across the United States were asked to compare costs for the same grocery list. Prices on the mainland average $22; in Hawai'i they average $32.35 or about 35 percent more. When Hawai'i's 4% excise tax is added the difference jumps even more.

To assure accurate comparisons each shopper bought the same brands and sizes. They were: lettuce from general display, not gourmet; least expensive 16 oz. loaf of white bread; Miracle Whip Light salad dressing, 32 oz. size; one pound ground beef, not more than 30% fat; Gerbers baby carrots, 1st food, 2.5 oz.; one dozen large eggs; one gallon whole milk, least expensive; one can Campbell's tomato soup, 10 -3/4 oz.; Mrs. Smith's Pumpkin Custard Pie, 1 lb. 10 oz.; Taster's Choice instant coffee, 4 oz.; six-pack Coca Cola Classic.

Foodland
Kihei, Maui, Hawai'i

Lettuce	.89
Bread	2.99
Salad dressing	4.69
Ground beef	1.79
Gerbers carrots	.63
Dozen eggs	1.85
Gallon milk	4.59
Tomato soup	1.09
Pumpkin pie	6.49
Instant coffee	6.69
6-pack Coke	4.19
Total	35.89
State tax	1.43
Total	**37.32**

Safeway
Kona, Big Island, Hawai'i

Lettuce	1.19
Bread	1.69
Salad dressing	4.75
Ground beef	2.29
Gerbers carrots	.59
Dozen eggs	1.99
Gallon milk	3.79
Tomato soup	.99
Pumpkin pie	4.89
Instant coffee	6.89
6-pack Coke	2.99
Total	32.05
State tax	1.28
Total	**33.33**

Safeway
Kapaa, Kauai, Hawai'i

Lettuce	1.59
Bread	2.79
Salad dressing	4.39
Ground beef`	2.29
Gerbers carrots	.75
Dozen eggs	2.09
Gallon milk	4.99
Tomato soup	1.39
Pumpkin pie	4.90
Instant coffee	6.89
6-pack Coke	1.95*
Total	34.02
State tax	1.36
Total	**35.38**

* Only 12-pack available. $3.89 cost was halved for comparison purposes.

Daiei
Honolulu, Oahu, Hawai'i

Lettuce	1.29
Bread	1.18
Salad dressing	3.99*
Ground beef`	1.48**
Gerbers carrots	.57
Dozen eggs	2.19
Gallon milk	3.95
Tomato soup	.87
Pumpkin pie	5.39†
Instant coffee	4.24††
6-pack Coke	2.29
Total	27.44
State tax	1.10
Total	**28.54**

* Regular, lite not avail.
** In bulk pack
† 2lb. 5 oz. size; smaller not avail.
†† Price calculated on 7oz. size

FOOD

Bashas Market
Phoenix, Arizona

Lettuce	1.29
Bread	.99
Salad dressing	2.69
Ground beef	1.79
Gerbers carrots	.31
Dozen eggs	.98
Gallon milk	1.99
Tomato soup	.85
Pumpkin pie	3.79
Instant coffee	4.69
6-pack Coke	1.49
Total	**20.86**

Albertsons
Tallahassee, Florida

Lettuce	.99
Bread	1.29
Salad dressing	2.49
Ground beef	2.09
Gerbers carrots	.37
Dozen eggs	.99
Gallon milk	2.88
Tomato soup	.59
Pumpkin pie	3.29
Instant coffee	4.79
6-pack Coke	1.99
Total	**21.76**

Meijer
South Bend, Indiana

Lettuce	1.49
Bread	.99
Salad dressing	2.49
Ground beef	2.59
Gerbers carrots	.43
Dozen eggs	.87
Gallon milk	1.49
Tomato soup	.43
Pumpkin pie	3.00
Instant coffee	4.89
6-pack Coke	2.49
Total	**21.16**

Hughes Market
Malibu, California

Lettuce	1.29
Bread	1.99
Salad dressing	3.29
Ground beef	1.29
Gerbers carrots	.39
Dozen eggs	2.89
Gallon milk	3.58
Tomato soup	.65
Pumpkin pie	2.50
Instant coffee	5.39
6-pack Coke	2.19
Total	**25.45**

Shop and Stop
Cleveland, Ohio

Lettuce	.99
Bread	1.52
Salad dressing	2.19
Ground beef	1.15
Gerbers carrots	.20
Dozen eggs	.99
Gallon milk	2.35
Tomato soup	.59
Pumpkin pie	3.49*
Instant coffee	4.99
6-pack Coke	2.29
Total	**20.75**

* Pumpkin not available. Price is for Mrs. Smith's frozen fruit pies.

Albertsons
Reno, Nevada

Lettuce	.99
Bread	1.79
Salad dressing	2.19
Ground beef	1.31
Gerbers carrots	.36
Dozen eggs	1.11
Gallon milk	2.99
Tomato soup	.49
Pumpkin pie	3.59
Instant coffee	5.29
6-pack Coke	1.99
Total	**22.01**

Prices reflect days shopped and are for comparison only — the price may change weekly or daily greatly in supermarkets. One week, it's a "loss leader" item offered at $3.39 a gallon, a bargain designed to bring in shoppers; the next week it's back up to five bucks. Bread usually costs at least $2 a loaf and brand names can go as high as $4. In recent years, Price Costco shopping club has become a popular place to "stock up" on groceries, in part because it retains consistently low prices on necessities like bread and milk.

Fruits and vegetables are very costly and sold by the pound instead of by the dozen as in mainland markets. Most produce is flown in at considerable cost — consider how bulky and heavy apples and oranges are and how perishable lettuce is. Locally-grown produce usually costs more since growing anything here is costly due to scarce land and high labor and utility costs.

One of the greatest contributors to Hawai'i's high food cost is the state excise tax, (four percent at this writing). In most states, food is exempt from sales tax or is applied only to luxury items like cookies and candies. Hawai'i's tax is assessed on all groceries, even those necessary to sustain life and nurture children: milk, vegetables, cereals, everything.

➤ **TIP: You can control food costs.** You have choices. You can forego expensive packaged cereals and prepared foods. You can shop at weekly farmers' markets and swap meets where seasonal vegetables and fruits are sold for as low as one third of grocery store prices. On most islands you can buy in bulk at warehouses or wholesale "clubs" such as Costco and Sam's Club. If buying bulk means buying more food than you can use, consider sharing costs and quantities with a neighbor or friend.

➤ **TIP: Avoid small markets** in tourist areas. Prices for staple items tend to be higher in such markets.

➤ **TIP: Stay away from roadside stands**, unless you know the prices are low. In Hawai'i, most roadside stands cater to tourists and rarely offer bargains.

➤ **TIP: Go to the source for your food.** If you do not fish, hunt or grow your own food, talk to friends and neighbors who hunt, fish, and garden. Ask them to sell you their surplus.

➤ **TIP: Consider growing some of your own produce** if you live in a house on the part of an island on which it rains frequently. Even a small garden in Hawai'i produces abundantly because the growing season is constant. And plants such as papayas reach maturity quickly. But be sure to take a class in gardening before you begin. Hawai'i's garden insects and unique conditions can be a challenge.

Housing

Renting a home

On the windward side of O'ahu, retired pilot Terry Davies and his wife Dale lease a large, recently renovated three-bedroom, two-bath house on a secluded ocean beach. From their small back *lānai* (porch), they walk four steps through white sand to Queen's Bath, a section of shoreline protected by ancient-looking stones.

The house would cost at least $500,000 to purchase; but the Davies are paying only $1,700 a month rent. By a rent calculation used commonly on the mainland (one percent of the total value monthly) their rent should be about $5,000 a month. But rental markets are over-loaded in some parts of the islands, so the Davies enjoy a bargain. Such deals exist; but expect to spend more than a day or so searching. Terry Davies looked at several homes over several weeks before finding theirs.

Matt Thayer

Honolulu high-rise condominiums and apartments are costly, but range widely in price depending on location in the building.

The search

Plenty of very decent rentals are available on all islands — you should be able to find exactly what you're looking for, eventually. Searching for apartments on O'ahu is relatively easy — more than 60 complexes are listed in the O'ahu phone book and some of those offer short term leases. A twice-monthly magazine, *Rentals Illustrated*, is also available on O'ahu. It showcases both homes and apartments for rent, mostly from private owners.

Searching for rentals on neighbor islands is difficult because most apartments within a complex are owned by individuals rather than one large corporation. That means to find apartments or homes for rent, you must search daily newspaper classified ads and talk to many individual owners instead of one building manager. This can make home-hunting tedious and time-consuming. It also can complicate keeping a rental, since individual owners tend to change their situations more often, for example, deciding to sell or occupy the property themselves.

The cost

You can spend anywhere from $600 to several thousands of dollars monthly for apartment and home rentals in Hawai'i — and you can live a dream come true, like the Davies, or a nightmare in an O'ahu slum with all-night partying and drug dealings. Interestingly, rents in these "low income" areas are usually no less than rents in more peaceful areas. Landlords simply cater to the ignorance of tenants who don't keep looking.

In general, expect to pay a minimum of $600 a month for a one-bedroom apartment and at least $900 for a two-bedroom on the outer islands or in an O'ahu suburb. You may pay slightly more in Waikīkī and downtown Honolulu. Those prices would be for a small apartment, unfurnished or partly furnished with major appliances, without an ocean view. You'll pay much more for penthouse apartments or apartments on the ocean. Well-furnished apartments usually cost about $100 to $200 more; because so many apartments are rented short term to visitors, they may come completely furnished down to cutlery and pans.

On any island, renting a house will cost from about $1,200 up per month. And you will need a security deposit, usually amounting to one month's rent. Most homes are unfurnished, but include appliances. Compared to buying a house, rents are a bargain — much less than mortgage payments would be for the home if it were purchased with a 20 percent down payment.

➤ **TIP: Plan to rent a home** during your first year here, while you get to know the islands. That will give you time to decide whether you will remain in Hawai'i, stay on the island you've chosen, and which town or neighborhood you prefer.

➤ **TIP: Do you know which neighborhood** you want to live in? Check shopping center bulletin boards or real estate offices in that locale. Pick up a real-estate-for-sale magazine and call realtors in that area. Most know what's going on in their neighborhoods and may be able to direct you to places for rent or rental agents. Also check small weekly newspapers and free publications at supermarkets and coffee shops.

➤ **TIP: Before bringing your pet,** consider that very few landlords allow them. If you plan to rent it may be wiser to leave your dog or cat on the mainland.

➤ **TIP: Leases tend to be shorter here** than on the mainland. Ask for a six-month lease or a month-by-month lease while you search for more permanent living arrangements or while you decide on which part of the island you want to live.

➤ **TIP: Apartments are rented either fully or partially furnished** (partial usually includes kitchen appliances — stove, refrigerator, dishwasher).

Steve Strand

Townhouse complexes like this one dot the islands. Aimed at the local market, they provide reasonably-priced housing, by Hawai'i standards, often under $200,000. They are also popular rentals.

And fully furnished means just that, often down to such details as silverware, can openers, and pots and pans.

➤ **TIP: Quiet by day can be less-than-peaceful by night** when residents are home from work and school. Visit the apartment or home you are considering at various times of day and night so you'll have no surprises after you move in.

➤ **TIP: Avoid houses or apartments that are for sale.** The owner or rental agent may tell you that for-sale properties stay on the market for many months before being sold, which is true. But how will you feel about potential buyers traipsing through your home? Or having to move within 45 days? (State law says your landlord must give you at least that much notice.)

➤ **TIP: Share.** Many people are hesitant to share living quarters, but sharing apartments or homes is simply a way of life here — a way to survive high costs. Sharing is particularly beneficial when you first come, to keep costs down while you find a job and establish yourself.

Buying a home

Hawai'i's high home prices are notorious, easily two-and-one-half to four times as much as you would pay for similar houses in the middle, South or Northeastern part of the United States, but on par with what you'd pay in higher priced areas such as southern California or in expensive cities like New York, Washington, D.C., or Boston.

At this writing, the median home price in the rest of the nation is $120,500; in Hawai'i, it is $347,000 — nearly three times as much. That $347,000 median price would buy a mansion in many parts of the U.S.

"It's recently down to $347,000," says Mike Haxton, president and chief executive officer of the non-profit Hawaiian Credit Counseling Service. "That's almost three times the national average. It's a great time to buy, a buyers' market...but look at the downpayment. Just the (20 percent) down payment is what some people pay for a whole house."

The good news

Good news: Houses on neighbor islands or outside Honolulu can be much less expensive than the $347,000 median. They begin at just under $200,000, which would buy an approximately 1,000-square-foot new house in a development of small houses on a tiny lot. (Hawai'i zoning laws sometimes allow houses to be built on "zero lot lines" — pushed up within about six feet of your neighbor's land — meaning you'll be within breathing distance of each other.) Or $200,000 may be enough to purchase a larger "fixer-upper" in need of repair or remodeling, on a bigger lot.

Condominium and townhouse prices vary greatly depending on location, views, quality and position in the building (usually the higher up an apartment is, the more it costs). Condominiums cost less than new homes, but condos can be costly over time as you consider maintenance fees and, if they are purchased as leasehold, land lease fees.

'Ohana and cottages

Many homes in the islands, in all price ranges, include *'ohana* (family) units, small attached studio apartments or separate cottages for elderly parents to live near their children, according to Hawaiian and Asian customs. With the high cost of getting started in life and the scarcity of well-paying jobs for young people, the situation these days is apt to be reversed: adult children living in their parents' *'ohanas.*

Matt Thayer

Cottages and houses on small "flag" lots, tucked behind other houses, are common in older residential neighborhoods.

In some neighborhoods, it is common for an extended family — parents, children, *tutus* (grandparents) and even aunts and uncles — to share the same house or to live in several separate houses on the same lot. In fact, Hawai'i has the most crowded houses in the nation. U.S. Census Bureau statistics show 15.9 percent of all homes in Hawai'i are officially classified as "crowded" or having more than one person per room.

Nationwide, the average new house has more than 1,920 square feet; the average new single family home on O'ahu has only 1,342 square feet. Average condo living space here is just 711 square feet.

➤ **TIP: Make paying your mortgage a sure thing**. Consider buying a three-unit property — a home with an attached studio, plus a cottage. Such properties are available on most islands starting at about $300,000. Rents might be, for example, $1,100 or $1,200 a month for the main part of the house, $500 to $700 for the studio and $700 to $900 for the cottage, enough to help pay the mortgage. So many people and their cars on small lots can make for crowded neighborhoods — but shop around; some multi-unit properties are well positioned and landscaped for privacy. "When we build a multi-unit property, we consider privacy. We never build with windows facing windows or doors facing doors," one contractor says.

Construction quality

The quality of construction here, or lack of it, surprises some mainland builders. Most houses have no basements, little insulation and are built on cement slabs or long stilts cemented into the ground. Unpermitted additions are illegal, but common. Construction regulations are somewhat more strict throughout the state since Hurricane 'Iniki devastated Kaua'i in 1992. For example, new construction must include "hurricane clips" bolting the roof to the house.

➤ **TIP: Hire a home inspector.** Your mortgage company will send an appraiser to verify the value of the home it is financing, but before you negotiate a price or sign a contract you should hire your own home inspector. He or she should spot any potential problems, avoiding costly surprises later. Use the inspector's report to help bring the sales price

Ask for "comps"

Computers put information at your realtor's fingertip that can help you ascertain the value of your purchase. Ask your agent to pull a list of comparable homes for sale in the neighborhood and also a list of homes recently sold, including both the prices at which they were listed and the prices at which they actually sold. If you are considering a condominium, ask to see a list of all the condominiums for sale in the complex, so you can compare prices, and also ask for a list of all the sold apartments, with their final sales prices, going back two years. That information should give you a good base for an offer on the property.

down. The inspector's fee may range from $100 to $500 — a bargain if you can negotiate the house price down by a thousand dollars or more.

State of the market

Housing bargains (bargains by Hawai'i's costly standards) abound throughout the islands, both in used and new housing. Unfortunately (or fortunately, depending on your situation) a declining economy forces some to sell their homes below market value. The real estate market varies greatly from island to island and can fluctuate from month to month. From 1996 to 1997, Honolulu home owners experienced an overall loss of 6.3 percent in market value, the largest drop in the nation, according to Runzheimer International.[1] Meanwhile, single family home prices rose in Kaua'i by about nine percent. At this writing, home sales on all islands seem to be on their way back up.

➤ **TIP: Consider foreclosures.** Banks often are anxious to sell properties they have repossessed when mortgagees could not afford payments. Foreclosured houses often sell for 15 to 20 percent less than their market value, says a banker. The discount on condominiums is even greater, from 15 to 50 percent, he says. Foreclosure auctions are usually listed in the classified section of major daily newspapers, along with procedures for bidding and times when properties are open for viewing. It would be wise to talk to an attorney on your island before bidding the first time.

Leasehold or fee simple?

Homes, condominiums and commercial property on the Hawaiian islands are sold as fee simple or leasehold. Fee simple means you own the land on which the home or condominium is built. In a leasehold situation, you usually own the building, but rent the land on which it stands. Much of O'ahu land is leasehold; relatively little of the outer islands' property is leasehold.

Among Hawai'i's issues is leasehold conversion — the court-mandated sale of land that has been leased to homeowners for decades. From about 1930, private residences, condominiums and commercial buildings were constructed on leased land, usually owned by the large estates like Campbell, Castle and Cooke and Bishop. This made homes and buildings less expensive, but inevitably led to disputes as lease agreements ended or lease fees were renegotiated and raised. In recent years, the state has stepped in, forcing leasors to sell land on which private homes are built at market value. Still in question are the condominium and commercial plots. The issue seems to be slowly resolving itself through voluntary negotiation. However, if you are considering buying a home, you should either 1.) stay away from leasehold property entirely, or 2.) consult an attorney and learn as much about leasehold properties as you can.

Most realtors will also answer your questions honestly, if you know which question to ask. At the least, inquire:

1.) How much the lease costs each month

2.) When the lease is due to be renegotiated

3.) Whether it is possible to purchase the land now

4.) Whether any of the owners have been able to purchase their land rights. (Once a landlord sells to one tenant in a project, he must be willing to sell to all.)

Home insurance

Hurricane Iniki, which devastated Kauai in 1992, is still affecting home insurance costs throughout Hawai'i. If you are paying about $200 a year for home insurance where you live now, expect to pay about $700 here for a similar home, says Cindy Nobriga, vice president of risk management services at Finance Insurance, Ltd. on O'ahu.

The good news is that you can even get home insurance these days. 'Iniki cost insurance companies about $1.6 billion; at least two major companies declared bankruptcy, others refused to write policies, and still others demanded astronomical rates. Things have calmed down, Nobriga says. Insurance rates have declined, but remain high compared to the rest of the nation.

Matt Thayer

Add the price of termite treatment to the cost of owning a home. Most specialists recommend tenting a home every five years. An odorless gas kills all insects and leaves no residue. "Tenting" for a 2,000 square foot home costs approximately $1,000.

94 Landscaping

You probably appreciate the islands' lush tropical greenery, many flowering shrubs and stately palm trees. That beauty is expensive. In dry parts of the islands greenery must be watered. In wet areas (like Princeville and Kilauea on Kaua'i) plants grow fast and must be regularly cut, trimmed and protected from fungi and insects.

You may be able to maintain a yard yourself, but if you are elderly or expect to be working a great deal, don't count on it. Count instead on adding at least $100 per month to your bills for gardening and $30 or $40 a month for watering.

Palms must be trimmed regularly, usually by islanders highly skilled at climbing the slender towers and whacking off the coconuts and old fronds for $20 to $100 a tree. Figure on trimming each palm at least twice a year. It's a must if your trees are near walkways; a falling coconut could mean a lawsuit.

Toni Polancy

Gardens abound in paradise, where anything grows if it's watered regularly, gardeners say. Keep in mind the cost of maintaining that tropical garden.

➤ **TIP: You don't need a large garden** and a big lawn to enjoy Hawai'i's beautiful flowering trees and shrubs. They are everywhere. Live in a condo or a house on a small lot, take a walk and enjoy someone else's gardening efforts.

➤ **TIP: Remember also** that lush gardens can be breeding grounds for mosquitos and rodents. Think before you plant.

Transportation

If you live in Waikīkī, downtown Oʻahu or some of its near suburbs, you can save a lot of money by NOT having a car. Oʻahu is the only island with regular, dependable bus service. TheBus goes all over the island and most routes are serviced every half hour. Fares are low: just $1 per ride and monthly passes, student passes and two-year passes for the elderly make it even less expensive. While buses tend to be crowded — standing room only during rush hour — they are cool, well maintained and a real bargain versus the cost of maintaining a car.

Neighbor islands have little or no alternative means of convenient mass transportation. At this writing, the Big Island has once-a-day bus service across the island; Kauaʻi has subsidized van service around the island in operation regularly but it is in danger of running out of funding; Maui has various tourist shuttles, but no mass transit; Lanaʻi has shuttle service every half hour from its two major hotels to Lanaʻi City, but it's geared towards tourists; and Molokaʻi has no service. If you are planning to live and work on a neighbor island, you will need a car.

Autos

Honolulu is the eleventh most expensive metropolitan area in which to drive a car. On the average, it costs $7,100 per year to drive a car in Honolulu.[1]

Gasoline, maintenance and insurance, as well as license, registration fees and annual depreciation were calculated in 80 cities by the management consulting firm Renzheimer International. Their analysis was based on a 1997 midsize car driven 15,000 miles a year within a 50-mile radius of a city and traded in after four years. (Los Angeles at $8,762 was the most expensive city and Sioux Falls, S.D., was the least costly at $5,710).

Cheaper on Oʻahu?

Talk to auto salespeople and you will hear several stories about how much island living adds to the purchase price of a car. Some sellers say it makes no

Consider a "Hawai'i cruiser"

"Hawai'i cruisers" are used cars, usually showing a bit of wear, and selling for less than $4,000 or $5,000. You don't have to buy an old car, but here are four good reasons to consider buying a used car:

1. Cars depreciate quickly from the ocean salt and your new car is likely to take on an old patina soon anyway.

2. An older, less attractive car is less appetizing to thieves and is less likely to be broken into or stolen, common problems on these islands.

3. People leaving the islands sometimes don't want to take their cars with them, so used car bargains abound.

4. Life is laid back here. You don't need to impress anyone with a fancy car.

difference, since autos usually must be shipped to dealers anyway; others say their markup from the MSRP (manufacturer's suggested retail price) differs only from mainland dealers by the cost of freight to ship cars to Hawai'i, $300 to $600. And they quickly point out that if you bought a car there and shipped it yourself, the freight cost would be higher. (Shipping an auto from California, Washington state or Oregon costs approximately $850. See the chapter: Moving, page 270)

Are autos less expensive on busy O'ahu than on the neighbor islands? Yes. Honolulu dealerships are larger, sell more autos, and their overhead is therefore spread over more sales. If you live on a neighbor island and buy a car on O'ahu, expect to pay about $175 to ship the car inter-island. Young Brothers Shipping is the only inter-island carrier. While calculating the price of your new car, remember to include your flight cost to and from Honolulu if you live on a neighbor island (about $100 round-trip air fare via Hawaiian Air or Aloha Airlines).

In truth, most of the car dealerships on all islands are owned by the same few owners, so it's hard to judge just who you are dealing with. However, dealers will negotiate their prices with savvy buyers, several Honolulu auto salesmen say. "The dealer may not if you are looking at a real popular car, in great demand, and he doesn't have enough of them. But for other cars, we negotiate," commented one of the salesmen.

➤ **TIP: Get quotes from O'ahu in writing.** If you call O'ahu from a neighbor island to inquire about car costs, you are sure to be quoted a very low price, said one neighbor island salesman. But be sure to get that quote in writing before you travel to O'ahu to buy the car, he advised, or you may find that particular car sold when you arrive at the dealership.

➤ **TIP: You don't have to travel to O'ahu to buy your auto.** If you know exactly what you want, the transaction can be completed via phone, fax, and mail. The dealer will arrange for the car to be shipped to your island.

➤ **TIP: Negotiate inter-island shipping.** Two O'ahu auto salesmen who prefer to remain anonymous offered this tip: Most O'ahu auto dealers will pay the inter-island freight cost as part of price negotiations.

➤ **TIP: Shop with information in hand**. The best way to buy an auto here is the same as on the mainland: refer to consumer books and magazines or the Internet for suggested prices and markups. Visit various dealerships with information in hand and try to negotiate a price. "Intellichoice" is one of many Internet sites that contain useful auto buying information.

Auto insurance

Hawai'i's automobile insurance rates are the second highest in the nation (New Jersey's are higher) and have long been the topic of heated debate among both legislators and constituents. The average insurance rate on the islands, two agents confirmed, is about $600 every six months — or $1,200 a year. That can be as much as twice what you are paying now, depending on where you live. Why so high? It's easy to blame no-fault insurance laws but Hawai'i set a record in 1997 for the highest profits on auto insurance in any state during this decade, and takes the number one spot in the nation for overall auto insurance profitability. The figures came from the Auto Insurance Report, a California-based auto insurance industry publication.

But agents insist there's more to the story. Insurance is also costly because these islands have one of the highest auto accident rates in the nation. And we also have very high medical and litigation costs.

Big earners, big debts

You might think Mike Haxton, president and chief executive officer of the non-profit Hawai'i Credit Counseling Service, meets mostly deadbeats. Haxton's clients are referred by banks and lenders including the U.S. Department of Housing and Urban Development and the Department of Hawaiian Homelands.

Haxton is busy. About 30 percent of Hawai'i's almost 1,200,000 residents cannot meet their financial obligations. That's double the 15 to 18 percent in the rest of the nation.

And his clients run the gamut. "From attorneys and surgeons to people who live on the beach," he says. After all, the more money you earn, the more credit you are eligible for... and the more debts you can accumulate.

Highly paid professionals — doctors, attorneys, engineers — who move to Hawai'i from the mainland get into financial trouble, Haxton says, because they are accustomed to having and spending money without worrying about it.

He offers a scenario: An executive family has been living in high style on the mainland and is transferred to Hawai'i.

"In California, they have a home, real estate, and maybe they have not been able to sell, so they have tenants. But the tenants do not pay enough to meet the mortgage, so several hundreds of dollars have to come out of pocket."

The family moves here and begins to live in the style to which they are accustomed.

"They usually get into a $2,000 or $3,000 (per month) rental house, upper-middle class," Haxton says. "And suddenly there are all these bills. Now what used to be a fabulous income isn't; now they find themselves short."

Maybe one spouse was able to stay home with the children. Now both spouses must work, so ego comes into play, too.

"It's a kind of humility/reality check," Haxton says. "And, believe me, it hits people at all economic levels."

Auto insurance rates vary, not only from state to state, but also from county to county, says Walter Von, an agent with Allstate Insurance in Honolulu. For example, at the time of our interview, six months of minimum coverage insurance on a 1990 Honda Civic would cost $1,091 in Waikīkī; $1,031 on Maui, Lāna'i and Moloka'i; $1,087 on the Big Island; and only $770 on Kaua'i. Von says several factors determine rates, including miles of roads on each island, the number of claims previously filed and individual driving records.

At this writing, the state legislature and government leaders are seeking solutions to high auto insurance costs. Recent reform is touted as cutting costs by about 10 percent, but that varies.[2]

Rush hour in downtown Honolulu.

Matt Thayer

TRANSPORTATION

Gasoline

Gasoline, like most products, is imported. Gasoline refiners and dealers are reluctant to compare costs, but reasonable estimates would be about 30 to 35 percent more on O'ahu than the Mainland and another 10 percent additional on neighbor islands.

The islands are too young to have natural deposits of crude oil, so Hawai'i is 90 percent dependent upon imported oil to provide its energy, more than any other state. On the mainland, many refineries are connected to their crude sources by underground pipelines, but in Hawai'i all crude oil and refined products must be imported by tanker.

Hawai'i has two main oil refiners, BHP Hawai'i and Chevron USA. Gasoline products are manufactured and stored on O'ahu, then transported

A van, for free

Imagine getting a free van just for picking up a few people on your way to work every day and taking them back home at night. In a program aimed at cutting the number of autos using Hawai'i's busy highways, Vanpool Hawai'i offers drivers full-time use of new Ford Windstars, Dodge Caravans and Chevrolet Astros, among other vans.

The program works like this: Several commuters agree to travel together, choose a driver and share parking and gasoline costs. Vanpool supplies the van and collects from $150 to $300 a month from the group. Riders and driver share the cost — the more people who ride, the less the cost — and the driver can also drive the van for personal use. Vans carry seven to fifteen passengers.

The program is run by a private business, VPSI, Inc. in Troy, Michigan, and is federally subsidized with tax dollars, according to Teresa Whitfield, account executive. O'ahu has over 100 Vanpool vehicles on its roads; the Big Island, 18; Lāna'i, 5 and Maui, 2. Call **(808) 596-8267**

➤ **TIP: Ask Vanpool to give you** the names of two or three drivers who have been operating a pool for at least six months. Ask the drivers for any suggestions they may have to make your group function more smoothly and ask how they handled problems like commuters who show up late or are delinquent paying. That way, you can structure your group to avoid problems.

via barge to outer islands. Stafford Kiguchi of BHP cites another reason for our high gasoline costs: we have fewer roads and limited opportunity for travel, so fixed costs (such as stations, pumps, employees) must be spread over fewer actual gallons of gasoline sold.

➤ TIP: **Avoid gas-guzzling traffic jams** at peak travel hours on O'ahu, Maui and Kaua'i. Ask your boss to cooperate. Can you travel to work an hour earlier or later to miss the rush?

➤ TIP: **Try to arrange your life** to avoid traveling long distances, for example, by living in the town in which you work, or by working from home. Bicycles and motorbikes are common on all outer islands. So is walking, although that's not always practical — distances can be long, even on small islands.

Shopping

If you are one of those people for whom shopping is a relaxing hobby, think twice about moving to an outer island with just one or two department stores, a couple of discount stores and numerous tourist boutiques carrying bathing suits. It's not difficult to find the clothes or items you need; it's a matter of not being able to shop as often as you might like.

Residents of all islands quickly learn a little rule: if you see something you want, buy it now; it could be sold out by the time you make up your mind and waiting for more to arrive by barge may be futile.

Clothing

Hawai'i's lifestyle is very casual, which keeps clothing costs down. For nearly all but the most elite professions, slacks and good-quality "aloha" shirts suffice for men. Women's clothing tends to be simple and colorful, in cool fabrics like washable rayons and cottons. Unfortunately, *mu'umu'u*, the traditional loose dress, is seen less frequently, even on Aloha Fridays when shop and office workers are encouraged to dress "island style."

Most resorts and hotels include boutiques geared to tourists, and their markup is high. Residents visit such boutiques only during annual sales. Each of the major outer islands has at least one large shopping center that caters to residents' more modest needs. For many years, **Liberty House** was the only upscale department store offering popular designer items. (Liberty House is a subsidiary of Amfac, one of Hawai'i's original Big Five companies.) With stores on all four major islands, it has kept prices at national levels for most name brands and has several sales during the year that rival any on the mainland.

Sears Roebuck and Co. also has stores on all major islands, although its Kaua'i store does not offer clothing. **JCPenney Co.** has stores on Maui, O'ahu and the Hilo side of the Big Island, but not on Kauai.

Honolulu shopping

For the cost of a *kama'āina* airfare (about $100 round trip), outer islanders can fly to shopping heaven. Honolulu's Ala Moana Center is one of the largest shopping malls in the world. It includes several American department stores and an interesting Japanese department store, Shirokiya. Ala Moana also has almost every mainland chain store — The Gap, Laura Ashley, Ann Klein, Banana Republic, etc — plus some upper-end boutiques such as Chanel and Gucci, and a sprinkling of touristy island boutiques and specialty stores.

O'ahu also has discount and outlet shopping. Waikele Center in western O'ahu offers 20 to 50 percent discounts in a wide variety of outlet stores including Saks' "Off Fifth" Avenue.

Within the past few years, discounters like WalMart and Kmart have established O'ahu and neighbor island stores, promising to sell at mainland prices. When Kmart opened near downtown Honolulu a few years ago, eager shoppers created traffic jams on busy Nimitz Highway.

Sam's Club (O'ahu) and Price Costco (O'ahu, Maui, the Big Island) shopping clubs, featuring everything from cauliflowers to computers, also debuted to big crowds and thousands of memberships. Here, as on the mainland, the arrival of large chains and wholesalers has had a devastating effect on some small businesses, but they have also cut living costs.

Furnishings

Furniture in most households is simple and easy to clean. Light colors are popular, but not always practical. The islands' famous red dirt makes it difficult to keep upholstered furniture and carpeting fresh. For the same reason, fewer knickknacks and small collectibles are seen in the average home. Much furniture is traded via household and garage sales or used furniture stores. There is a preponderance of inexpensive boxed furniture such as that sold by Kmart and WalMart.

Upscale furniture on the neighbor islands is usually purchased through interior decorators, although two or three small furniture stores operate on Maui, the Big Island and Kaua'i. People who are serious about furnishing their homes usually travel to Honolulu to shop or hire an interior decorator.

➤ **TIP: Many Honolulu stores will pack and deliver large items** — without cost — to the Honolulu wharfs to be carried interisland by Young Brothers. (A large couch costs about $50 to ship from Honolulu to Kaua'i.)

➤ **TIP: Consider thrift stores and consignment shops** instead of high priced retail stores. These shops, numerous on the islands, include interesting furniture and clothing from all over the world at big savings.

Keeping in touch

"I spend $2,000 to $4,000 a year on travel," says a successful O'ahu business-woman in her forties. "I either visit my family on the mainland or help them come here. This is money that should be going into a retirement fund. But I figure, what the heck, you only live once and family is important to me."

When you are calculating expenses, be sure to add the cost of keeping in touch. If you can afford it, you'll probably travel often to see mainland friends and relatives and to assuage "rock fever" — a confined feeling some people experience from living on a small island.

➤ **TIP: Track airline costs.** Since flights to the east coast of the U.S. can range from a few hundred dollars to well over a thousand, depending on time of year and "specials," it is beneficial to keep tabs on rates. Ask a friendly travel agent to keep you advised of airline specials. Or search the Internet for travel bargains. Try **www.ttinet.com**.

➤ **TIP: Book flights for the Christmas** holidays at least three months in advance for best rates.

➤ **TIP: Island business people** used to swear by their toll free phone numbers; now everyone loves computer e-mail, the least expensive and most convenient way to stay in touch with other parts of the world. E-mail is ideal for islanders who are five or six hours behind mainland time. Enjoy unlimited access time for about a $160 annual Internet fee.

➤ **TIP: Long distance phone rates vary widely.** Since phone companies rarely volunteer their lowest rates, you'll need to watch advertisements. And don't just quit your current phone company to switch to another; discuss your rate with a company sales representative. Often your current long distance provider will try to meet a competitor's rates. That saves the inconvenience of switching accounts.

➤ **TIP: Watch your phone bills carefully**. Once you've switched to the least expensive long distance provider, make sure your bill is calculated at the rate you expect. Inter-office miscommunications can cost you big bucks.

Lana's story: You can afford paradise

Lana Stuart was in her carefree early 20s when she left New Zealand and took a job on a freighter to see the world. She had already visited parts of the United States and Canada when a friend suggested she could support herself picking flowers in Hana, a remote tropical village on the western tip of Maui.

She packed a hammock and a hammer and a tarp in her knapsack and used her last few dollars to fly 3,000 miles to Maui. Tiny, quaint, rural and rainforest green, Hana was everything Lana had imagined. She hung her hammock between two palm trees near a black sand beach and nailed up the tarp as a roof.

"I lived in my little hammock for a week," Lana beams. "And I ate bananas and liliko'i (a seedy, delicate-tasting fruit that grows wild). It was over Christmas time and there was a storm, but I stayed perfectly dry. It was gorgeous."

Lana picked flowers at a flower farm; then a friend told her that a room came with a job at the Hotel Hana Maui, the only large resort on that part of the island. By then, Lana had no clothes worthy of wearing to an interview so she stopped at a little church to meditate about how to solve her problem. She noticed a lovely, lacy altar cloth and decided that God would not mind loaning it to her. She wrapped it around herself as a pareo or sarong and wore it to the interview. She was hired, supplied with housing and given a $500 advance for clothing.

After a few years, Lana began driving 50 miles for pottery lessons. She supported herself selling glazed platters, cups and bowls to tourists at craft fairs. Eventually, she opened her own small gift shop in Hana.

Hundreds of people leave Hawai'i each year, decrying its high costs. But Lana insists you can live your paradise dream on these islands. She lives in a cottage near the ocean for which she pays $450 a month.

"I have the same bills as anyone else. Car, utilities, car insurance, health insurance. But you survive here if you live simply," she says. "You don't need that much here because we live in abundance. Outside of our precious material home is a world of the most beautiful and fulfilling life."

G Brad Lewis

The Self-Employed,

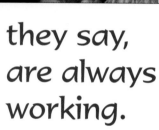

Toni Polancy

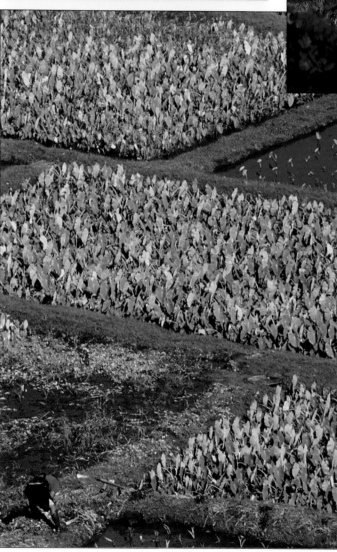

Matt Thayer

they say, are always working.

A young man collects shells for jewelry early one Honolulu morning. He sells them at the weekly swap meets at Aloha Stadium. A woman fashions souvenirs from natural materials at Dolly's Hale (house) at Maunaloa, Moloka'i. A taro farmer bends to his task on the Keane peninsula, Maui.

Homes:
You can pay a little or a lot... or a lot more

Kailua-Kona, Big Island $3,330,000

Princeville, Kaua'i $335,000

Kīhei, Maui $327,500

Portlock, O'ahu $5,500,000

Hawai'i Kai, O'ahu $345,000

Photos courtesy of *Homes & Land* magazines, O'ahu, Maui, The Big Island and Kaua'i.

Kōloa, Kaua'i $189,000

Kīhei, Maui $197,000

Napili, Maui $3,995,000

Kailua-Kona, Big Island $3,330,000

Na'alehu, Big Island $38,000
No Electricity and no city water

Some jobs

Matt Thayer0

need workers

Steve Brinkman

Matt Thayer

...more than others. A good bartender can usually find employment, at least part time. Tour boat workers, especially those speaking German or Japanese, should be able to secure work. Positions in the Honolulu police force are usually available.

Taxes: Coming down, slowly

While you are lolling in one of Hawai'i's many beach parks, admiring Honolulu's carefully cared-for government buildings, driving O'ahu's breathtaking Pali Highway, ask yourself this: How much is all this worth to you?

According to the Tax Foundation of Hawai'i, in 1998 the average Hawai'i family paid out about 42 percent of its income in state and federal taxes. Those who earned $50,000 had on the average only $29,000 to spend on necessities like food, shelter and transportation. In fact, in 1998, Hawai'i had the fourth highest state taxes and fees in the nation, behind Alaska ($5,964); Washington, D.C. ($4,824) and New York ($4,310.) The state Legislature in 1998 approved personal income tax cuts that will kick in during the next few years and should supply some relief. The

How much are you willing to pay for paradise?

Legislature steered clear of a rise in the state's most controversial and costly levy: the excise tax.

The excise tax

A four percent excise, collected on virtually every purchase made by the state's nearly 1.2 million residents and nearly 7 million annual visitors, provides the elephant's share of state general fund revenues — about 44 percent. Designed in part to make sure tourists help pay for parks and roads, the tax eats relentlessly at the pocketbooks of residents who must purchase food, services and medical supplies.

It is not a sales tax; it is an excise tax assessed over and over again along the production and wholesale chain (sometimes at a lower .04 percent at the manufacturing stage) and, some economists maintain, it equals a 16 percent actual sales tax.

The excise tax is regressive, says Lowell L. Kalapa, president of the Tax Foundation of Hawai'i, because it hits hardest at those earning the least. The poor spend a larger share of their money on taxed necessities like food and rent. Even nursing homes pay the excise tax, tacking it on to elderly clients' bills. The wealthy spend less of their income on necessities, as little as 30 percent, often investing or saving the rest.

In 1998, amid constituent protests, the state Legislature declined to raise the excise tax, as recommended by a governor-appointed Task Force on Economic Development.

Real estate taxes

The counties (islands) administer and collect real estate taxes. Property is assessed at 100 percent of its "fair market value." Hawai'i has unusually low real estate taxes, among the lowest in the nation, and people who reside in their homes are also entitled to homeowner's exemptions. Exemptions vary by county, from $40,000 to $50,000. For example, if your house is assessed at $300,000, you would be taxed on only $260,000. As the you grow older, the exemption increases, in most counties, peaking at $100,000 or $120,000 (Honolulu) when you reach the age of 70.

State income tax

A very high state income tax has for years provided about 33 percent of the state general fund revenues. Hawai'i income tax is collected at a graduating rate and, until 1999, peaks at 10 percent for individuals earning more than $20,500 per year and couples earning more than $41,000.

In 1998, the Legislature approved state personal income tax cuts of about 25 percent to take effect over four years beginning in 1999. That was expected to eventually add $1,893 to a family of four's annual paycheck. Tax in the top brackets will be assessed at 8.75 percent in 1999 and 2000, dropping to 8.5 percent in 2001 and to 8.25 percent in 2002. The top income bracket for joint returns and "head of household" will kick in when income reaches $80,000 and $60,000 respectively. Under the tax revision, payers will not be assessed the highest rate.

Tourist taxes

Hawai'i has a couple of extra levies designed to cash in on the tourist business. The nearly 7 million visitors pay $2 each day for every car they rent; they also pay 6 percent (hiked to 7.25 percent as of 1999) on every room they rent.

Where does it go?

The state general treasury operating budget is $2.99 billion a year. Where does all that money go?

About $700 million goes to teach Hawai'i's children, but the Department of Education suffered severe cuts in the 1998 budget, including funds for computers and instructional materials.

About $55 million is spent on tourism promotion. The 1998 increase in hotel room tax will go directly to promotional spending, deemed extremely important to Hawai'i's future. By 2010 the tourism industry is expected to account for 1 in every 2.6 jobs in this state ; up from 1 in 3.2 today.

Hawai'i also supports a high, but not unusually high, number of public employees for its population size. Legislators have made attempts in recent years to cut costs and employees, but Hawai'i's strong labor unions fight privatization and job cutbacks that could save money.

➤ **TIP**: **Newcomers are often** the most vocal and active reformers on these islands. And their efforts often bear fruit. Hawai'i's small resident (voter) base means legislators are very sensitive to the desires of their constituents. Here, it pays to let your government representative know exactly what you think. Take an active role in fixing Hawai'i's tax situation. Also consider supporting the Tax Foundation of Hawai'i, a non-profit, non-government watchdog.

The shadowy halls of government, Honolulu

Matt Thayer

Maui commercial artist Beth Marcil camps out with a portable computer.

ka hana

work

Are you

willing to

change

occupations?

He's successful

In some places in the world, a college graduate who has been a bellhop for over 20 years might consider himself a failure. Not in Hawai'i. Not Daryl Davis.

Daryl, polished, polite and professional, beams as he pushes a brass luggage trolley through the lobby of the Renaissance Wailea Beach Resort in Maui.

"The rest of the world might think of this as a low-paying job," Daryl, 51, says. "But things are different here. Here it doesn't matter what you do. It's who you are and what you contribute to society, to your community."

To survive in Hawai'i's limited job market, you have to be flexible, and Daryl has certainly been that. A Vietnam veteran raised on the islands, he taught school in California for a while, then returned to Honolulu in 1974. No teaching positions were available, so he took a job as a parking lot attendant at a Waikīkī hotel.

A year later, he moved to Maui and became swimming pool manager at a resort, then a bellhop. It was supposed to be a temporary job, but Daryl quickly learned, " I could make as much as a bell-hop for 40 hours as I could working as a teacher for 100 hours." That was 20 years ago; now he's looking toward retirement, planning to take advantage of perks like discounted rooms at his hotel chain's resorts around the world.

In his spare time, Daryl has had a few other jobs. He started two taxi cab companies, a jeep rental company, a wedding service and a bicycle tour company. He sold all of the businesses, which still function. Meanwhile, a friend helped him build several homes which he rents out.

Daryl illustrates an important point echoed by job specialists interviewed for this book: to support yourself in Hawai'i you must be flexible and open-minded, ready to accept a job that pays less than you are earning now or willing to accept a position in a totally different field. You must be ready to start at the bottom and work up, clever enough to find an additional source of income, or able to live happily with the fact that you may never progress financially.

Working

Coming to the islands? Put your master's degree away in a drawer, don an apron or snorkel gear and head for the nearest hotel, upper-crust restaurant, resort or tour boat.

Hawai'i's is a tourist and service economy — it's becoming more so every day. That's where the money and jobs are now and, economists say, in the future. Positions other than in tourism are scarce on these islands, and even those jobs can be difficult to secure during the spring and summer months when the number of visitors dwindles.

A study in the American City Business Journal says the Hawai'i job count fell 2.3 percent to 530,600 during the mid 1990s, while the nation expanded its employment base by 11.8 percent.

White-collar positions

A recent federal report says Hawai'i professionals earn up to 30 percent less than mainland counterparts.

"We get a lot of calls from the mainland," says Hank Sotelo, a recruiter at Dunhill Search of Hawai'i. "I'm very truthful. First of all, I tell them if there is an equally experienced or talented person here on the islands, preference will be given to him. Don't think an employer is going to pay your way out here."

> **"Don't think an employer is going to pay your way out here."**
>
> —Hank Sotelo,
> O'ahu job recruiter

The high turnover of new residents here is partially responsible for that, he says. Many recruits stay just a year or two and contract "rock fever" — grow tired of living on a small island — and leave their jobs at the time they are becoming most valuable to their employer.

At HR Pacific, another Honolulu recruiting firm that specializes in executive help, Nita Williams, co-owner, put it even more forcefully: "Tell them not to come for years. The job opportunities are extremely limited. We have too many people here and there are not enough jobs for them all."

Williams advises would-be residents, "Come here and enjoy it on holiday, and if you really want to look at Hawai'i from an employment standpoint, consider not only the (lower) pay but the increased cost of housing versus the size of the house."

Are any white-collar jobs outside the tourist industry available on the islands now or in the near future?

At the time of our interviews, Sotelo had a need for a chemical engineer at an oil refinery. Both Sotelo and Williams mentioned a need for computer software programmers, but stressed they must be very experienced with specific backgrounds to exactly fit clients' needs.

Jobs 'tight'

A state labor specialist, asked where the jobs are in Hawai'i, responded emphatically, "They ain't nowhere!

"The economic situation is such that jobs are really tight here. Look at the newspaper ads. The travel industry requires you to speak Japanese. Construction is dead," she lamented.

"People who move here just up and move. They come with very little resources; they don't do research. They (come to see us) and are very upset. You try to tell them how hard it is but they don't believe you. They say, 'Well, you're living here!' And we say yes, but we are from here. We have families here. It's easier."

She had a message for people who read this book: "Tell people that jobs pay less here. Also they should know that in some professions requirements are high. For example, for a social worker we recruit with master's degree.

"And truck drivers are appalled when they learn we have strict licensing requirements and it costs over $100 to get a license. Even (office) clerks must know computers, plus type 50 to 60 words per minute and know Lotus software. And their pay is only $1,200 a month. It's not a question of where the jobs are; it's a question of what you are willing to settle for."

Multiple jobs

The cost of hiring employees is very high in Hawai'i. For example, if you work 20 hours or more for more than four consecutive weeks, your employer

Maybe we should all work 'ukupau'

Ukupau philosophy is an interesting concept, popular on these islands, but not unique to them. *Ukupau* is a Hawaiian word meaning "finished pay." An *ukupau* system allows workers to complete the task assigned for that day and go home — no matter how short or long it takes.

According to *A Newcomer's Guide to Hawaii:* The *ukupau* attitude can be traced back to ancient Hawai'i when clock time did not exist, only work to be performed. Later, some plantations allowed workers to do an expected amount of work no matter how long or short it took. *Ukupau* also carried connotations of pitching in, working together to accomplish something that needs doing."

Today, *ukupau* is just about *pau*... gone, although a few offices and delivery services still use the concept; so do refuse collectors in Hawai'i and some mainland cities and towns. Hawai'i's refuse collectors finish their day in about three or four hours, a county personnel manager says.

Ukupau may be almost *pau*, but the attitude that spurred it remains. On these islands, where an ocean and warm breezes beckon, work is secondary to play.

must provide health insurance, according to state labor laws. The employer may withhold 1.5 percent of your gross monthly wages to help pay for that insurance.

Altogether, health insurance, worker's compensation and employer's share of social security, as well as other costs, add as much as 45 percent to the cost of hiring an employee. For that reason, many jobs in Hawai'i tend to be part time and "occasional." And many people hold two or three such jobs to earn a living.

Redefine priorities

Many people from other parts of the world have been taught to define their worth by their professions — but the islands have a limited business base, almost no industry, and a small population that needs only so many doctors, attorneys, scientists, journalists, bankers, CEOs. Many newcomers complain that top spots in those professions go to people who have lived here for a long time and have connections in the islands.

"You can work very hard to get ahead here," says one woman executive, "and you will bump your head on that glass ceiling whether you are a man or

Average Pay Rates
for selected jobs (in dollars)

Annual Rates	1992	1997
Clerk, entry level	15,588	18,833
Cashier	20,592	25,503
Secretary	24,072	28,020
Switchboard operator	19,596	24,503
Bookkeeper, full-charge	24,660	32,137
Engineering drafting technician	30,924	35,298
Hospital attendant	19,800	N/A
Staff nurse	44,280	N/A
Hourly Rates		
Housekeeper	8.94	11.07
Cook, general	10.92	13.24
Wait help	5.07	6.03
Laborer, light	8.48	9.38
Carpenter, maintenance	14.06	16.01
Electrician, maintenance	15.58	19.73
Automotive mechanic	13.56	16.04
Truck driver (trailer)	10.59	13.65

Source: The Hawai'i Employers Council, Pay Rates in Hawai'i

Industrial earnings
hourly average (in dollars)

Hourly Earnings	1991	1996
Construction	21.14	25.72
Manufacturing	11.39	12.79
Food and kindred products	9.66	11.39
Communications and utilities	16.58	20.69
Trade	9.28	9.75
Wholesale trade	10.67	12.03
Retail trade	8.70	9.24
Eating, drinking places	N/A	7.31
Banking and credit agencies	9.65	10.48
Hotels	9.97	12.10

Source: Hawa'i State Data Book 1996 quoting Hawai'i State Department of Labor and Industrial Relations, Labor Force Data Book and Internet site http://www.hawaii.gov/workforce.

a woman. There just isn't room in the middle, let alone at the top, and you're lucky to have a job in some of these professions at all.

"So pretty soon you say, Okay, why bother? I'm not going any further and I'm going to either move back home or stay here and relax and enjoy life here like it is. Change my priorities. Learn to live with less. Share a home with one or two people."

If working in these islands requires a change in the way you view your life — well, what's wrong with that? Where is it written that a job must be repetitive, dirty, or unpleasant? Why not work taking tourists on sunset cruises from Honolulu Harbor? Or scuba diving near Molokini islet? Or riding bicycles down Haleakalā Mountain? Or steering a rubber raft into Kaua'i's cliff-side caves?

Tourism wages

Although wages for most occupations are the same or lower than on the mainland, wages in the tourist industry are higher. For example a waiter, including tips, can earn as much as a middle manager in some white-collar positions. *Honolulu* magazine quotes $70,000 for a "career" waiter.[2] But be warned: working up to a top wait position in an upscale restaurant can be like moving up the hierarchy of a law firm — seniority counts. Newcomers may be given fewer working hours or shifts that net less tips.

Another reason service people earn more here: many belong to unions — in fact, 30 percent of all Hawai'i workers belong to unions — which wield a lot of power. Consider also that some people under-report their earnings to avoid taxes — and the remuneration for resort jobs can be substantial.

Turnover: 25%

"There's a huge wash of employees [in the resort industry], a big turnover," says Sandy Marr, employment coordinator at Turtle Bay Hilton Hotel on O'ahu's North Shore. "People, especially young people, come in and are brand new on the island. They come out here thinking they can live on $100 a week. And we find that after about a month they leave, after they find out the costs here."

Turtle Bay's annual employee turnover is 25 percent, about average for positions in the tourist industry. The food and beverage department has the highest turnover, Marr says. "We feel like we're a winner if we can keep (an

Retail Employment
annual average (in dollars)

Retail Trade	No. of establish-ments	Average employ-ment	Total wages ($1,000)	Average wage
Total	7,345	114,248	1,898,468	16,617
Hardware stores	57	1,037	31,679	20,910
Retail nurseries and garden stores	22	147	2,565	17,488
Department stores	53	11,069	177,229	16,012
Misc. general merchandise stores	75	682	10,898	15,970
Grocery stores	380	11,427	217,942	19,072
Meat and fish markets	52	349	5,552	15,924
Candy, nut, and confectionery stores	39	327	3,308	10,127
Retail bakeries	125	1,205	16,283	13,511
Misc. food stores	74	628	8,285	13,187
New and used car dealers	84	3,784	133,903	35,387
Used car dealers	20	128	3,896	30,415
Auto and home supply stores	178	1,599	38,182	23,874
Gasoline service stations	294	3,353	52,757	15,735
Motorcycle dealers	18	171	4,122	24,154
Men's and boys' clothing stores	71	961	13,020	13,543
Women's clothing stores	258	2,293	35,684	15,565
Women's accessory & specialty stores	91	773	17,528	22,682
Children's and infants' wear stores	30	209	2,127	10,177
Family clothing stores	162	2,167	33,780	15,588
Shoe stores	113	1,309	25,219	19,261
Misc. apparel and accessory stores	183	1,274	20,199	15,852
Furniture stores	96	740	20,451	27,627
Floorcovering stores	33	264	7,199	27,295
Drapery and upholstery stores	12	36	807	22,373
Misc. homefurnishing stores	54	371	6,003	16,166
Household appliance stores	56	266	5,922	22,293
Radio, TV and electronic stores	82	601	12,157	20,234
Computer and software stores	56	488	11,765	24,117
Record and prerecorded tape stores	42	584	6,701	11,468
Musical instrument stores	14	112	2,310	20,621
Eating and drinking places	2,525	46,914	602,570	12,844
Drug stores and proprietary stores	171	3,706	94,021	25,370
Used merchandise stores	51	223	3,280	14,724
Sporting goods and bicycle shops	167	1,432	22,336	15,593
Book stores	63	658	9,115	13,851
Stationery stores	22	302	6,189	20,475
Jewelry stores	318	2,192	51,587	23,539

Source: Hawai'i State Data Book 1996.

For updated statistics see http://www.hawaii.gov/dbedt/index.html

employee) six months to a year. We do hire military wives, so they tend to stay two years or less," she adds.

Surf's up; attendance's down

Turtle Bay, like many hotels, restaurants and resorts, has a large pool of "casual employees" who fill in for absentee workers. "We have a saying, 'Surf's up; attendance is down'," Marr says. "A lot of people come here to play."

"Casual employees" are on-call to fill in. They include people who don't expect to work regularly, but may be available as needed. "They can't make a living as casual employees, but they are invaluable to the hotel," Marr says.

A resort concierge says his company is beginning to seek middle-aged and retired people instead of relying on youthful waiters and waitresses. "Older people are more dependable. They don't take off when the surf is up," he says. "Also, they don't have to rely entirely on their wages. They don't mind being on-call or working just a few hours a day."

Jim, in his late 30s, is on-call as a waiter in addition to having a full-time day profession. "This is a real play environment," he says. "People just don't apply themselves. It's not a super environment for work, for competition that drives people.

"You can look at it two ways," Jim reflects. "You can say, 'Well, okay we live for other things than work. To enjoy the place; that's why we're here.' And on one hand, that's an advantage for people who are serious about their work. It's easier to get ahead because you are taking the job seriously and those around you aren't."

➤ **TIP: Among the most desirable positions** at resorts are some you might not think of: in the property operations department. Charged with keeping the mechanics of the hotel running smoothly, the operations department includes many long-term employees. To be hired, they must be highly skilled in at least two "specialty trades" such as electricity and plumbing, Marr says. The job pays over $16 an hour plus benefits, as opposed to $10 for housekeeping and dishwashing and $12 for front desk help.

Jobs with a future

selected fast-growing Hawai'i occupations to the year 2005

Occupation	EMPLOYMENT		CHANGE IN EMPLOYMENT	
	1994	2005	Number	%
Ushers, lobby attendants, ticket takers	860	1,150	290	33.7
Physical therapists	340	440	100	29.4
Medical secretaries	630	810	180	28.6
Radiology technologists	350	450	100	28.6
Dental hygienists	530	680	150	28.3
Medical assistants	1,160	1,480	320	27.6
Dentists	510	650	140	27.5
Dental assistants	1,210	1,540	330	27.3
Physicians	1,610	2,030	420	26.1
Legal secretaries	1,290	1,620	330	25.6
Respiratory therapists	330	410	80	24.2
Food servers	1,500	1,860	360	24.0
Registered nurses	7,530	9,300	1,770	23.5
Home health aides	570	700	130	22.8
Hotel desk clerks	1,760	2,160	400	22.7
Medical/clinical lab techs	750	920	170	22.7
Paralegals	670	820	150	22.4
Maids & house cleaners	9,190	11,240	2,050	22.3
Nursing aides & orderlies	3,500	4,270	770	22.0
Counter & rental clerks	2,290	2,790	500	21.8
Licensed practical nurses	1,840	2,240	400	21.7
Travel agents	1,150	1,390	250	21.7
Baggage porters, bellhops	1,210	1,470	260	21.5
Housekeeper supervisors institutional	940	1,140	200	21.3
Laundry, dry cleaning	1,320	1,600	280	21.2
Aircraft pilots, flight engineers	1,010	1,220	210	20.8
Travel clerks	1,120	1,350	230	20.5
Pharmacists	490	590	100	20.4
Transportation agents	1,290	1,550	260	20.2
Flight attendants	2,240	1,690	450	20.1
Other health service workers	50	900	150	20.0
Lawyers	2,020	2,420	400	19.8
Receptionists, information clerks	4,780	5,720	940	19.7
Switchboard operators	1,130	1,350	220	19.6
Parking lot attendants	930	1,110	180	19.4
Food service &lodging managers	2,740	3,270	530	19.3
Dining room & bartender helpers	3,410	4,060	650	19.1
Cooks, restaurants	6,510	7,720	1,210	18.6

Employment figures were rounded to nearest ten. Includes only occupations with 300 or more employees in 1994. From Employment Outlook for Industries and Occupation, *Dept. of Labor and Industrial Relations*

Where the jobs are

Here are 15 occupations in search of workers. You may fit into one of them. Workers are recruited from elsewhere for a few of these positions: teachers, multi-lingual dive instructors, some nursing assignments.

Artists and craftspeople

Two things draw artists to Hawai'i: the natural beauty and the 6 to 7 million tourists who come each year, eager to take home reminders of their visit. Painters, sculptors, carvers and craftspeople ply their trades in home studios throughout the islands and peddle their products at a galaxy of galleries and shops, via Internet sites and at weekly arts and crafts shows. Some artists, like internationally known Christian Riese Lassen, own their own galleries. Maui is touted as the nation's second largest fine art market (behind New York City). But, be warned: only the best artists and craftsmen or those with exceptional marketing savvy make a substantial living. Others settle for a pleasant, pressure-free lifestyle or let their arts and crafts supplement income from other jobs.

Advertising

It has been said that Hawai'i has the largest collection of free curbside literature in the nation. Tourist-oriented brochures and publications overflow racks throughout the islands, most designed by graphic artists and written by copywriters, usually freelancers. In addition, Honolulu's many advertising agencies hire account executives. Nationwide, the advertising field has been flooded with newcomers in the last decade, and competition for these jobs is as stiff here as elsewhere. But a graphic artist with sophisticated technical skills — computer design and Internet skills or an artist who can follow an assignment through from design to printing — is ahead of the game. So are creative writers willing to do research. Pay is commensurate with ability and reputation.

Government, civil service

Government budget decreases mean civil service jobs have been cut in recent years, but cities, counties and state continuously recruit for many positions, especially in the police and fire departments. Highly unionized, Hawai'i's state, city and county pay poorly when the cost of living is taken into account, but benefits are substantial, including paid vacations, health care, sick leave and generous retirement plans. The 24-hour job lines below describe available civil service positions. Some applicants claim you must live on the islands for generations or "know somebody" to get hired in state or county positions, but persistence pays here. Some newcomers get these jobs too.

State 24-hour job line: **(808) 587-0977**

Honolulu City and County: 24-hour job information line: **(808) 523-4301**

Federal Job Information Center: **(808) 541-2791**

Police

Honolulu's city and county Department of Personnel accepts applications for metro police recruits on an ongoing basis. The road from application to uniform had a reputation of being long and grueling — less than half of the original applicants graduated from the six-month-long academy — but the process is being eased because the department can't keep cops. They move on to better paying jobs on the mainland. Recruits earn $2,481 per month; after one year, they can be promoted to metropolitan police officers at $2,679. They receive numerous benefits, including 13 paid holidays (14 in an election year), 21 vacation days and 21 days sick leave each year, a human resources clerk says. Unused sick leave can be converted to retirement credits.

Note: You must be a Hawai'i resident to apply for a police position. No length of time of residency is required, but you cannot live in another state and apply for a position.

For police recruit information: **(808) 529-3171**

On the Internet: **http://www.co.honolulu.hi.us/depts/per**

Grocery stores

About 40 to 50 people each month leave positions as grocery store cashiers, clerks, meat cutters and wrappers and delicatessen workers, and new workers take their place, says Pat Loo, president of the United Food & Commercial Workers Union, Local 480. The union represents workers on all islands in the state's largest markets: Foodland, Star, Safeway and Sack-N-Save. Compensation for service help averages $13.26 an hour; meat cutters make more. Several smaller chains and markets also tend to hire more frequently, but pay slightly less, Loo says. It may also be possible to transfer from the mainland to a job here, he adds.

United Food and Commercial Workers Union: **(808) 942-7778**

High tech industries

Hawai'i's hopes for job diversification hang on high tech industries such as telecommunications, advanced computer applications and multi-media production. Some of the employers in those fields say it is hard to keep talent in Hawai'i because jobs elsewhere pay more. Businesses tend to develop here, only to move away to locations where the cost of doing business is less. However, positions are available for highly skilled programmers, analysts and designers, recruiters say. The key word is "skilled" — recruits must match specific employer needs exactly. Some entry level jobs are also available. Try **http://www.mrtc.org/~hpd/hpdindep.htm**

Health care

Hawai'i ranks high in quality of health care. Despite entrenchment in the health care industry, many positions are available. At Kaiser Permanente, one of the state's largest providers, Gayle Condo, management assistant for employment and recruitment, says people are constantly being sought to fill a variety of positions: nurses, case managers, physicians' assistants, advanced care nurses and physical therapists. Entry level clerical positions are also usually available. At Straub Clinic & Hospital, Inc. a recorded job line recited a need for nurses aides, physical therapists, telecommunications operators, licensed practical nurses, medical assistants and systems analysts.

Kaiser Permanente personnel office on O'ahu: **(808) 539-5500**

Straub Clinic & Hospital, Inc. and other health care providers job line: **(808) 592-9675**

Nature Scott

Scott Hemenway, 30, came to Moloka'i in 1993, one of 50 new teachers. From upstate New York, he had never been to Hawai'i. Scott looked down from the island hopper at the majestic Maunaloa Mountains, at neatly planted fields of pineapple, groves of coffee trees, at the ocean surrounding it all like a sparkling blue blanket...and thought he was about to land in heaven.

With just under 7,000 population, Moloka'i is bucolic and quiet. There are no movie theaters. No bowling alleys. No fastfood places.

Kaunakakai, the island's only real town, barely four blocks long, looks like a setting for a cowboy movie — false-fronted buildings and cars that pull up perpendicular, like tethered horses. Most of the kids hang out at the commu-

Courtesy Scott Hemenway

nity pool and gym, a block away. Evenings the adults, old and young, gather at the Pau Hana Inn to dance and listen to guest artists, some of whom drop in from other islands. On the way home, it's tradition to line up in the alley behind Kanemitzu Bakery. Knock on the door and a friendly baker will serve up, by the slice, baked bread, warm from the oven, with cream cheese, honey, peanut butter, jelly. Then it's time to wrap up, to return home to small plantation houses set in clusters overlooking stunning views.

Weekends, there's an ocean to swim in, mountains to climb, fish to catch and deer to hunt. Moloka'i's deer are so tame they stop and stare at you, interrupting their graceful ballets in fields misty with early morning light.

Still, the alluring charm and peace tend to wear thin after a spell. Five years after he arrived, Scott is the only one of those 50 teachers still on Moloka'i. The rest left, most having gone back to a less costly life on the mainland, or to O'ahu or Maui, where life is more exciting.

Not Scott. Scott teaches eighth and ninth grade science at Moloka'i High. In his spare time he umpires little league and interscholastic baseball. On weekends, he conducts tours at the Nature Conservancy, where volunteers call him "Nature Scott."

Scott's mom once visited Moloka'i. She noted how happy Scott seemed and the night before she left she looked at him wistfully. "You're never coming home, are you?"

"No." Scott shook his head. "I'm staying. As long as they will have me."

Nurses

Terri Peterson, with Kahu Malama Nurses, Inc., a statewide medical recruiting firm, says jobs are available for nurses in certain specialties. At the time of our interview, the company was seeking critical care and emergency room nurses for Oʻahu. Permanent jobs are more scarce on the outer islands, but temporary nursing positions are usually available, she said.

Kahu Malama: **808-951-0111** or **1-800-553-0367** from neighbor islands

Photography

Hawaiʻi not only provides wonderful scenery for photographers — it also provides jobs. There are local, national and international markets for tropical photography, but also much competition. Commercial photographers are hired by resorts, magazines and ad agencies. Novice photographers usually shoot lūʻaus and weddings. The best photographers build portfolios of scenic, sports action and other photographs to sell worldwide.

Real estate sales

Real estate is one of the few professions where successful people can earn more here than on the mainland. "It's not a situation of who you know here, but what you know," says one leading broker. "Success is based on how hard you work, your aptitude for sales." You are in effect starting your own business, he points out, and the start-up costs are very low compared to most other businesses. But, if you are a newcomer, be warned: The hours are long. Hawaiʻi's real estate laws and requirements are complex. And you may be dealing with foreign investors, requiring special knowledge and skills.

Hawaiʻi Association of Realtors: **(808) 737-4000**

Maui Board of Realtors: **(808) 242-6431**

Hilo Board of Realtors: **(808) 935-0827**

Kona Board of Realtors: **(808) 329-4874**

Kauaʻi Board of Realtors: **(808) 245-4049**

Retail sales

Well-groomed, friendly people can usually find jobs in retail sales, including management and assistant management positions in boutiques, dress shops, gift shops and art galleries. The pay may be low (see charts) and hours part-time. Managers or salespeople who work on commission can usually earn more than those receiving hourly wages. Shops in tourist areas prefer clerks who can speak at least some Japanese. Art galleries and tourist activity booths throughout the islands also hire frequently; pay is usually based on commission.

Resort positions

Once it was relatively easy to pick up a job as a waiter or waitress, cook or busperson, maid or maintenance personnel most anywhere in Hawai'i. That's not necessarily true today. This is a tourist economy and the need for people to fill these jobs can vary greatly throughout the year. (Busiest seasons are from Christmas to the end of March and summer months when families with children travel.) Pay is slightly higher than on the mainland, however, and many positions include hospitalization and other benefits. A very few include such perks as reduced rent. (See the Lanai section of the Which Island chapter.)

Teaching

A high turnover of public high school and elementary teachers means positions are often available, especially in rural areas on outer islands. The average new teacher stays on the job two years, says Ray Hart, past president of the Hawai'i State Teachers Association on Maui. Only ten percent of Hawai'i's teachers have been in their jobs longer than ten years. There are fourteen steps on the salary scale negotiated by the Hawai'i State Teachers' Association. Wages range from $27,623 (for a person with a bachelor's degree and no experience) to a maximum of $54,147. Hawai'i ranks 22nd among the states in pay, a spokesperson for the Hawai'i State Teachers' Association said, but warned that ranking does not take into account the high cost of living here. At this writing, the state Department of Education was recruiting teachers for special education, secondary math, secondary science and industrial arts. Counselors and librarians were also needed. The job market for elementary teachers was very tight, a D.O.E. spokesman said. Teachers interested in working in this state can call the recruitment office toll free during Hawai'i business hours.

Department of Education job availability:

1-800-305-5104 (toll free) or **(808) 586-3420**

Or write, Personnel Management

Department of Education, Certificates Section

P.O. Box 2360,

Honolulu, HI 96804

Hawai'i State Teachers Association: **(808) 833-2711**

Tour operators, divers

Newspaper classified sections are dotted with jobs for dive instructors, tour van drivers and tour boat operators. Those we talked to reported earning $40,000 to $60,000 a year; most had full benefits since the work includes an element of risk. All seemed happy with their work, possibly because they are outdoors doing what they enjoy. One commented, "Some tourists can be a pain, but most are having a good time and so my job is like going to a party every day." Another said he appreciated the fact that his clients "change daily, so you are always dealing with new people. There's no baggage to deal with." Being multi-lingual is a major advantage — and often a requirement in this line of work — noted a dive instructor who minored in Japanese and German at college. He said he is constantly getting job offers. Most of these positions require certification or additional licensing.

Truck drivers, delivery persons, warehouse workers

Licensed commercial drivers are needed, a state job counselor says, but stresses that truck driving and warehouse jobs on an island are very different from those on the mainland. Short distances and small companies mean a driver must be willing to load and unload goods as well as drive; warehouse workers often must have a commercial driver's license. A job recruiter commented, "Drivers say to me, 'Well, I just want to drive' and I say, 'Where are you going to drive to? The island's only 50 miles wide!'" Most companies are so small they have only two or three trucks. Even sales representatives must sometimes drive trucks.

Job lines

These 24-hour pre-recorded phone lines give lists of available jobs.
- Health care: **(808) 592-9675**

  (Several Honolulu hospitals and health care-related businesses)
- State Dept. of Education: **1 (800) 305-5104** or **(808) 586-3420**
- Hawai'i state: **(808) 587-0977**
- Honolulu City and County: **(808) 523-4301**
- Federal Job Information Center: **(808) 541-2791**

Additional job information:

Attorneys: Cruise the Internet. Try http://www.aloha.net/~hlcvls

Doctors: The first time we called, a recruiter at LAM Associates, Honolulu, a medical recruitment firm, said, "We've just filled ten or twelve jobs and have nothing at the moment. I've got Guam, do you want Guam?" A few months later, a spokesperson said there was a need for short term doctors on all islands to fill in for physicians on vacations and attending training.

LAM: **(808) 947-9815**

Physician's Associates: **(808) 941-0530**

G. Brad Lewis

Waikīkī Beach: As long as they keep coming, all those tourists mean jobs. In addition to the obvious positions in hotels, restaurants, souvenir and apparel shops, add pleasure boat operators and water craft rentals.

B.Y.O.B.
(Bring Your Own Business)

There's one way to make sure you have a job on these islands: bring your own. For many reasons, Hawai'i blooms with opportunity. New businesses are started in Hawai'i almost daily, many by people bringing new ideas from other parts of the world, and many of those businesses succeed. Overall job counts in Hawai'i have fallen for the past few years, from a high of 591,300 in 1992 to 576,200 by the late 1990s, but the number of self-employed people has risen.

Choose your business and its location carefully, bring plenty of money, and plan to work very hard for several years.

The advantages

Entrepreneurs in Hawai'i have some unique advantages.

1. THE STATE IS AT LEAST TWO YEARS BEHIND the mainland in business trends — and on some islands that time lapse can be as much as four or five years or more. An entrepreneur has the opportunity to create a business today with the knowledge of yesterday. There is no excuse for saying, "If I'd only known then what I know now." Things that happened years ago, opportunities missed, are occurring here, now.

2. THE ISLANDS ARE STILL GROWING and developing. New towns are being established; old ones are increasing in size and changing character. Businesses are needed. A 31-year-old highly successful graphic designer insists he has a list of "at least 100 businesses I could go into right now, any one of which would succeed." (He declines to share the list.)

3. COMPETITION MAY BE RELAXED. The key to his own success, says the young artist, has been applying mainland concepts surprisingly rare on the islands: serious work and regular hours." A savvy person willing to put the time in will succeed here," he says. And several other business owners agreed.

4. HAWAI'I'S EXOTIC APPEAL — and the 7 million people from around the world who visit annually — provide special opportunities for small business people. For example, Hawai'i is probably one of the few places in the United States where:

- Little-known artists and craftspeople can make a living selling their wares.
- New products can find a worldwide market without leaving home.
- Many resorts and lounges employ entertainers. Talent is encouraged and nourished.

The problems

Don't expect establishing a new business to be easy. Hawai'i is the most expensive state in the country in which to do business, according to a survey by Regional Financial Associates in Pennsylvania,[1] with the highest labor and energy expenses in the nation and the second highest state and local taxes (behind Alaska). Hawai'i also has a higher than average failure rate for new business. Bob Johnson, president and chief executive officer of the Maui Economic Development Board, Inc., in a *Maui News*[2] article, provides a reason for the failures.

"Many [people] come here to visit, have liked it here, and without a great deal of research and analysis, start a business," he says. "They run into trouble."

"The plan may have worked somewhere else, but if it fails to consider the state's tax structure, the legislation affecting workers and the permitting process, it likely will [not succeed]."

The Maui Economic Development Board refers entrepreneurs to information and research sources, so they can make a wise decision before starting a business.

Meanwhile, Sam Slom, state senator and president and executive director of Small Business Hawai'i, a private organization of 3,000 business owners, cites several disincentives for business. Most begin with Hawai'i's centralized state government, which wields extremely strong powers.

1. MANDATED EMPLOYEE BENEFITS such as heath care, workers compensation, unemployment compensation and temporary disability insurance. Coupled with federally mandated employee costs, they add 35 to 45 percent

to the cost of hiring employees. "A worker who complains he's only getting $7 an hour, is in fact earning $10 or $11 in actual compensation," Slom points out. And the cost of benefits increases as the pay goes up. A person earning $12 an hour costs his employer at least $16 an hour. The result is tough on both employers and employees since it keeps wages low and the actual cost of employment high. Many small businesses hire fill-in or temporary employees rather than pay the high cost of permanent, full-time employees. There is some good news: worker's compensation rates are coming down. They have been cut drastically in the past few years, saving business about $100 million.

2. HIGH COSTS FOR COMMERCIAL SPACE. All rents are high in Hawai'i compared to many places on the mainland, but the cost of commercial space, especially in high traffic areas, is especially dear. Meanwhile, the price of land and construction makes owning your own business property impossible for many small businesses.

3. HIGH FREIGHT AND IMPORT COSTS. If your business requires material from the mainland or another country, freight costs by sea or air can double the price of the materials.

4. EXCESSIVE TAXES. The 4% state excise tax is collected over and over again from businesses at various stages of production and service and is also added to rent. It is collected so often that some economists say it amounts to an actual (sales) tax of 16 to 18 percent. For example, construction contractors, restaurants and real estate agents are licensed by the state. Like all businesses, they must pay the excise tax. If they fail to do so, their business licenses can be withheld. Since the strong state government administers this tax, there is little or no recourse, no way to argue disputes or correct errors.

5. SCARCITY OF EMPLOYEES. In some businesses, finding and especially keeping good employees is a problem. A former car rental agent tells about being solicited almost daily by other car rental companies seeking employees. "They would come over and say, 'We'll give you $2 an hour more'... and some people would just quit and walk over to the other company."

She learned: take nothing for granted

When Holly Lang, 32, bought a home-operated business and moved to Kaua'i, the first thing she did was the first thing most people do: look for somewhere to live. She signed a condominium lease at Princeville Resort on the northern tip of the island. Then she got ready to go to work on her small magazine — and the problems began.

First, she learned there was no home postal delivery to the 5,000 people on the North Shore of Kaua'i — a real inconvenience since much of her business depended on the mail. Princeville residents could pick up their mail at the local post office, but there was a year-long waiting list for a post office box.

"I said to the man at the post office, 'For heaven's sake, they're just post office boxes! How hard can it be to put in enough of them?'" Holly recalls. "But he just stared at me like I was crazy."

The Hanalei post office was just two miles away, but neighbors warned her that heavy rains can wash out the bridge to Hanalei, so she headed to a new post office eight miles in the opposite direction, at Kīlauea. The waiting list was three months, her mail could go to general delivery in the meantime.

Steve Strand

Holly encountered another problem when she purchased a computer for her business: she could find only one service technician on the island who dealt with MacIntosh systems which her business required. "It is a little scary," she says. " If something goes wrong and he's off the island, I'm in trouble."

Installing phone and fax connections presented another obstacle: each apartment in her complex could have only one phone line. Holly resolved that issue by using a cellular phone and assigning the condo phone line to her facsimile machine and computer.

"It never occurred to me to ask about mail and phone service. On the mainland, those are all things you just take for granted," she says. "When you first come here, it's like you are blind — walking around bumping into things. Anyone setting up a business anywhere on these islands had better ask questions in advance. Take nothing for granted," she advises.

7. LIBERAL LAWS. "I can't grow my business," says a Hawai'i dress shop owner. "I'm scared to death to hire employees because they have so many rights." The state Supreme Court ruled in 1997 that employees who suffer stress as a result of disciplinary action can collect worker's compensation benefits. Since almost any employee is disciplined at some point and any discipline is stressful for employees and employers, the law is frightening for employers. "Lawmakers must correct that provision. If the employee deserved to be disciplined, he should not receive compensation for stress," the *Honolulu Star Bulletin* has editorialized.[3]

Business owners mention a lesser problem, too. Hawai'i's isolated location puts it far from other markets. And the time difference means, says one, "You must start your day at 4 a.m. if you do business on the mainland. If you sleep in until six, you miss people who are out to lunch and their business day is half over." But one business person's problem can be another's advantage. If you do business in Asia, Hawai'i's time difference allows you a few more business hours.

➤ **TIP: Keep it small.** Leroy Laney, chief economist at First Hawaiian Bank, advises that to survive in these islands businesses must be very small or very large. A small business can avoid much of the overhead, such as the cost of employees and commercial building. A very large business has the resources to survive them. A Hawai'i accountant agrees, "Keep your business small, with just yourself or family as employees. Keep it in your home. That way you avoid some of the overhead and the extra costs of doing business in this state. There's a huge amount of underground business being done on these islands," he says. "Employees being paid under the table. People working from their homes despite zoning restrictions, people trading goods for services or services for services — anything to avoid the high cost of doing business here. And you can't blame them. I never advise my clients to cheat, but sometimes it's the only way they can stay in business."

➤ **TIP: Know your island.** Be sure you understand the island on which your business will be located. Each island's economy and business climate is unique and offers its own problems and opportunities. It might be very difficult to maintain a business on Lāna'i, or in rural

Hana, Maui, for example, because of the small population. And it would be difficult on Moloka'i for two reasons: many of its 7,000 people are jobless and residents often fight development. But there are no absolutes. A charming combination restaurant/gift shop/vacation rental business in isolated Hana thrives; so do some businesses in Kaunakakai, Moloka'i's main town. And a hardware store opened recently on Lāna'i. These are carefully chosen businesses that serve specific needs.

➤ **TIP: Look for business opportunities** when you first visit the islands — while new experiences make the greatest impression. What service or product did you enjoy in your country, state, or hometown that is not available here? Would it succeed here? Get some opinions from accountants, bank advisors and other business people.

➤ **TIP: Buy an existing business.** Business owners sell out here for all the same reasons they do on the mainland, plus an added one. Some owners get "island fever" — they grow tired of being in slow-paced paradise and are anxious to sell and return to the mainland.

➤ **TIP: Get in the business business.** If you have a strong track record of building successful businesses, consider starting businesses and selling them. Many people want to move to Hawai'i and most of them are looking for ways to earn a living. Some brokers specialize in selling currently operating businesses to foreign investors, especially those who want to move to the United States. Specific regulations and requirements apply; be sure to get full details and work with a reputable business broker knowledgeable in this field.

➤ **TIP: Subscribe to** *Pacific Business News*, a weekly newspaper. This publication includes lists of business bankruptcies and foreclosures statewide. If you spot a bankruptcy in a business similar to the one you are considering, attempt to talk to the owner. What went wrong? What went right? What advice does he or she have for you? (Subscriptions: P.O. Box 833, Honolulu, HI 96808).

➤ TIP: **Join Small Business Hawai'i**, a private, independent non-profit statewide organization dedicated to improving Hawai'i's business climate. **(808) 396-1724** or fax **(808) 396-1726**

➤ TIP: **Bring enough money** to keep your business afloat for four years. Expect to be in the red your first year or two, then break even for another year or two before making a profit. This is typical for a new business. Many new businesses fail because they do not have enough resources to survive this period.

➤ TIP: **Obtain advice**. Many of the business world's top people retire or visit here; some of them volunteer their services through agencies like SCORE. In addition, most islands have business development centers. Start with the resources listed on the next page. Also, take at least two courses in running a small business in Hawai'i. These are offered regularly through local Chambers of Commerce and community colleges.

Billboards are forbidden in Hawai'i and limits on sizes of signs make it hard for small businesses to advertise. A Maui restaurant painted its location on the side of a truck and parked it near a busy corner. Police eventually stopped the practice, the owner said.

BUSINESS

All islands

- For a free workbook "Starting a Business in Hawaii":
  Business Action Center, **(808) 586-2545**
  This branch of the Hawai'i Dept. of Business, Economic Development and Tourism provides entrepreneurs with information, business forms, licenses and permits.

- Access the Internet: **www.Hawai'i.gov/dbedt/**

- Hawai'i Dept. of Commerce and Consumer Affairs, **(808) 586-3000**

- High Technology Development Corporation, **(808) 625-5293**

- Professional and Vocational Licensing Division, Department of Commerce and Consumer Affairs, Maui, **(808) 586-3000**

- Small Business Hawai'i **(808) 396-1724**

- *Island Business* magazine **(808) 524-7400,** fax **(808) 531-2306**

- *Hawaii Business* magazine **(808) 537-9500**

Maui

- Small Business Development Center and The Business Information Center,
  590 Lipoa Parkway
  Kihei, HI 96753
  (808) 875-2400
  E-mail dfisher@maui. com
  E-mail corn@maui.com or sonia @maui.com

Kauai

- State Department of Labor and Industrial Relations, employment
  service division,
  3100 Kuhio Highway, Suite C-14
  Lihu'e, HI 96766
  (808) 241-3421 Fax: (808) 241-3518

Hawai'i

- Hawai'i Island Economic Development - **(808) 966-5416**

- Research and Development - **(808) 961-8366**

- Kailua-Kona Chamber of Commerce - **(808) 329-1758**

- Hawai'i Island Chamber of Commerce - **(808) 935-7178**

Also see pages 282 - 287

'ohihana
koa

the military

Look before

you leap into

Assignment: Paradise

Military in Hawai'i

Military Personnel, Dependents & Families

	Personnel & dependents	Dependents in Hawai'i	In Housing Units
State Total	98,356	55,337	27,890
O'ahu	97,867	55,056	27,711
Hawai'i	105	63	42
Maui	77	48	29
Kaua'i	307	170	108

Source: Hawai'i State Department of Business, Economic Development & Tourism, Military Personnel and Dependents in Hawai'i, 1995 and 1996

Civilian Employment in Military

	1990	1996
State Total	19,350	16,800
Airforce	2,300	2,050
Army	5,600	4,950
Navy	11,450	9,800

Source: Hawai'i State Department of Labor and Industrial Relations, Labor Force Data Book, May 1997, p. 11; and calculations by Hawai'i State Department of Business, Economic Development and Tourism

Cutbacks

	1989	1996
Total Personnel and Dependents	116,644	98,356
Military Families	31,652	24,667

Source: Hawai'i State Department of Business, Economic Development & Tourism (DBEDT), annual survey of local commanding officers. Military personnel and Dependents in Hawai'i, 1995 and 1996

The military

Assignment: Paradise

Exiting Honolulu's busy Nimitz Highway and swooping into Hickam Air Force Base is leaving one world, one time, and floating into another. Honolulu's rush and noise subside; peace is the order of the day. Palm trees stand at attention. Broad lawns and flowering trees almost obscure a neat, tan family housing complex where a few swing sets hang motionless in the afternoon heat. The sole indication of strife comes from an electronic sign, just inside the gate, flashing an ad for marriage counseling.

Hickam, one of the largest of Hawaii's 17 military installations, is a 10,000 population town plunked in the middle of paradise. Following tourism, the military is most important to the state's economy, contributing more than $2.6 billion a year and employing 27,000 civilians. More than 55,000 active duty military personnel and 65,000 family members are on the islands at any one time, according to *Your Military in Hawai'i*, a resource book for military newcomers. State statistics show somewhat less; still, that's about 10 percent of the state's total population. The state's mid-Pacific location is vital to United States security; military cutbacks that slashed funds and closed some mainland installations did only minor surgery here.

Look up into the clear blue sky. Inhale the scent of newly cut grass. Close your eyes and try to imagine this quiet place on Dec. 7, 1941. Japanese planes rumbling overhead. Bombs pounding Pearl Harbor just across the bay.

Today, you have to look hard to find the tanks and other tools of war partially hidden beyond patches of lawn, back behind the kiawe trees, across from the golf course. These days, Hickam is a prime assignment — an all-expense-paid trip to paradise. There's a theater, PX, gyms, playing fields, pleasure boat launches, in addition to 1940s-style hangars and barracks. A posh oceanfront restaurant — all you can eat buffet $5.95 — looks out on a wide bay with sailboats, two pools, a private beach.

MILITARY

The perks

For families who accept Assignment Paradise, a wide array of services is provided — everything from sponsors to help with settling in to legal advice and a chance to earn a graduate degree. From opportunities for fun to employment and abuse counseling. Among the services and perks:

- **Wai'anae Army Recreation Center** has one of the finest beach facilities on the island, cabins with full kitchens and a club and water sports. Some of the military installations even have their own golf courses with driving ranges and putting greens.[1]

- **The Fort DeRussy Armed Forces Recreation Center** in the middle of Waikīkī Beach with lifeguards, tennis courts, picnic areas, and 1,500 feet of beach.

- **The Hale Koa Hotel**. This military-operated first-class luxury resort is exclusively for active duty, retired military, and Department of Defense civilian personnel. Located on 66 acres of prime Waikīkī beachfront property, it has 814 posh guest rooms with private balconies, includes live entertainment as well as buffets and Sunday champagne brunches, dinner shows and a sunset lu'au on the beach. Room rates — from $53 to $143 a night depending on pay grade and status, as well as room locations — are about half that of civilian hotels. Reservations are made on a first come, first serve basis, a spokesperson says, but rooms are typically reserved up to a year in advance. Interestingly, Hale Koa is self-supporting — no tax dollars are used in its operation.

- **Tripler Army Medical Center**. As you leave Honolulu's main airport and head toward downtown, you'll see a large pink building sitting up in the hills to your left. That's the Tripler Army Medical Center, the largest medical treatment facility in the Pacific, providing health care needs to every branch of the military in all parts of the Pacific. Over 850,000 people are eligible for health care at Tripler, which is also a teaching hospital in conjunction with the University of Hawai'i.

- **Legal assistance.** Legal assistance is available at all military bases for numerous routine matters: taxes, divorce and child support, auto title transfers, landlord/tenant disputes, wills, powers of attorney. Active duty personnel, as well as their family members and retirees, are eligible.

- **Child care.** Subsidized child care centers are available at several of Hawai'i's military bases. For example, working military parents and Defense Department employees can bring children ages six weeks to five years to Hickam Air Force Base's Child Development Center from 6:30 a.m. to 5:30 p.m. Staff to child ratio is low — one caregiver to every four infants or every five toddlers — so the center is often filled and has a waiting list in some age categories, its director says. Call Hickam's Child Development Center at **(808) 449-9880.** (That number will also lead you to phone numbers for child care centers on other bases.)

The problems

The perks can be misleading; military life in Hawai'i is not all leis and sunshine. Families whose breadwinners are transferred to paradise face tough decisions: jeopardize their finances by coming along or be separated for long periods of time during the usual three-year tour of duty.

The kindly staff at the Hickam's family services building produces a very thorough informational packet for newly assigned families. A bright yellow flyer is imprinted in heavy black type:

THE COST OF LIVING IN PARADISE

Living in Hawai'i is enjoyable, but very expensive. Please read this very carefully and make sure you can afford it before accepting the assignment.

The cost of living in paradise is at least 35% higher than it is on the mainland. You should figure out what your expenses and credit debt are per month. Multiply your expenses by 35% and add it to your current budget. Will your pay support that? Do you have enough now in savings to take care of emergencies such as car repair? Do you have an extra $3,000 to rent an apartment here and cover unexpected expenses? If you must take advance pay, add that figure into your monthly expenses. The island is beautiful, but for many, the beaches and fine weather are not worth financial bankruptcy.

...A two-bedroom condo/townhouse rental unit will run $900-$1200 (without utilities) per month; $1100-$1200 for a house rental. It is very hard to find housing at the lower rates. The rents have been flat for the past five years and are not expected to increase in the near future. The current waiting list for junior enlisted members (E-1 to E-9) to receive on-base housing can be 1 to 10 months, maybe longer. For junior officers it's about a 4-12 month wait.

...Landlords require first month's rent and an amount equivalent to the first month's rent for a security deposit. You will need a minimum of $1800-$2400 just to rent your house or apartment.

...Utility costs will generally be paid separately from your rent. Security deposits on utilities can be waived. The appropriate waiver forms are available at your command. Estimated cost of electricity for a family of two living in an apartment without air conditioning is $74 (per month) and for a family of 4 it is $126. Estimated water and sewage is $60 per month for a family of four. Estimated cable TV service is $25 per month for standard cable. Telephone connection services are $46 and estimated $20 per month for basic service. If your rental doesn't have a phone jack, the installation charge is $95. Long distance rates are similar to the mainland.

...Car insurance is higher than on the mainland. Estimate at least $100 per month. Driving record and at-fault accident can cause the premium to increase dramatically. One speeding violation can increase cost to $135 per month; two speeding violations raises the amount to $208; and a single DUI increases the rate to as much as $600 per month.

...A spouse can easily find employment here, but generally pay is lower than on the mainland and more than half the jobs are downtown. Parking rates can run from $120-$200 a month and gasoline costs $1.63 per gallon on base for the lowest grade. Gas for the second job can run your expenses up an extra $40-$60. A bus pass is $25 per month (student pass is $12.50). Senior citizens (65 and up) pay $20 for a two-year pass.

...Child care costs are very high on O'ahu. It will cost you between $229-$446 per month depending on your household income. Our Child Development Center is considered the best in (the Pacific Air Force) and is currently expanding to accommodate more children. The Hickam Family Day Care Providers Program offers licensed care ranging from $300-$380 per month. The local school system's after-school A+ program is $55 per month. Children on free or reduced lunch program pay substantially less.

An employed spouse may find that the net return for working a full-time job is only $100-$300 per month once the costs of child care, parking, gas and lunches are factored in.

The typical family may find that they must adopt a firm budget to remain free from financial worries. There may be no room in the budget for life's unpredictable emergencies. If your spouse worked on the mainland and you have accumulated the debt of a two-income family, you may find yourself in serious trouble trying to pay your creditors, especially if you are only receiving one income in Hawai'i. Please call the Family Support Center's Personal Financial Program Manager to work on your "Aloha" budget upon arrival.

Housing

There are thirty-seven government housing areas on O'ahu, ranging in size from a few units to hundreds. Much of it has been renovated recently, but housing for military families still can be a problem, says a relocation specialist for Community Homefinding Referral Relocation Service. The service finds off-base housing for military families. Base housing may not be available, depending on the time of year, or may be in such poor condition that families reject it and decide to rent off base. Or the only available housing may be on the other side of the island, like Barbers' Point, fifteen miles away through heavy traffic. Or housing may be in a less than desirable school district.

And life

Military life anywhere can be rough on dependents. In recent years, at least four O'ahu military personnel or their spouses have been charged with killing their young children in fits of anger. These cases put military family life under a microscope and expose a mass of problems: spouses stationed worlds away, young parents raising children alone far from family and friends.

It's a stressful life, even in paradise. Maybe especially in paradise, where high living costs can add to anxiety.

➤ TIP: **Be sure to communicate with family counselors** at the base you will be assigned to well in advance of your arrival. Many services are available to help you settle in, such as "Aloha kits" including dishes, ironing boards, irons and baby furniture for rent at reasonable rates or free. Complete packets of information, sent to you in advance of your move, include coupons, maps, school data, and a useful book, *Your Military in Hawai'i* by Hart Publishing, Honolulu, available only to military personnel. If you do not receive a copy of *Your Military in Hawai'i*, contact the publisher directly.

Hart Publishers Inc.
1110 University Avenue, Suite 304
Honolulu, HI 96826
(808) 943-1676
Fax: (808) 949-0966

➤ **TIP: After you've received** your orders for Hawai'i, begin making arrangements for housing. Submit a DD 1746 (an Advance Application for Housing) to the appropriate personnel on your base or to:
Community Homefinding Referral Relocation Service
3189 Nimitz Road
Honolulu, HI 96818-3676
(808) 474-2343
CHRRS aides help families find off-base housing, even going as far as providing transportation for the search. They can also supply a list of hotels for temporary housing.

➤ **TIP: Temporary housing.** Several O'ahu hotels specialize in temporary lodging for military families; at least two, The Plaza Hotel (Best Western) and the Holiday Inn, have special military liaison persons and Wednesday evening "Welcome to Hawai'i" programs. Call (808) 836-8889 or (808) 576-6637.

➤ **TIP: Leave bulky furniture at home.** Ranges and refrigerators are provided in base housing and are included in most rental apartments and homes. Additional furniture can be purchased inexpensively at household sales, thrift and used furniture stores or discount stores.

ho'omaha retirement

"It is important for us

to utilize our *kupuna mano'o*

(the wisdom of our elders)

because after they're gone,

who will teach us?"[1]

—Richard Kalolo'okalani Keaulana

Courtesy Josephine Falk

"On the mainland, in many places, I think the elderly are made to feel like a nuisance. Here, it is a custom, because of the Oriental and Hawaiian cultures, to appreciate and respect old people. And it carries over to how everyone treats you. You feel it."

—Josephine Falk, 86, O'ahu

A change of life

In 1978, Josephine Falk, then 66, came to O'ahu to visit her daughter and family, who were living here temporarily. It was her first visit to the islands. She disembarked at the Honolulu airport, savored the warm fragrant breezes, smiled up at the sunshine and promptly called her family back in snowy Pennsylvania.

"Rent out my apartment," she said. "I'm never coming back."

Many tourists fall in love with the islands and decide to stay, but Josephine faced a stiffer challenge than most. She had no pension with which to support herself — only her social security check of a few hundred dollars a month.

For a few weeks, she lived with her daughter's family in Kailua, a half-hour drive from Honolulu. She learned all she could about life in the islands by reading and talking to residents and she found that Hawai'i is one of the kindest states in the nation to retirees. People who retire here collect all standard federal benefits such as Medicaid and Social Security, and the state offers other incentives for seniors. All pension and social security income is tax exempt.

> Josephine was 66, alone, and had only her social security when she "retired" to Honolulu.

Honolulu, the state's largest city, is ideal for healthy retirees — convenient, clean and, in most areas, relatively crime free. And there's plenty of activity for those who wish it — easily accessible beaches, free entertainment at hotels and shopping centers, and pleasant places to just sit and watch the crowds go by.

In Hawai'i, she could expect to live longer, and she was hoping the warm weather would ease her arthritic pain, enabling her to live a more active life.

Another boon to seniors is TheBus, Honolulu's extremely efficient public transportation system, which makes it easy for elderly residents to relinquish their drivers' licenses and still stay mobile, traveling all over the island to social events and free meals at senior citizen centers. Seniors 65 and older pay only $20 for a two-year bus pass.

Important, though less tangible, says Josephine, is the gentle aloha spirit and the respect for the elderly so evident in Hawai'i.

"On the mainland, in many places, I think the elderly are made to feel like a nuisance. Here, it is a custom, because of the Oriental and Hawaiian cultures, to appreciate and respect old people. And it carries over to how everyone treats you. You feel it," she says.

Josephine hoped for a job in one of Waikīkī's many gift shops, where today employees earn as much as $15 an hour plus commissions; but shop owners prefer employees who can speak at least a little Japanese. She had extensive child care experience in her hometown, so she answered a newspaper ad for a nanny and was quickly hired to care for the two sons of a Chinese couple in a fashionable section of Honolulu.

Next, she went apartment hunting, answering more than twenty ads before finding a first floor apartment within her budget near Waikīkī's Ala Wai Canal. The mainland owner wanted a tenant who would keep the apartment clean and safe, so the rent was a bargain. At $400 a month, it covered only her landlord's maintenance fees and utility costs. In effect, she was "house-sitting," a common way for responsible people to cut their housing costs. Wealthy people from all over the world buy Hawaiian homes and condominiums as part-time residences or as investments. Thefts and break-ins are common so absentee owners occasionally offer reduced or free accommodations to trustworthy people who guard and maintain their residences.

At the same time, Josephine put her name on a three-year waiting list for a federally subsidized apartment in one of several O'ahu senior citizen complexes.

Her daughter soon moved back to the mainland, but Josephine remained in Honolulu. Though alone, she was happy. She made friends. She walked a few blocks to the beach each day after work. On her days off, she took long bus rides, exploring the island.

"Oh, I missed my family," she says. "But I could call them. Or take out the albums with the family pictures and reminisce. And they visited often."

She took lessons in Hawaiian culture and hula, offered free to senior citizens. She also studied Japanese. When the children she was caring for outgrew her, Josephine got a job in a Waikīkī gift shop and began dating the uncle of the gift shop's owner. She was over 70 and still working full-time, but she is quick to say, "Enjoying it too. I like meeting people from all over the world."

Eventually an apartment became available in a new federally subsidized complex for the elderly. Airy, with a large living room/kitchen combination, bedroom and ample storage, it is close to markets and malls.

In her mid-70s, Josephine stopped working at the gift shop and for several years, took part in a federally funded "grandparent" program at a school for handicapped children. She continued in that role until she was 81. Today, at 86, she is completely retired but still rides TheBus daily, striking up conversations with travelers from all over the world, and she swims often.

"I know if I lived elsewhere, especially where it's cold, I would be bedridden or confined indoors during the winter," she says. "Here, each morning I get up to sunshine and I can't wait to get out and enjoy the day."

She has, she feels, adequate medical care in Hawai'i, at least as good as she would have in Pennsylvania, and she has just begun taking advantage of subsidized housecleaning help and van services. Like most elderly people, Josephine wants to be self-sufficient, living in her own apartment as long as she can. Apartment complex managers assess her physical and mental capabilities each year and she worries that they will someday decree that she must leave her home.

During her twenty years on the islands, she has seen her circle of friends shrink. What happens to elderly *kama'āinas*, far from family, when they can no longer live alone? Some eventually need help with day-to-day living chores and move back to the mainland to be near relatives. Others who can afford it move to more costly comprehensive care facilities (see next story). Still others go to private nursing homes.

Caring for the kūpuna

As on the mainland, the trend here is to help seniors live on their own for as long as possible. On most islands, seniors who need it have access to free or very low-cost assistance with housekeeping; daily meals delivered to their door by programs such as Meals on Wheels; community meals served daily at least one senior center on each island and at several sites on O'ahu; van service to doctor appointments, grocery shopping and to the many senior centers for recreation and socializing.

Living in Honolulu is convenient for seniors and they may be able to live on their own longer there than on neighbor islands where there is no mass transportation and health care is limited.

Hawai'i's Department of Business, Economic Development and Tourism projects that by the year 2020, persons aged 65 and over will account for twenty percent of Hawai'i's population. Traditionally, Hawaiian and Asian *'ohana* (family) cared for their *kūpuna* (elderly), usually at the family home. Even today, fewer than two percent of Hawai'i's 65-plus population lives in long-term care facilities.

But economics and customs are changing. Today, some 63 percent of Hawai'i's women, the customary caregivers, work outside the home and society is providing more of the services once supplied by relatives. When people are no longer able to care for themselves, they rely on government agencies for placement in nursing or extended care homes. And they are at the mercy of health insurance and what it will provide, says Leilani Hayes, a physical therapist who works with the elderly. On the neighbor islands, where large professional nursing homes are scarce, that could mean boarding in a private home.

For example, Hayes points out, a stroke or heart attack victim may have to live in a household run by an ethnic group other than his own. Some Filipino and Japanese families accept boarders, but the cultural and dietary differences can be a culture shock for seniors, making them feel even more alone and isolated.

Housing the elderly

Hawai'i, and especially the neighbor islands, lag behind the rest of the United States in elderly housing options. The neighbor islands are just now beginning to offer assisted living complexes, where seniors can get help with housekeeping, daily meals, baths and medication. Maui, the Big Island, Kaua'i and Moloka'i all are constructing or considering such complexes.

"Until now, those complexes have been too pricey for the average retiree," says Mildred Ramsey, director of gerontology, Child and Family Services for Hawai'i. Some complexes, like Honolulu's Arcadia, involve an admission fee. Newer complexes, like The Ponds at Punalu'u on O'ahu, which opened in

1997, are geared to lower and middle-income seniors. No buy-in is required and monthly costs are $1,250 to $1,800.

At Punalu'u, "The person has their own apartment with their own furniture and support services are right there. Showers you can wheel into, aides to assist only as much as you need," Ramsey says. "An assistant will give medication, shots, and can handle some nursing tasks. As your needs go up, so does the cost."

Within the next decade, Ramsey predicts, such complexes will be common throughout the islands. "Middle-class seniors who can afford $2,000 a month may never have to go into a nursing home," she says.

Still, many transplanted elderly opt to return to their hometowns before advanced old age sets in. "Once you get to the point where you hardly leave your apartment, you might as well be in inexpensive Duluth (Minnesota) or Sun City (Arizona) or someplace in Florida," says one caregiver. "And (if your family lives on the mainland) it sure will be a lot easier for your family to visit and help out."

Moving parents here

Another scenario comes into play on these islands. Since 1970, Hawai'i has experienced a 54 percent increase in population. Many of those who moved here are middle-aged now, heading for retirement themselves — and back on the mainland, their parents are becoming old and need the care and security of adult children nearby.

"We get many, many calls from family members thinking of moving mom out here," Ramsey says. "It is very traumatic to bring them out here

RETIREMENT

• **Hawai'i Senior information line (808) 523-4545.** This hotline provides a multitude of information and will even connect seniors with emergency if they need it.

•**The Senior Information and Assistance Handbook**, published by the city and county of Honolulu and American Savings Bank, includes a very complete list of services and phone numbers. Call the Senior information line at **(808) 523-4545** or write Elderly Affairs Division, 715 S. King Street, #500, Honolulu, HI 96813

• **AARP**
(area code 808)

Big Island	**334-1212**
Kaua'i	**246-4500**
O'ahu	**526-4500**
Maui	**661-0159**

and expect them to make such adjustments. They have been living, maybe most of their lives, in familiar territory, maybe with old friends. Their activity level is set. It can be very sad," Ramsey continues. "Some seniors retire here. Sell their home on the mainland. Ship all their furniture, put all their money into a new home or high rent. Then they want to return and it's so expensive, their retirement savings are used up."

➤ TIP: **Ask yourself a few question** before you decide to retire to Hawai'i. If you are part of a couple, do both of you really want to come? Will it be forever, or just for a few years? Would it be wiser to live here a few months of the year and closer to your family or old friends for the rest of the time? What provisions can you make for later years, when you are no longer able to care for yourself?

➤ TIP: **Remember that services vary greatly** from island to island. Contact the Office of Elderly Affairs in each island for specific information:
Big Island (808) 961-3418
Kaua'i (808) 241-6400
Maui, Moloka'i and Lāna'i (808) 243-7774,
O'ahu Retirement information **(808) 586-1660**
Senior citizens' programs **(808) 586-0100**

A resident peers from the eighth floor of a building at the Makua Alii Senior Center, a subsidized housing complex in Honolulu.

A sampling of island retirement residences

Retirement living options for a variety of incomes are available on O'ahu. On neighbor islands, choices are very limited, but several developments are planned. The selection below is a sampling of a few of the living situations; it is not a complete list. Prices and waiting periods quoted here were accurate at press time, but may change. Call or write for detailed information.

O'ahu

Makua Alii Senior Center. Complex of three high-rise buildings with rent-subsidized apartments for seniors. Two blocks from Honolulu's convention center. Near shopping, grocery stores, bus service. Tenant pays approximately 28 percent of his or her income. There are about 8,000 people on a four-year long waiting list for all subsidized housing on O'ahu and the waiting period for subsidized elderly housing can be a year or more, a Housing and Urban Development spokesperson says. 1541 Kalakaua Avenue, Honolulu. Applications: **(808) 832-5960**; rent subsidy: **(808) 832-6040**

The Arcadia. This downtown Honolulu high-rise complex is owned and operated as a non-profit corporation by the United Church of Christ, under an endowment. Open to persons of all faiths. Resident pays a one-time lifetime lease fee (from $84,100 for smallest unit to $500,000 for penthouse suite) plus a monthly maintenance starting at $1,233. Apartment reverts to the corporation when resident dies. Studios, alcoves, one-bedroom and double units, each with kitchenette and *lāna'i*. Indoor and outdoor recreational facilities. Monthly charge includes meals, some laundry, maid service, utilities and building maintenance. Health care at nominal cost is available in the Medicare-approved health care center on site. Alzheimer's unit. Skilled nursing unit. Waiting list is three to seven years for some apartments. 1434 Punahou Street, Honolulu, HI 96822. **(808) 941-0941**

One Kalakaua. Luxury high-rise near Ala Moana shopping center and the Honolulu convention center. Buyers own their condominium units, have full rights and can will their apartments to heirs. One bedroom, $257,000; two bedrooms, $402,000. A $1,400 monthly fee for one person or $1,800 for two includes a daily meal, weekly housekeeping, all utilities including cable TV. Non-denominational chapel. Health club. Heated pool. Game rooms. Library. Restaurant. Full staff. Doctor and nurse on call. Thirty-six bed health center for convalescing. Residents may have guests for up to 30 days. 1314 Kalakaua Ave. Honolulu, HI 96826. **(808) 949-1111**.

Pohai Nani Good Samaritan Kauhale. (Translates as "village surrounded by beauty.") Owned and operated by Evangelical Lutheran Good Samaritan Society, Sioux Falls, S.D. Retirement village on 16 acres near Kāne'ohe Bay on windward O'ahu. Cost: Non-refundable admission fee of $3,000 to $4,000 and monthly fee from about $1,500 to $2,900. Includes three meals, housekeeping, all utilities except phone and cable. Buildings include 22 cottages plus a fourteen-story high-rise with studios and one and two-bedroom apartments. View of Ko'olau Mountains from most *lāna'i*. Heated pool. Golf course nearby. Downtown Honolulu 20 minutes away by bus. Jacuzzi, exercise room. 42 bed nursing facility. Six-month waiting list on average, but waiting list is flexible, since some applicants are waiting to sell their homes, says a marketing director. 45-090 Namoku Street, Kāne'ohe, HI 96744. **(808) 247-6211**.

The Big Island

Lyman Gardens. Community of fee simple one and two bedroom condo homes (from $129,000 to $238,000) overlooking Pukihae Stream near Hilo. A $690 monthly fee for one person or $895 for a couple includes all utilities and weekly maid service. Dining room, library, beauty salon, van transportation, workshop, fitness center, pool and spa on site. Pets allowed. 245 Wainaku Street, Hilo, HI 96720. **(808) 9696-7600**.

Maui

Kalama Heights. A 240-unit senior rental community is planned on nine acres in South Kīhei. The initial phase would include 90 retirement residence suites and 30 assisted-living suites. The retirement residences would be designed for seniors in good health who want prepared meals, housekeeping, transportation, social activities and recreation programs. The assisted-living units would be for elderly in need of some nursing and personal care, according to John Min of Chris Hart & Partners, the developers. The project was still in the early developmental stage at the time of this writing and no cost estimates were available.

Kaua'i

The Harry & Jeannette Weinberg Hale Kupuna. A nonprofit 28-unit project for people 62 and older with limited incomes. In rural Kalaheo, it is less than one-third mile from shopping, churches, a senior center and medical and professional help. The project consists of one-bedroom, one-bath units arranged in four-plex clusters on 3.5 acres. [1]

Līhu'e Theater Project. The Kaua'i Housing Development Corp. has renovated the historic downtown Līhue Theater, converting it to a 20-unit project that will serve up to 40 low-income seniors.

A resident and the complex's mascot enjoy the scenery at Pohai Nani Good Samaritan Kauhale, a retirement village in Kāne'ohe, O'ahu.

Photo courtesy Pohai Nani Retirement Center

8 good reasons to retire to Hawai'i

1. **Longer life span.** On the average, you should have four more years of life here than on the mainland. And you may be thinner and more active. Hawai'i has the fewest overweight people in the nation.

2. **Tax exemptions.** Hawai'i is one of only two states that exempts all pension and Social Security income from state income taxes.

3. **Low property taxes.** Hawai'i senior homeowners also enjoy exemptions on the state's already low property taxes.

4. **Stimulating friends and activities.** Hawai'i retirees are among the world's brightest and most successful people. Talented retirees and visitors often share their gifts through classes in writing, painting, dance, languages.

5. **Warm weather, better health.** Hawai'i's warm weather is kind to some ailments associated with aging, such as arthritis. Temperatures hover in the mid-70s to mid-80s on most parts of the islands during the day. They rarely fall below 65 on the shorelines, even at night.

6. **High respect for elderly.** Respect for elderly tends to be high in Hawai'i, due to the strong influence of Hawaiian and Asian cultures.

7. **Mobility.** People age 65 and older can ride TheBus all over O'ahu almost free. That could mean you'll stay mobile and active longer. (At this writing a senior bus pass costs $20 for two years.)

8. **Plenty to do.** Bountiful beaches, golf courses, parks, senior centers — and senior citizen discounts on many activities.

8 good reasons NOT to retire to Hawai'i

1. **Loneliness.** Once the thrill of living in paradise wears off, it's possible you'll miss your family and old friends more than you imagined.

2. **Helplessness.** You may become ill far from family, perhaps before you've had time to make reliable friends.

3. **Housing.** Inexpensive elderly housing and assisted living is difficult to find. Assisted-living arrangements exist in Honolulu, but they are very costly at this time. It can take two years or more to secure government subsidized housing on some islands.

4. **Distance.** Ideally, your annual budget should include a few thousand dollars each year for travel, to reinforce ties with family and friends and to help children and grandchildren visit you.

5. **Costs.** Food and medical costs are high and include a four percent state excise tax.

6. **Poor public transportation.** On the neighbor islands, public transportation is almost nonexistent. Seniors who relinquish their driver's licenses must depend on cabs, van service, or friends and relatives to transport them.

7. **Lack of care homes.** On some islands, boarding homes for the elderly tend to be operated according to ethnic backgrounds. If it became necessary, could you adjust to living in a household with customs and diets different from your own?

8. **Limited medical care.** Seriously ill patients must be airlifted to Honolulu for many sophisticated procedures.

Also see chapter: General Information, health section, pages 75-78.

Matt Thayer

chapter 8

nā keiki
the children

We cherish

our toddlers,

but shortchange

our school kids

Breanna turns one

When Breanna Haulani Aki Gaddis turned one year old, her grandmother's whole Waikapū neighborhood knew it. So did 400 of her family's friends. Breanna's birthday party lasted for six hours, longer than most weddings, and included three bands, tables of catered food, and a room full of presents. It cost more than $4,000.

It was quite a party, well befitting one of Hawai'i's favorite traditions, the baby lū'au. Custom calls for a huge event, often sponsored by the baby's grandparents, to which friends, relatives and co-workers are invited. And for good luck, the party must be held on or after the child's birthday, never before, since it celebrates the fact the infant has survived the dangers of infancy.

Breanna's grandparents, Matthew and JoAnn Aki, had a home and yard large enough to host the affair; but lū'aus are usually held in halls or community centers, her mom Brandy says.

"For Breanna's party, we got a little carried away," Brandy adds. "We invited everybody who took the time to ask about my pregnancy or her birth. Usually people come to see you at the hospital and then they never see the baby again, so we wanted everyone to come."

Bob Fijal

Breanna and her mom

Usually, it's adults who party the hardest at baby lū'aus; in Breanna's case the sunny toddler joined right in, dancing in the arms of guests and laughing at the bands.

No one is quite sure which of Hawai'i's many ethnic groups originated the baby lū'au, but Breanna would qualify no matter which. Her ancestry includes Japanese, Hawaiian, Chinese, Irish, English and French — and that's just on her mother's side.

"Her daddy (Beau Gaddis) is everything else," Brandy laughs. "Breanna is real chop suey!"

From cradle to college

To a young child, Hawai'i can be an ideal place to grow up. There's grass to run barefoot in, fruit and flowers to be picked, the same sports and activities as on the mainland plus those provided by nature, by liberal government funding, and by a caring community. Kayak teams to paddle on. Mountains to hike. An ocean to swim. Olympic-sized swimming pools. Skateboarding facilities. Small towns that are, for the most part, safe and convenient.

Interestingly, Hawai'i children take less Ritalin than any other children in the country. Nationwide 1.5 million young people ages 5 through 18, or almost three percent of U.S. school-age children, take the drug for relief from attention and hyperactivity disorders, researchers reported in Pediatrics, the journal of the American Academy of Pediatrics. [1]

An added bonus for children of traditional families here: they are cherished. Just as Hawaiians and Asian cultures value their elderly, so they pamper their young. In some families, the child may not always have two parents, but he will usually have everything he wants or needs and more, even if *tutus* (grandparents) and aunties and uncles must help provide it. Toys. Love. Attention. In the Hawaiian tradition, a child belongs as much to his greater family and to the community as he does to his parents.

> **If you want your child in a rarefied environment, well — that's not what Hawai'i is about.**
>
> –O'ahu school principal Lea Albert

Here, a huge *lū'au* marks the child's first birthday, celebrating the fact that he or she has survived the first, delicate year of life.

As the Hawaiian and hapa-Hawaiian (part Hawaiian) child grows older, he or she may study hula, Hawaiian language and traditional chants and perform at family get-togethers, at weddings and *lu'au*, at

Kid care

Childcare is big business in Hawai'i where few employers offer child care assistance. Most centers these days call themselves pre-schools, with the emphasis on school. Aides at ten centers we called were anxious to discuss learning programs.

Most pre-schools accept children at age two; only a few accept babies as young as eight weeks of age. Most are open from 6 or 7 a.m. until 5 or 6 p.m. Prices range from $390 to $450 per month, including lunch and snacks. Babies under age two cost extra: a total of $151 per week at one facility that accepted them, $575 per month at the other.

The O'ahu day care center servicing Kapiolani and Straub hospitals employees is open to the public; its fees decrease as the child grows older and more able to care for himself. At eighteen months to two years, the fee is $580 for employees and $710 for others; at age 2, it's $490 and $595 (deduct $30 if the child is potty trained). At age 3 and up the fee is $425 and $500.

hotels and shopping centers and other public places. Someday the child may be able to support herself by entertaining, thereby enabling her to stay and live on the islands where jobs are scarce.

Young Caucasian children share in this good fortune. Young *malihini* may suffer a few taunts from classmates, but overall they usually have little trouble adjusting during the first few school years. For the offspring of a traditional two-parent or extended family, Hawai'i is truly a young child's idyll.

Unfortunately that's not the case for every child in Hawai'i today. Here, as on the mainland, times are changing:

• About 27 percent of Hawai'i's children are born to unwed mothers. Traditionally, there is little stigma to that in Polynesian cultures, but these children are more apt to live in poverty. Hawai'i has four times more children living in emergency shelters than the national average.

• Even if a child has two parents, they each may be holding down two or more jobs to make ends meet in Hawai'i's costly environment and have little time left for their child. That can be particularly difficult for newcomers who have no relatives or extended family to help with child care. If the child encounters problems adjusting at school, there may be no adult available to help overcome the difficulties.

A lifeline for parents

Your toddler Tim has been having temper tantrums. What should you do? Call **Parent Line** and get professional advice. Dial **526-1222** from O'ahu or **1(800) 816-1222** from any neighbor island and child and adolescent development professionals will answer questions about kids from birth through 17 years. Topics include, but are not limited to, single parenting, sibling relations, discipline, homework, eating concerns, breast feeding, divorce and death. The line also welcomes calls from students. The confidential line is staffed by the state Department of Health from 8 a.m. to 6 p.m. Monday through Friday and 9 a.m. to 1 p.m. Saturdays.

• As a child grows older and enters junior and senior high school, his life becomes more complicated, just as it does on the mainland. And here the child has some special problems: an often-overcrowded public school system and a mix of cultures that can be stimulating but also frightening. It takes a special kind of teenage *malihini* to adjust with ease.

Hawai'i's schools

When Mary moved to O'ahu with her teenage son a few years ago, it seemed every longtime resident she met had a warning for her. Your son, they said, must attend either a private school or one of two public high schools with good reputations — in Kāhala and Hawai'i Kai, both upper middle-income enclaves. Since Mary could not afford to live in those neighborhoods, she "borrowed" a friend's address to register her son at the Hawai'i Kai area school. Five years later, she was very satisfied with her son's education.

"At some schools you can get an education," a psychologist/father says, "others are nothing but trouble and drugs. The kid goes to school and comes back beat up. The teacher speaks pidgin... and you wonder why they are not getting an education?"

Put hundreds of young people of various races and ethnic backgrounds together. Factor in youthful tensions. Add a highly transient population and rapid growth that overcrowds school facilities. Figure in a single state-wide school board making decisions for communities miles away. Consider a large turnover of teachers on some islands — and you'll calculate the tremendous challenge facing Hawai'i's public school system, parents and students.

Public school or private school?

About 16 percent of Hawai'i's students attend private schools which have very good reputations but are costly — from about $1,000 to $10,000 annually. Is it necessary for your child to attend a private school to get a good education in Hawai'i? Not absolutely. The quality of public school education varies greatly from school to school. And school assignments can be bolstered by additional attention from parents with homework and assignments, teachers advise.

O'ahu journalist Patrick Williams, 26, reflected on his experiences in both Hawai'i public and private schools. He attended Punahou School, considered one of Hawai'i's finest private high schools, on scholarship.

"I went to public school until seventh grade and then to Punahou. In public school, I was always the brightest kid in the class. School was a cruise, easy," Williams remembers. "But when I went to Punahou, I just bombed. I had to start all over. I had to learn to study, how to take notes, and I did. But that was the difference. A big difference."

Of the 135 private schools in Hawai'i, 44 percent are parochial. Here is a sampling of some of Hawai'i's private schools and their costs.

School	District	Grade	Pupils	Tuition
Punahou School	Honolulu	K-12	3,700	$8,600-$9,200
Iolani School	Honolulu	K-12	1,781	$8,750
Waldorf School	Honolulu	pre-12	272	$4,700-$8,375
Holy Trinity School	Honolulu	K-8	151	$3,250
St. Andrews Priory	Honolulu	K-12	500	$7,965-$8,235
Ko'olau Baptist Academy	Oahu	K-12	140	$2,100
Seabury Hall	Maui	6-12	370	$9,375
St. Anthony Jr./Sr. High	Maui	7-12	360	$4,800
Hawai'i Preparatory Academy	Big Island	9-12	688	$15,800-$20,200
St. Joseph High	Big Island	7-12	78	$3,400-$4,100
Island School	Kaua'i	K-9	165	$6,150-$6,500
Kahili Adventist	Kaua'i	K-12	170	$3,537-$4,312

[1] Source: Telephone interviews with the schools.
[2] Pacific Business News, Nov. 10, 1997

It's no wonder 45 percent of Honolulu's public school teachers send their children to private schools, according to a 1990 U.S. census. On the mainland, only 12.1 percent of public school teachers' children attend private schools.[2] Overall, 16 percent of Hawai'i's elementary, intermediate and high school students chose private schools, compared to 12 percent in the rest of the nation.

What tests say

Scholastic Aptitude Tests, which compare students throughout the nation, score Hawai'i at close to the national norm in math (482 to 482), but considerably below in verbal skills (407 to 482).

A Department of Education report said the percentage of students needing special education of some sort, including instruction in speaking English, has risen 42 percent since 1990.[3] Educators usually blame the verbal scores deficiency on the students' wide variety of ethnic backgrounds.

At the same time, the National Assessment of Educational Progress ranks Hawai'i's eighth graders as among the worst science students in the nation. Their tests determine knowledge of science and ability to use what is learned to solve problems. Only students in notoriously poor school districts like Washington, D.C., Guam, Louisiana and Mississippi score lower.

"We still have a long way to go to improve student achievement," says Greg Knudsen, director of communications for the state board of education. "We have a large share of people who do not speak English as their first language and pidgin English is a factor here."

Some defenders of the status quo argue that Hawai'i's public school students are getting another, important kind of education: in human relations. Students benefit from playing and working with people from a variety of cultures. The world is becoming homogeneous as more countries are opened to international business, and Hawai'i's young people may be better equipped for life in the new global community.

One school district

The structure of Hawai'i's school district is sometimes blamed for its problems. Instead of each community having financial responsibility for its own schools, there is one centralized school board on O'ahu with jurisdiction for the entire state. Hawai'i is the only state in the nation with such an autonomous one-district system.

Ideally, this centralized concept equalizes the schools. Teachers and funding are allotted per student and are the same whether you live in highly populated Honolulu or rural Hana. Kindergarten through second grade is allotted one teacher for every 20 students; grades three and up get one teacher for every 26.15 students. (Actual classes in some areas are much smaller and sometimes are much larger with an aide helping out.)

"When you have real economic downs, like Hāmākua [sugar mill] closing, the community is depressed, but the schools are not affected. The basic funding continues," Knudsen points out.

The Kamehameha Schools

Kamehameha Schools are unique to Hawai'i. About 90 percent subsidized by the estate of Bernice Pauahi Bishop, the Kamehameha Schools gives preference to students with Hawaiian blood and tuition is low: $500 for preschool to $2,500 for a boarding high school student. With three campuses on O'ahu and one each on Maui and the Big Island, the schools serve approximately 4,300 students.

Too many students?

Hawai'i's schools are the largest in the nation in individual enrollment. Until 1998, when enrollment began to level off, the Hawai'i school system had increased by an average of 3,000 more students each year for several years. A Department of Education school performance review found one-third of the state's 243 schools overcrowded. Forty percent lack library and office space. Kamali'i Elementary, a new school built to relieve overcrowding in Kīhei, Maui, one of the nation's fastest growing towns, was packed by its second year. Enrollment surpassed planning estimates by over 130 children. Principal Sandra Shawhan was dealing with an overload of students whom she said were "coming from everywhere" — from a nearby public school, the island's expensive private schools, the mainland and places as far away as Austria. She had to move two teachers, originally scheduled to teach special subjects like computers and music, to regular classroom duty.[4] Two classes that boost children's interest in learning were eliminated.

David Scull / Honolulu Advertiser

Children skip up the steps to Maunaloa Elementary School on Moloka'i. Principal James Fuchigami says an intensive reading and writing program is helping students at the old plantation town overcome language and literacy problems. Students have several reading periods throughout the day and at least two or three chances to write; then each child takes a book home every night to read with his or her parents.

Kamali'i is set to become one of the state's first multi-tract schools, functioning year-round with students on various nine-month schedules; other Hawai'i schools may eventually follow suit to alleviate crowding.

High turnover

A high turnover of both students and teachers in some areas adds to problems. At O'ahu schools near military bases as many as 70 percent of students come and go within a year, Knudsen says. That means teachers must

Pay your child support, or else

Don't come to Hawai'i hoping to escape child support payments. Hawai'i is one of the toughest states in the nation when it comes to protecting children's support rights. The Child Support Enforcement Agency, a federal-state entity, can garnish wages, intercept tax refunds, report to credit bureaus, file liens against property or file a criminal complaint in court.

And a 1998 law tightens the noose: State licensing authorities can suspend, deny or refuse to reinstate deadbeat parents' vocational and professional licenses.[1] Under Act 293, more than 45 licensed professionals ranging from boxers to hearing-aid fitters must meet their child-support obligation or risk losing licenses.

The statute also gives the state the authority to revoke or suspend drivers' licenses and recreation licenses of a person in arrears for at least three months.

be constantly working to bring new students up to speed — and teaching suffers.

High teacher turnover also contributes to educational problems in some areas. About one-half of the 100 teachers recruited annually from out of state leave their Hawai'i jobs within a year.

And teachers cite another factor for high newcomer turnover: because all teachers in the state fall under one school system, teachers with seniority can "bump" new teachers to take jobs in most desirable locations. Teaching jobs in busy O'ahu or less rural parts of Maui are deemed more desirable than those, for example, on very rural Moloka'i or Lana'i.

Teacher wages

Teachers' wages are about average for the nation, enough to support a family in most mainland communities. But adjust that by 30 to 40 percent for the high cost of living here and the state's high taxes, and pay is among the lowest in the country. Many teachers hold second jobs, reducing after-school time they could spend with students. In the past, disgruntled teachers have protested low wages by refusing to perform after-school extras, advising clubs and supervising activities. Teachers sometimes even spend their own money to buy extras for their students.

Teachers are allotted a fixed amount of money each year for supplies and receive that money all at once. When it's used up, some go to weekend garage and moving sales to find supplies like paint and craft items. "I spent $2,000 (of my own money) one year," a teacher says. "I didn't realize it until I did my taxes."

Test scores improving

Hawai'i's schools are improving. National test scores have been rising during the past few years. And success stories twinkle like stars in a midnight sky.

An O'ahu school that almost closed a few years ago recently won a national award from the U.S. Department of Education. Momilani Elementary, in the highly transient Pearl City area of O'ahu, was cited for its high teaching standards, community involvement and student achievement. The State Department of Education had considered closing the school due to low enrollment; instead the curriculum and teaching style was improved to the point where the school draws 70 percent of its students from outside its immediate area.

About 200 of Hawai'i's 245 schools (including a total of 190,000 public school children) are taking part in a new program, School Community Based Management. Administration shares authority with teachers, supplementary staff, students, parents and community members. Knudsen says the key is to get the community involved. "We want people to relate to the schools as central to their community. If education played a leading role in everyone's thoughts, it would affect students' achievement."

Racial and ethnic incidents

Racial or ethnic incidents occur at some public schools. These range from teasing new students to teenagers in tougher neighborhoods being intimidated and threatened.

The State Department of Education agreed to pay $25,000 to a Maui intermediate school student. A suit, filed by the child's mother in 1995, claimed her son had been attacked by classmates numerous times since 1993 and charged that the school breached its duty to provide a reasonably safe and secure environment for the boy. As a direct result of the assaults, the child allegedly suffered injuries to his face, back, ribs and other parts of his body.[5] The mother charged that the attacks were racially motivated in part because her son is Caucasian.

The school's principal disagreed on the cause of the attacks. "I don't dispute the attacks. But I don't believe it was racially motivated," she told the

Consider home schooling your child

"Alternative" lifestyles are generally accepted in Hawai'i and, especially in more rural areas, some parents choose to take responsibility for their children's education. Approximately two percent of Hawai'i families home school their children.

"The [home schooling] laws in Hawai'i are some of the best, and the Department of Education is very supportive of families" who choose to educate their children at home, Gail Nagasaki of the Home School Support Group writes in her newsletter "Home School Adventures: Programs for Parents and Youngsters."

No special training or governmental approval is necessary, but parents must notify their local school principal and follow state procedures. The parent is responsible for the child's total educational program including athletics and must keep a record of the planned curriculum. After grades 3, 6, 8 and 10, children are required to take standardized tests.

How does a parent go about teaching a child?

"It depends on your philosophy of learning," writes Nagasaki. "On one end of the spectrum are families who believe in a school-like approach, with a teacher or tutors, assignments, regular hours and such... On the other end of the spectrum are those who believe children can't help but learn and that life and play are their best teachers....Most of us start with some sort of formal curriculum and eventually evolve into our own programs."

Support groups on all major islands offer opportunities for children and parents to meet, network, share ideas and offer each other support and encouragement.

Contact your local school administration office and ask for Form OIS-4140 or call the state school superintendent's Hotline on O'ahu at (808) 586-3587.

Maui News. Many Caucasian students attend this school and encounter no ethnic problems.

The mother of two teenage children says ethnic differences make it difficult to solve youthful problems. "Many of the parents who come from Pacific Islands have different rules for dealing with crisis, for dealing with problems, and it is not to talk it out or go to court. It's by yelling or threatening or fighting it out," she says.

"My son knows that saving face is very important in some of these cultures and he has learned to slide around. He related one episode where he just said, 'Hey man, it's okay. I didn't mean to push you. It's just a game.' So by him backing down the other kid was able to save face which was very important for his cultural standing."

Hawai'i's rich ethnic mix can mean problems at some schools, school communications director Knudsen admits. "I have one Caucasian family right now saying they want to transfer to another school because their child doesn't want to be the only *haole* in class. But we cannot transfer the student based on that. It's a race argument.

"Some people come here with very low tolerance for anything different than where they came from. Others thrive on the diversity," he points out.

The state's 39-page discipline code spells out discipline action for major offenses; individual schools can have their own discipline code for dealing with minor infractions. The centralized school system actually allows more freedom for principals to handle individual problems, Knudsen maintains.

What students say

Melissa McOmber, 17, who grew up in the Lāna'i schools, says she encountered some teasing, some prejudice, but not much, probably because as such a longtime resident she was considered a part of the island society.

Melissa sees a change in student attitude. "Going to school and growing up is different here now then when we were younger. Everyone knew everyone; we were very close; until third grade we were all brother and sister. Then it started to get different.

"I baby-sit for a few *haole* blonde kids who get it worse than me because they were not born here. I think kids are much more vicious [about ethnic teasing] now. There's probably more resentment now. Some kids don't have it as hard, but probably they all have it some ways."

A 14-year-old who prefers not to use his name came to the islands two years ago. He spent his first year at an intermediate school and his second year at high school. He sees no racial problems, just what he calls "ethnic differences."

"It's not like you're just walking down a hall and someone yells, 'White boy!' like that. People don't just yell, 'white boy' if they don't know you. It's more like if they know you. They don't have anything against the person... they are just joking around, trying to intimidate you."

Some schools celebrate their students' ethnic differences, which seems to diffuse problems. At Kahuku High School in windward O'ahu, where about 25 percent of the students are Caucasian, principal Lea Albert says most of her students benefit from the rich mix of cultures. Each year 3,000 to 5,000 people attend Kahuku's May Day celebration at the nearby Polynesian Cultural Center. Photos of Samoan, Tahitian, Tongan, Hawaiian, American and Ukrainian students in full costume dance across a bulletin board in Albert's office.

Albert suggests parents instill an attitude in their children that "you're coming to learn and to benefit" from the array of cultures. "There are many fine people in the world and in this school many parents want the multi-cultural experience for their children," she says. "That's the real world. If you want your child in a rarefied environment, well... that's not what Hawai'i is about. It's a multi-cultural society where we learn from one another."

Drugs and alcohol

In Hawai'i, as on the mainland, the use of tobacco and drugs is on the rise in schools. About a tenth of Hawai'i's intermediate and high school students need treatment for substance abuse, according to a survey by the state Department of Health and the University of Hawai'i.[6] The survey found that marijuana contributed most to the increase in illicit drug use; its use increased among high school students from about 36 percent in 1989 to about 45 percent in 1996.

Cigarette use has increased the most in sixth and eighth grades, the survey said. More than 10 percent of students tried alcohol and tobacco by fourth grade; about half had experimented with them by eighth grade.

One teacher compares drug availability in Hawai'i schools today to when she attended a California school in the 1960s. "The availability is the same," she says, "but it is starting much younger. Eighth graders are doing what we did in high school. But it's not just Hawai'i, it's a change of the times. From what I hear from new parents coming into the school district, the risk of gangs and drugs is higher there [on the mainland] than here."

Here, as on the mainland, absentee parents seem to contribute to the problems, she suggests. Hawai'i's high living costs mean many parents are working two or three jobs and have little time to listen to, talk with, and guide their children.

The A-Plus program

A special program, called "A-Plus" baby-sits 21,000 children of working parents in school after regular school hours. Started in 1990 when the state had a revenue surplus, A-Plus costs $20 million a year to operate. Only $5 million comes from the $55-a-month fee per child paid by parents. Fees are reduced for children from low-income families. But one parent criticizes the need for such a program.

RESOURCES

- Hawai'i State Teachers Association **(808) 833-2711**
- Hawai'i State Parent Teacher Association **(808) 834-772?**
- Hawai'i Department of Education super-intendent's hotline **(808) 586-3587**
- Teacher employment information **(808) 586-3420**
- Non-teacher employment recruitment **(808) 586-3422**
- Use the internet to find out more about The Hawai'i School district at **http://www.k12.hi.us**
- Learn more about Kahuku School on O'ahu at **http://www.pixi.com /~kahukuhi/**

"They have the A-Plus program for latchkey kids and it's 'Wow! Look what we are doing for you.' But if we weren't so heavily taxed by the government, if we didn't need two-income families to survive, we wouldn't have latchkey kids," he says. "It's like they stabbed you in the artery and gave you a bandage. And we're suppose to say 'Thank you very much for the A-Plus program!'"

His comments do not take into account that two-income families have become the norm on the mainland and in many parts of the world. A single mother defends the program: "For single parent families, which there is a growing number of these days, the A-Plus program is a godsend. How can one parent come home at three in the afternoon to care for a child after school? Even if you are lucky enough to work one job you still probably work until five. What are you going to do?"

Tips for choosing and adjusting to your new school from parents, students and their teachers

For Parents

1. Choose your school or community before you choose your home. Some schools have few problems; others have many. "You hear, 'I just chose the house with the Monier tile roof, the sunken living room' instead of 'a good school for my kid,'" an Oʻahu psychologist points out.

2. Visit several schools. Ask for a copy of the state discipline code and the individual school's discipline code. Ask how that code is enforced. How do school authorities handle drugs, fights, swearing and insubordination?

3. Ask your school counselor or registrar for any additional information or suggestions that may make your child's transition to a new school easier.

4. Attend parent organization meetings, if possible, both before your child enrolls and after. Is there a parent advisory system set up to help operate the school?

5. Suggest your child take part in sports and community youth programs. Most communities offer football, basketball, softball, volleyball, track, tennis, wrestling, surfing, soccer and canoeing. Some sports do not require much skill or equipment. If you move in summer, don't wait until school starts. Visit your neighborhood youth center soon; that way your child may already know some fellow students when he starts school.

6. Prepare your child for his or her new school. Explain that Hawaiʻi includes many cultures and your child may now be a minority. Tell your child he may be harassed or bullied. If he is, ask him to let you know and also to tell a teacher or counselor at school.

7. If you are concerned about ethnic differences or feel your child might not be able to handle them, discuss this openly with school authorities. Ask

for a list of incidents reported in the past year — how often were police called and for what reasons? If you are not satisfied with the answers, consider searching for a home in an area with fewer problems.

8. Try to be at home when your child returns from his first few days of school, even if he is in high school. Relax and talk about the child's experiences. If you cannot be there, try to have an older sibling, friend or relative at home to greet your child and converse about the child's experiences.

9. If your child has persistent problems, comes home crying or has been injured, be sure to see a school counselor immediately. Most schools have a system in place to handle such problems. Schools can't fix problems they don't know about, a teacher says. "Communication is the key in problem solving, from the first level up to the most severe case."

For Students

1. You are turning over a new leaf. Whatever your past experiences have been, moving and changing schools is a fine opportunity. Consider what went right for you at your past school and repeat this. What went wrong? Avoid those actions.

2. Don't overreact. Remember phrases like "white boy" or "*haole*" are not necessarily name-calling, but communication from a culture that is different from yours.

3. Keep quiet and observe during the first few days or weeks at school. Most of Hawai'i's kids and many cultures present in Hawai'i don't like show-offs. Kids who act up are especially looked down upon.

4. Avoid asking silly or obvious questions. Questions like "Wow, do you people eat raw fish?" may sound friendly to you, but may be intrusive to other children.

5. Avoid fights. Period. The cultural differences here make fighting dangerous. In some cultures, parents will back up their children and encourage them to fight. The truly strong person is sure of himself and does not have to prove his power. He walks away from conflict.

6. If you encounter problems of any kind, discuss them with your parents, a teacher or a school counselor immediately.

7. Relax. Open your mind to new experiences. It may not seem like it right now, but you really are lucky to be here. Soon you'll enjoy your new life.

Higher education

It's called "The Brain Drain". About 18 percent of Hawai'i's higher education students attend college on the mainland and an estimated 75 percent of them do not return. In addition, many students who attend college here move away, lured by the greater availability of jobs, better paying professional positions, and lower living costs. Neither colleges nor high schools track students after they leave and no one knows exactly how many students forsake their island homes.

"I wish [University of Hawai'i Students] would borrow more and enjoy their college years."

–Sumner J. LaCroix,
UH professor of economics

Often, families who can afford to send their children to the mainland for an education — and for good reason: the islands can be provincial. Students who attend Mainland colleges and return to Hawai'i bring a valuable perspective which will serve them well.

That's not to say the 82 percent of Hawai'i college students who attend college here do not receive a very decent education. The University of Hawai'i and its seven community colleges serve every populated island through direct programs and satellite hookups. Programs are designed to match island needs: oceanography, linguistics, food services, astronomy, Pacific and Asian studies and travel industry management, as well as more traditional courses. State spending for the University of Hawai'i is $341 million annually, about 21 percent above the national average and about ten percent of the total state budget.

Hawai'i students also have a choice of three private O'ahu colleges and universities: Chaminade, Brigham Young and Hawai'i Pacific, as well as several specialized institutes and colleges. But the majority of the nearly 10,000 college freshmen each year who attend college go to the University of Hawai'i, which has many points in its favor:

- **Tuition and fees** for Hawai'i residents who register as undergraduates are very reasonable: at this writing, $1,476. For non-residents, the cost is $4,714.70.

- **Undergraduate classes** are unusually small compared to mainland classes and Hawai'i students have easier access to faculty.

- **The main campus** at Mānoa has strong master's and doctorate programs, in addition to a very broad undergraduate program.

- **Hawai'i's unique geography** — Mauna Kea mountain on the Big Island, the Pacific Ocean, our tropical climate — makes UH a natural for research. Its research program is among the top 70 university programs in the nation, according to the Carnegie Foundation for the Advancement of Teaching.

- **The university's ocean location** makes it perfect for a strong Asian-Pacific business program at a time when that part of the world is emerging economically.

- **The graduate school** received an "acceptable plus" rating from the Gourman Report, which cites UH's programs in agricultural economics, anthropology and botany.

Still, UH has a relatively poor reputation. Test scores are low compared to national university averages and many faculty members choose to send their own children to the mainland for a higher education.

The Fiske Guide to Colleges says of UH, "Overall, the academic atmosphere is very laid back" and quotes an education major: "Everyone more or less does his or her own thing and tries to just get by with decent grades."

In *The Price of Paradise*, published in 1992, UH professor of economics Sumner J. LaCroix offers several reasons for the poor image. He pointed out that 90 percent of UH students hold jobs, compared to about 63 percent at mainland universities. That means UH students have little time for study and for the campus activities that add dimension to the college experience.

Fewer than 20 percent of students live in campus housing and so must waste valuable study and social time traveling to and from campus. The little campus housing facilities that exist often go to those from the mainland or other countries.

In an interview for this book, LaCroix points out differences and similarities in attitude. Hawai'i students differ from mainland students in that they don't want to come out of college with debt.

"So they work in addition to school and many work not 20 hours, as you would expect, but 30 to 35 hours per week. Almost full-time," he says. "I think they are afraid that after-college debt will force them to the mainland [to live]. And there is also a cultural aversion to debt here."

"I wish," LaCroix says, "they would borrow and enjoy their college years. They'd get more from their college years ultimately."

LaCroix mentions another factor for UH students. Some believe if they work at the "Sheraton three years, they've got a leg up when they graduate and can move into higher positions at their workplace."

LaCroix argues, fairly, that students who apply themselves and do research before choosing classes can, and do, get a solid education at the University of Hawai'i.

pili

ho'oipoipo

romance

Adam and Eve

started it all

in a place

called paradise

About 20,000 people marry in Hawai'i every year; that's 55 a day. Just about one half of them are visitors who come to the islands for its beautiful backdrops — an ocean sunset or Kaua'i's famous Fern Grotto. The rest are kama'āina, *often celebrating their new life in ways unique to these islands.*

Mabuhay! Emily and Rufino are wed

One by one four men rose from long tables that filled the Lahaina Community Center, raised glasses of champagne and saluted newlyweds Emily Maniago and Rufino Villanueva:

"Mabuhay!" "Okole maluna!" "Banzai!" "Cheers!"

The 800 guests at the Villanueva wedding toasted the second generation Filipino couple according to modern Hawai'i tradition—in Filipino, Hawaiian, Japanese and English, representing the islands' ethnic diversity.

According to Filipino custom, several "sponsors" helped plan and finance the huge event. Chosen by the couple's parents, sponsors are longtime family friends whose role includes premarital counseling and advice to the young couple.

Emily's religious heritage is Jehovah Witness; Rufino's Roman Catholic. At their wedding in the garden of an ocean-front resort, Rev. Piula Alailima of Polynesian heritage performed a non-denominational ceremony. Alailima is minister at Lahaina United Methodist Church.

Loreto, one of Rufino's six siblings, prepared food for the reception that lasted five hours. It included traditional Hawaiian *lū'au* food like *kālua* pig and haupia, a coconut pudding.

Photo courtesy of family and Beach's House of Photography

Family and friends contributed hours of entertainment to the wedding reception. Emily's brother Jerry performed a traditional Tongan slap dance, his friend a Polynesian fire dance. Emily's nephew Frederick Maniago, from Moloka'i, sang a solemn Hawaiian chant. Emily's three sisters Anna and Lorna Maniago and Brenda MacPhetridge performed a hula. According to Hawaiian tradition, the new husband sits in a chair as the new wife dances a wedding hula in front of him. The Villanueva reception put a new twist on that: Leilani, a family friend, performed the wedding hula in front of guests.

Altogether Emily and Rufino's wedding and reception blended at least six cultures. And formed a culture of its own: *Hawai'i hou*. New Hawaiian.

Dating, mating, wedding, wanting

In the 1900s, when male workers by the hundreds were being imported to labor in Hawai'i's burgeoning sugar industry, there were 223.3 men on the islands for every 100 women. Women were so scarce that "picture brides," chosen by their husbands from photographs or through matchmaking relatives, were imported from the Philippines, Japan and other countries. The ratio has closed and today the number of men and women is about equal.

Today, it's apt to be the romance of paradise, not work or the necessity of mating that draws people here. For many young, single people Hawai'i is an adventure, a time to wait table, surf and soak up sun before moving back to Minnesota, marriage and a desk job. For others, perhaps recently divorced, it is a place for fresh starts and new relationships.

Couples also come for romantic reasons: newlyweds starting a new life together, older-weds hoping to rekindle romantic sparks under the tropical sun or simply fulfilling a longtime dream in paradise.

> "You're white and you want that brown-skinned man. Or a man wants an Asian wife."
>
> —Jennifer Terrance, Compudate

Will those coming here for romantic reasons find what they are looking for?

Dating tourists

For anyone seeking short-term relationship, Hawai'i is a dream come true. The high number of tourists (about 150,000 are on the islands at any one time) means a constant influx of new people from around the world. Longtime bachelor Tom Guthrie, happily married now, remembers a roommate who was "popular with the ladies."

"I never knew whose slippers were on the doorstep," he says. "It depends on how guys want to play it here. If they just want to get layed there are planeloads of *wāhine* arriving every day. Some guys would hang out at the airport to catch them as they got off the planes. They'd have their surfboards on the car and just ask, 'Hey, you want to go to Hana?'"

Guthrie grows pensive. "What freaks me out," he says, "is that I know a lot of people in my age group who are alone. There must be something freaking them out that they don't settle in with one person."

Several single professional women said they rarely or never date tourists, primarily because the relationship would be brief.

"It's very easy to get dates with tourists. They are at hotel bars literally waiting to be picked up," a *kama'āina* in her 30s commented. "But, at my age, I am looking to get married. I don't want to leave Hawai'i and I would not marry a tourist. So why would I date someone who doesn't live here?"

Still, nearly everyone who visits Hawai'i wistfully considers moving here — and many do return to live. A businesswoman in her 40s is engaged to a mainland attorney she met in an upscale Hawai'i restaurant. He is planning to move to the islands after they marry. "I told him I would not leave the islands and he was willing to move," she said. "In the meantime, having a long-distance relationship is fine. It lets me concentrate on work when he's away and concentrate on fun when we are together."

Dating kama'āina

Both sexes complained that the islands have small *kama'āina* or resident populations, limiting choices. "Everybody knows your business," complained one neighbor island bachelor. "It's like living in a small town, except that on the mainland you could get in your car and drive away, meet new people. Here, you can't do that."

The small neighbor island population makes "cheating" risky. A bachelor in his 50s was "three-timing", emotionally involved with three women at the same time. They found out, called each other, and all three dropped him.

Hawai'i is a wonderful place to date, an O'ahu radio announcer in her 20s points out. There's so much to do here and most of it is free: romantic places to hike and swim and just talk.

But a 48-year-old medical secretary was leaving Hawai'i after five years. Never married, she did not exactly come looking for a man, she says. Still, she admits, it would have been nice to find one.

"Men and women come here for different reasons," she insists. "Women

Menage a trois — Maui style

A Maui bachelor tells this delightful story.

He and a female acquaintance had gone snorkeling together near Molokini crater. As usual on first dates, conversation had been friendly, but stilted.

Bikini-clad, his companion lie relaxing on a float in the water, her eyes closed, a dreamy smile on her face. He gazed at her longingly, wishing he could muster the courage to tell her just how lovely she looked.

Suddenly, she began to giggle. "Hey!" she squealed. "Cut it out. You're tickling me!" Chuckling again, she swatted at the water.

It appeared something was nudging her from under the raft — and, of course, she assumed it was her male companion — that he had dived into the water and was boldly engaging in amorous frolic.

A few seconds later, to their surprise, a dolphin poked his face up out of the water and peered at them — his large mouth curved in what seemed like a smile.

"That dolphin did what I didn't have the nerve to do," the bachelor laughingly recalls. "He made the first move and it really broke the ice. I knew just how far I could go without getting her mad — and it was a lot further than I thought!"

Some *kama'āina* who heard this story cast it in a mystical light. Dolphins, they say, are so tuned in to humans that they can read our minds. The cetacean Cupid, they contend, had sensed the man's yearning and was lending a helpful hand — or nose, in this case.

come here usually to change spiritually, to get closer to nature. A lot of single men, on other hand, come here to bum out, live on the beach, chase women, live on the edge.

"On the mainland I used to say, 'What kind of job does he have? What kind of a car does he drive?'

"Here it's 'Does he *have* a job? Does he *have* a car?'"

Meanwhile, a Honolulu twice-divorced father of two complains that Hawai'i's *haole* women are too independent.

"Well, it takes a certain amount of chutzpah to get here," he says. "Some of these women came alone, left friends and relatives. I met one woman who sailed over on a container ship, for god's sake! Another one had hitchhiked all over the world. These are very tough women. They don't need a guy. Some guys maybe think that's good. Not me."

From O'ahu singles: great (free) dates

"The absolute worst possible thing to do on a first date," says a bachelor in his 50s, is to go a movie. "You sit there for two hours, not talking, staring at the screen and wondering what your date thinks of you."

Hawai'i's idyllic ambiance is free — and dating provides some of the island's best bargains. Here are suggestions from O'ahu singles for romantic, free or inexpensive dates. Some ideas are applicable to any island.

- **Walk.** Take a moonlight walk, scheduled regularly at Waimea Falls Park (638-8511) or the Honolulu Zoo (971-7195). Under a full moon, parks assume a wondrous appearance. Sign up. Or, call the Nature Conservancy (537-4508) and ask for hiking and nature walk schedules.

- **Be romantic**. Stroll on any beach. Pick up a pretty shell or a piece of coral and offer it to your date as a souvenir. Or, tell your date you are taking it home as a reminder of the beginning of your relationship.

- **Check the *Honolulu Weekly*** or the entertainment and community sections of newspapers for free concerts or lectures. Choose any subject that will interest both of you. A lecture on relationships can be especially appropriate and provide topics of conversation.

- **Park.** The tops of Tantalus or Pacific Heights are great for enjoying the view. Or, drive out to the windward side of the island. Have a sunset dinner at the Crouching Lion Inn, then park at La'ie Point. Watch the waves, talk and get to know each other.

- **Hike.** Get up early — 5 a.m. or so — and drive to Makapu'u lighthouse with backpacks full of water, fruit, and food. Hike up to the lighthouse and watch the sun come up. Then hike over the cliff to the inlet and dive off the rock or bask in the sun.

- **Picnic.** Ka'ena Point Nature Preserve has sand dunes, endemic coastal plants, albatross nests, whale watching. Or rent kayaks, take along a lunch, and paddle to Mokulua islets off Lanikai/Kailua. Or trek up to Kapena Falls off the Pali Highway. Or try the easy hike up Makiki; it has plenty of romantic spots for picnics.

- **Enjoy free or inexpensive shows and entertainment**. Hawai'i's many performers appear at book stores, on shopping center stages, and in free or inexpensive resort shows. Perfect for a casual date.

- **Be spontaneous**. Call at 4 p.m. and suggest the two of you go down to the beach to watch the sunset at 6. Bring a bottle of champagne or wine and two glasses. For an extra romantic touch, tie long thin ribbons on the glasses or wrap the bottle in a flower lei.

Tropical fantasies

The relatively small population of the islands does make it difficult for some people to find a perfect match, says Jennifer Terrance, promotions director at Compudate, an 11-year-old O'ahu dating service with clients on all islands.

A few years ago, before military cutbacks nipped the number of bachelors pouring into the islands, Compudate had many more male clients than female, Terrance says. In the last few years, the ratio of men to women clients has been equal.

In Hawai'i, people use the dating services not because they are desperate, but because they are particular, she insists. They want to fulfill romantic tropical fantasies.

"You're white and you want that brown-skinned man. Or a man wants an Asian wife," she says. Or, conversely, a woman may dream about men like the ones she left behind, and buttoned-down East coast professionals can be difficult to meet here.

Tropical realities

Mixed race relationships are common here, where cultures blend so smoothly. Many lead to interesting and fulfilling lives, but fusing cultures can put added stress on a relationship, warned two social workers.

"Mainland young people come over here and are fascinated by locals. Maybe it's the dark skin," says one. "But about a year or so after they are together, things start to fall apart. I see this happening over and over. There is not a strong bond between men and women in some cultures. The guys like to be with their buddies and want to hang out with them and (some of them) don't treat women very well."

Men dominate in some Pacific Island cultures, where communal living is common, "so the wife is left to care for the children and just be with the women, and mainland women just aren't brought up that way," she says.

Social workers see much spousal abuse, she warns, and it is not limited to any particular race. In Hawai'i, on the average, one woman per month loses her life to domestic violence.

Cultures aside, commented the second social worker, the stress of everyday life rears its ugly head in any relationship. "With the added problems here of very high food and housing costs and low-paying jobs, that puts a strain on any relationship."

Escaping to Paradise

Not every woman is seeking a relationship; some are trying to escape them. Hawai'i, an ocean away from their troubles, seems a safe haven for women who fear for their lives.

"We get calls every week from women on the mainland who want to start their lives over again [here in Hawai'i], to get away from abusive relationships," says Carol C. Lee, executive director of the Hawai'i State Coalition Against Domestic Violence.

But, Lee says, "We need to let these women know how difficult life in Hawai'i is. How difficult it is to get jobs, how scarce affordable housing is, how expensive child care is here, that only O'ahu has inexpensive mass transportation."

Most shelters give preference to women in immediate danger, Lee says, and that means women who already live here, whose antagonist is on the island. A woman who moves here from the mainland would be away from immediate danger and might not be accepted if the shelter is crowded.

On the other hand, the coalition often helps Hawai'i women escape abusive situations in Hawai'i, Lee says. They are sheltered on the islands until they can escape to the mainland.

Domestic violence is a leading cause of homicides both on the islands and on the mainland. Of the 58 murders in Hawai'i in a recrent year, 40 percent occurred in homes, according to the Hawai'i State Health Department.

Expectations

Maybe, romantically, we expect too much of the islands. Some couples come hoping fragrant breezes, moonlight walks and the flutter of cool sheets will repair a rent relationship. A man now in his early 50s sold his family farm in the midwestern U.S. and moved his family to the islands several years ago because, he says, his wife was dissatisfied and dreamed of living here — and he wanted to save his marriage. The family found financial success in a business, but marital happiness nonetheless eluded the couple and they eventually divorced.

"Maybe it's the Adam and Eve thing," he muses. "After all, this is supposed to be paradise. You come looking for perfection. The expectations are too high. Or maybe it is people who are not happy who come here, looking for more in their lives. This is a wonderful place. I'm glad I came. But maybe if whatever you are looking for is not there, where you are, maybe it does not exist."

The trauma of divorce can be doubly difficult here, far from supportive family and friends. In some cases, there's an urgency to finding a partner, any partner who can help pay the bills, who can stave off loneliness and help you survive in paradise. A 42-year-old divorced attorney says, half joking, "It's so expensive here. I need to find a wife."

Homosexual relationships fare no better in paradise. A spokesperson for gay rights blamed Hawai'i's "play environment" for the break-up of many gay relationships shortly after the couple arrives in the islands. "One of them may be serious and working hard; the other is off playing and maybe meets someone else," he says. "I've seen it happen over and over again."

Seeking wealth

The islands are famous for being costly — and they are also well-known for attracting the wealthy. Among the singles here are those seeking rich spouses. There's a clichè: "You can fall in love with a rich man as easily as a poor one. You just have to find one first." And you'll find one faster in a neighborhood where rich men swing their golf clubs just a few feet from your *lāna'i*.

"Oh sure, such men exist," says an attractive 42 year-old woman. Hoping to find a wealthy husband, she lives in an upscale O'ahu resort where she admits she cannot afford the $2,100 a month rent.

Watching a male foursome tee off across sweeping greens, she adds, "But most of them have wives. And even if you do find a rich, available man, there are hundreds of beautiful woman here, many hoping to marry money. And even the poor men are dating women 20 years younger than they are."

Former lovers

Former lovers have a way of showing up in Hawai'i. Four single women related similar experiences. They had lived on the islands for several years when an ex-boyfriend or ex-husband sought them out and visited, hoping to rekindle youthful sparks on a romantic tropical isle.

"He was just a friend I worked with, and we had a very short affair. We kept in touch and when he was available he called and it all sounded very romantic — him coming to visit. But it had been eight years and we really didn't have anything in common anymore. I enjoyed showing him around the island, but that was it," says one woman

Another woman: "I knew as soon as I picked him up at the airport that it wasn't going to work and I said, 'Uh, oh, what am I in for?' So I had to be honest about it and just tell him, 'No. Sorry. We're just friends.'"

"Actually," says a third woman, "I think we're better preserved in Hawai'i. Seeing a paunchy old mainland flame can be a bit of a shock."

The fourth woman enjoyed a happier encounter. She and a recently-divorced man she dated in college over 20 years ago are planning a long-term relationship.

Finding a mate

In Hawai'i, as elsewhere, a potential perfect mate is likely to appear when you aren't looking, when you are satisfied with yourself and your situation. In exotic paradise, many people meet their mates in very ordinary ways, at churches, at civic and business organizations, at work.

Beth and Doug — and "their tree"

Beth Holiday, 45, and Doug Baughman, 48, were both working when they met at the Maui County Fair. She was staffing a booth inside a hot, sticky tent. Doug was stationed at a booth outside, near a shady tree. Beth bought a soda and took a break under that tree. They struck up a conversation, continued talking for the four days of the fair, and communicated often by phone for three weeks before a first date.

One year later, they married at the fairgrounds.

"There's a lot more to it

than running into each other," Beth says. "We both worked on ourselves and were ready to be in a relationship. We were both happy and enjoying our lives. The only reason to take on a partner was to augment our lives, make them even better."

Sometimes looking — and praying — helps. Photographer Steve Strand prayed for a beautiful Christian wife for several years before meeting Valeria Franco, a Brazilian immigrant at his church. They married within a year.

It's the law:

Marriage

If you are living with your spouse without the benefit of a legal ceremony, think twice about coming to Hawai'i. Common law marriage is not officially recognized here.

In common-law marriage, a couple lives together as husband and wife and displays to the community that they are bound together as such, but are not married according to the laws of their jurisdiction. In other words, they have not applied for a marriage license or gone through a legal ceremony performed by an authorized person.

Whether your marriage will be recognized in Hawai'i depends on where you are coming from. If you are from a country (other than the United States) where common law marriages are recognized, Hawai'i will also recognize the marriage. But if you are from a state which recognizes common law marriages, Hawai'i may not consider you legally wed.

Those whose marriage is not valid by Hawai'i law do not have rights which the law gives to legally recognized spouses. They may not have a claim to their spouse's social security or other benefits. However, children born to unwed couples enjoy full rights.

Ironically, although Hawai'i does not recognize common law marriage, it is the first state in the nation to institute a "Reciprocal Beneficiary Relationship" law allowing unmarried couples many of the same benefits as those in official marriages. These include the right to shared medical insurance, joint property ownership and inheritances. The law, in a test stage at this time, is generally considered full of loopholes. Legislators and political groups are seeking ways to clarify the issue.

Divorce

Hawai'i is no place to bring a shaky marriage. Hawai'i has a "no fault" divorce law, but you must live in Hawai'i for a year before you can file for divorce and three months before you can file for legal separation. Simple uncontested divorces can be granted a few weeks after filing. Complex or contested cases can take much longer, but about 95 percent of divorces in Hawai'i are uncontested cases, handled amicably, according to Attorney Peter J. Herman in *A Practical Guide to Divorce in Hawai'i*.[1]

About 5,500 people get divorced in this state each year. It is not necessary to find fault with a spouse or to prove adultery, cruelty or desertion. The person seeking the divorce must simply show the court either that:

1) the marriage was irretrievably broken, or

2) the couple has had a legal separation in Hawai'i for two years and have not reconciled, or

3) the couple has a legal separation from another state and the time has expired or

4) the couple has lived apart without a formal separation for two years and there is no chance they will live together again.

Do-it-yourself divorces are legal in Hawai'i, although author Judith R. Gething,[2] strongly recommends that attorneys be consulted by both sides if children are involved.

➤ **TIP: Don't look for a potential mate**; just look for good friends of either sex, Beth Baughman advises. "You find people when you are giving — that's when you make bonds with people."

➤ **TIP: Become involved in activities** that will put you in contact with people whose interests are similar to yours. Join an investment group, a Toastmasters (speakers) club, or go on a Sierra Club or Nature Center hike, join a paddling team, visit the local Internet coffee shop.

RESOURCES

Send for:

• *Getting Married*, a pamphlet from the Hawai'i State Health Department, 1250 Punchbowl Street, Honolulu, Hawai'i 96813.

• *Marry Me on Maui*, a pamphlet from the Maui Chamber of Commerce, 250 Alamaha Street, N16A, Kahului, Hawai'i, 96732

ka pilikia
trouble

From the

unpleasant

to the illegal

Residents flee 1946 Hilo tsunami.

Nature's Fury

The seven Hawaiian Islands, floating like a tiny lifeline in the center of the vast Pacific Ocean, look vulnerable — and they are. Those yellow sirens on tall poles in and around beaches are designed to alert residents of approaching hurricanes and worse, tsunamis.

Tsunami

What is a tsunami? Imagine an ocean giant taking an enormous breath and inhaling miles of water, then spewing it back in a gargantuan wave traveling 500 miles an hour, crashing over people, homes, even towns. Tsunamis, the stuff of legends, occur only rarely, usually decades apart; but they can cause many deaths and much damage.

> **"Hawaiians know it's no good you live right on the ocean. More safe live back in town."**
>
> –elderly woman, Big Island

Hawai'i telephone books include a section devoted to tsunami evacuation routes. If those yellow sirens sound, you are instructed to get away from the ocean as quickly as possible, and head for the mountains.

Major tsunamis hit Hawai'i in 1946 and 1960. The 1946 tsunami caused 159 deaths and over $26 million in damage, much of it in Hilo on the Big Island. Survivors describe residents flocking to the ocean in awe to watch the water recede, then running for their lives as a tremendous wave swept onto shore, swallowing people and structures.

Considering the dangers lurking out there, some locals find it puzzling that newcomers pay millions of dollars for oceanfront homes. "Hawaiians know it's no good you live right on the water," says one elderly Big Island resident. "What for you do that when water all around us? You can look at it everyday anyway. More safe live back in town."

Hilo waterfront after 1946 tsunami.   Hawai'i State Archives

Hurricanes

As dangerous weather goes, hurricanes seem almost tame. Unlike tornadoes, which pop up in unexpected places with little warning and can take hundreds of lives, hurricanes usually announce themselves well in advance of their arrival. Whirlwinds form out in the vast Pacific and head toward the islands, spin offshore from one island to another, a dervish dancing this way and that, finally hurtling off to dissipate somewhere in the ocean. Meteorologists track these strange ballets for weeks. And longtime residents have seen the scenario played out so many times they tend to grow nonchalant.

In September, 1992, Kaua'i watched Hurricane 'Iniki perform an eerie pirouette offshore of the Hawaiian islands, threatening first the Big Island, then Maui. Just as it was poised to strike O'ahu, 'Iniki turned and roared straight into Kaua'i, its eye passing directly over the island. Winds of up to 165 miles per hour pummeled the island for five hours, causing $2 billion in damage.

While 'Iniki's arrival was devastating, advance warnings helped save lives. On Kaua'i, four people died as a result of 'Iniki: one from a heart attack, one by flying debris, and two fishermen at sea. Residents had plenty of time to evacuate oceanfront homes and condos and head for shelters. The democratic hurricane ravaged homes all over the island, chewing up mansions as well as cottages. Residents cowered under mattresses in bathtubs or crowded together in windowless staircases, listening to debris torpedo their homes.

Those who did not witness the devastation have had a difficult time relating to it. In 1993, a year after 'Iniki hit Kaua'i, Maui residents were ignoring a hurricane hovering off their shores. A Ha'iku resident summed up the attitude: "Relax, if it's going to hit here, the tsunami sirens will sound. We'll have plenty of time to go to a shelter."

➤ **TIP: Rent an inland bank safety deposit** box for family photos, small heirlooms and all important papers or keep them in sealed waterproof (plastic) boxes that can be easily carried and taken with you to a shelter.

➤ **TIP: Prepare.** Each summer assemble a hurricane kit including flashlights, batteries, medical supplies, canned food and water. Extensive instructions and evacuation routes are printed in the front of Hawai'i phone books. Be familiar with them.

➤ **TIP: Live a few blocks inland.** While modern technology makes it easier to track tsunamis and issue warnings, some people feel more comfortable living at least a few blocks from the ocean — and home insurance costs less.

➤ **TIP: Mortgage and homeowner's insurance** (costly here, in part due to 'Iniki) is a must. State law also mandates flood insurance in some areas. If you rent and your important belongings cannot be quickly packed and taken to a shelter, purchase renters insurance.

See also volcanoes and vog in the Big Island section, chapter 11: Which Island? pages 251 - 252.

This article, by Kaua'i writer and media producer Mary Earle Chase, first appeared in Kaua'i's *The Garden Island News*.

Don't fool around with Mother Ocean
by MARY EARLE CHASE

The headline read: "Fisherman drowns off Kīlauea." The article went on to tell, in a few paragraphs, of the death of Eric Myers, age 28, off Waikalua Beach.

We see these stories all too often here on Kaua'i. Someone swallowed up by our waters. Usually, it is the unforgiving ocean, but recently lives have been lost in the mysterious "blue room" in the West Cave and in the pool beneath Wailua Falls. Water has its way with us; its power too strong even for our willful ways.

The difference in this drowning was that I knew Eric Myers. He was not a fisherman. He was a computer graphics designer and programmer, one of an elite few on the Mainland hired by cutting edge technology companies to blaze new trails in the cyberbush.

He came to Kaua'i whenever he could to escape the world of glowing computer screens and embrace nature, raw and unprogrammed. He fell in love with a piece of land on the ocean at the end of Waikalua Road and managed to buy it. He put up a teepee.

A local fellow showed him how to place nets to catch lobsters on the reef by his secluded beach. He took two of his friends there one Saturday to help him. The ocean was rough but he seemed to know where to go and where not to. His friends followed.

Something went awry, and Eric and his friend Glenn found themselves struggling against a ferocious current. His other friend, John, tried to help, but before he could reach the two of them, Eric slipped away. He was found later with an obvious blow to the head. Waves, rocks, currents, they will have their way — even with experienced fishermen.

Many of us on the island know people who have been taken by the sea. Perhaps we have waged our own brief battles.

Eleven years ago, when my husband and I were visitors here, we unwittingly snorkeled into a swift current at Mākua (Tunnels) Bay. My brand new snorkel filled with water and I could not purge it. Choking, I grabbed at coral, but the current ripped me away. I panicked.

Fortunately, my husband Bill grabbed me and said, "Swim!" If I hadn't he would have knocked me out. When we made it back to the beach, a couple of local folks were standing at water's edge with surfboards, telling us they had been ready to go after us.

I thanked God they didn't have to.

Since then, I have maintained the utmost respect for the waters of Kaua'i. Perhaps I am overly cautious, doing most of my ocean swimming in summer when Hanalei Bay is like a lake. I hover around my children as they snorkel on boogie boards and watch nervously as my older son tries out his surfboard. When I hear sirens or see the fire-rescue truck speeding toward Hā'ena, my stomach churns and I pray.

Mother Nature's love is not unconditional. She demands that we stay awake, respectful, and in awe of her power.

Crime

Lloyd Yonemura, registrar at Moloka'i High and Intermediate Schools, is greeting 75 public school registrars from around the state. They have come to the quiet island of Moloka'i for a weekend conference that includes an optional mule ride to a leprosy colony and a hike through a rainforest.

"If you leave your car anywhere, don't lock it," he advises attendees. "Take everything out, okay? Take your purses and cameras with you. Leave your car unlocked and the windows down."

That way, he explains, thieves will know there is nothing to steal. They can rifle through your car conveniently, without having to jimmy open the glove compartment or the trunk. Or, they may bypass it completely, assuming it contains nothing of value.

> Hawai'i doesn't have much violent crime, but burglary's a breeze even for amateurs.

Hawai'i doesn't have much violent crime. As in the rest of the United States, violent crime rates are dropping. In fact, one study showed Hawai'i remains safer from violent crime than 41 other states and the District of Columbia.[1]

But robberies and non-violent crimes continue to climb.[2] Hawai'i's sliding doors, easy-open jalousie windows, and trusting lifestyle make burglary a breeze for even amateur bad guys. Most burglaries occur during the day, while people are at work.

"You are far more likely to come home to a ransacked apartment than get shot waiting for a bus," *Honolulu* magazine reported.[3]

That's comforting — unless you happen to be in the apartment when it's targeted, like Sharon, 28, was. She and a friend, sleeping in the third-floor loft of a condominium, left the sliding doors to their second floor balcony open. The loft looked directly down on the doors. And, after all, they were on the second floor. How could anyone break in?

"Easy," said a policeman who came to investigate the theft of Sharon's purse from a kitchen counter. He placed one foot against the exterior wall and hoisted himself effortlessly to the balcony. Then he showed

'A disaster from the civil rights standpoint'

In Hawaii, police can hold suspects for up to 48 hours without charging them or allowing them to post bail. That is longer than any state in the union, according to Honolulu attorney Eric Seitz, who called the State Supreme Court ruling allowing the holding "a disaster from the civil rights standpoint."[1] Civil rights attorneys argue that holding suspects without bail violates their constitutional rights.

Sharon and her neighbors a large footprint that indicated the thief had done just that.

Sharon's purse contained her credit cards, driver's license and car keys. Her car was gone from the parking lot.

"You don't have to get physically beaten to be mugged," Sharon mourned. "I feel violated."

Police blame the rising property crime rate on the burgeoning population. Much of the stolen property never turns up again. Carefree tourists make especially easy marks.

Pakalōlō (pot) and other drugs

A car stops for a light in a relatively busy Maui roadway. A disheveled man, about 40, comes up to the car window. "Pakalōlō...you want?"

It's the only time in the six years I've lived here that anyone has offered to sell me pot, but visiting friends say they are approached often to buy marijuana and other drugs. It is so common it becomes part of the tourist scene, an anecdote to scribble on a postcard and send home to friends. On most islands, community attitude toward pot is relaxed and in some quarters a strong sentiment exists for legalizing marijuana.

Locals warn visiting friends — and each other — not to hike too deep into Hawai'i's mountains alone, to obey *kapu* (no trespassing) signs. Occasionally lone hikers do not return and *kama'āina* look at each other with raised eyebrows. Did the hiker get lost, fall from a cliff, tangle with a wild boar... or wander upon someone's *pakalōlō* patch? Police make occasional raids on private gardens and stashes.

DUI laws: guilty until proven innocent

Hawai'i is dead serious about stopping drunk drivers. When you accept your driver's license you are agreeing to Hawai'i laws governing driving and liquor ingestion. If officers suspect you have been drinking, they do not have to read you the Miranda rights. Under the implied consent law,[1] you have already consented to submit to breath or blood testing. You do not have the right to remain silent, nor the right to counsel prior to taking the breath or blood test.

A first offense conviction can result in mandatory counseling, suspension or restriction of your driver's license, community service, time in jail, and/or a fine that ranges from $150 to $1,000. In Hawai'i you are legally intoxicated with a blood alcohol level of .08 percent. If you are in an accident, you can be charged with drunk driving if your alcohol level is .05 percent — for some people as little as two drinks.

Alcohol: *a legal drug*

A legal drug kills many island residents each year and because our neighbor islands have small populations, serious and fatal accidents hit home harder. Many longtime Maui, Kaua'i or Big Island residents know someone who has been killed or injured in an accident involving liquor.

Hawai'i has the fourth highest number of alcohol-related fatalities in the nation. Alcohol is involved in 55 percent of all traffic fatalities — 12 percent more than the national average.

It's not that Hawai'i's laws are lax; in fact, they are among the toughest in the nation and periodic road checks are conducted to weed out drunk drivers. But the islands' easy-going lifestyle encourages partying... and to many that means drinking. Not all drinking is celebratory. Alcoholism tends to go up as employment goes down and on some Hawaiian islands, jobless rates are high.

Murder

When murder occurs, in Hawai'i as on the mainland, police look first to family and friends. Family violence is also on the rise here, in part because of drug and alcohol abuse.

Family Court in Oʻahu allegedly has a zero tolerance policy toward domestic violence. Offenders who violate the terms of their parole can be sentenced to serve time in Hawaiʻi's cramped prisons, including tents at Oʻahu's Hālawa prison.[4]

Bars and brothels

Hostess bars are legal on Oʻahu; prostitution is not. "Korean" bars or hostess bars — all with the word "club" in them — are generally understood to be strip bars. They are legal and well-attended by both locals and tourists. In fact, they are so numerous that Honolulu has no red-light district to which prostitution is contained; bars are scattered throughout the island. The state legislature has at times considered how to deal with the problem of prostitution; crack-

Nothing illegal here — just another form of diversion on Oʻahu

downs are common. While prostitution is visible in Waikīkī, Chinatown and a few other parts of Honolulu; it is much less obvious — and probably somewhat less prevalent — on neighbor islands.

The crime, a petty misdemeanor, carries a fine of $500 and up to three days in jail for a first conviction. Like drugs, prostitution is considered by some visitors as just another tourist attraction; to others it is offensive. Whatever your attitude toward prostitution, it is not so rampant that it should in any way affect your decision to live here — unless you are planning to run a bar or other nighttime entertainment.

Speaking of sex, convicted sex offenders must register with local police. In 1996 the Oʻahu police department's identification unit registered 302 sexual offenders.[5]

Here are some rules you should know about:

- Front seat drivers and passengers must wear seat belts whenever the car is moving. At this time, failing to use a seat belt carries a $27 fine.

- Stop for pedestrians at designated crosswalks and intersections. Failing to yield to a pedestrian carries a $42 fine. It is also illegal to pass a vehicle which is stopped at a crosswalk.

- Children under three years of age must be in approved child restraint seats when they are in a moving car. Fine, $82.

- Littering — throwing any debris from a car, moving or not — is a crime.

- You must turn off your car's engine if you leave the car. You must also lock the ignition, remove the key and set the parking brake.

- Jaywalking carries a $40 fine.

Gangs in paradise

Hawai'i has about 1,000 documented gang members,[6] says Honolulu gang prevention police Officer Dean Shear. The word "gang" evokes images of crime and brutality, but gangs can vary from a bunch of kids spray-painting walls to armed villains extorting money and dealing drugs. A gang, by police definition, is a group of three or more who

1.) associate on a regular basis;

2.) has a name;

3.) claims territory or "turf";

4.) engages in criminal behavior.

Shear has seen Polynesian gangs from the mainland whose sole purpose is to deal drugs. "We're positive they have family here, and it's only a matter of time before there's trouble," he told a gathering of Windward O'ahu parents and educators. He sees illegal drugs, particularly "ice," (crystal methamphetamine) as the major gang problem.

Sidney Rosen, author of *Toward a Gang Solution*, counts about 50 gangs on O'ahu. Rosen says there is gang activity on all islands and it's no different on the mainland. Gangs vary from graffiti groups whose primary activity is defacing property, to gangs that deal in drugs, steal, extort money from students and instigate inter-gang violence that can end in injury or death.

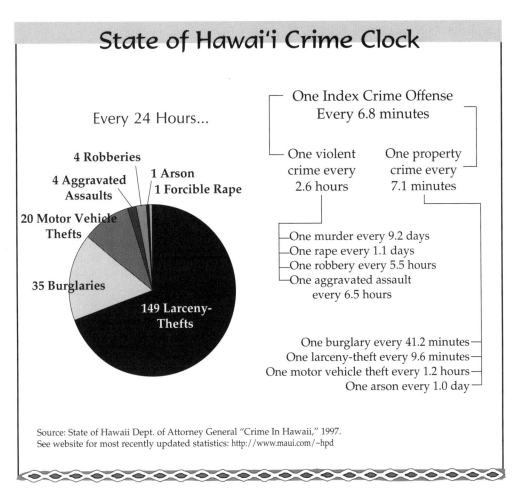

Every 24 Hours...

4 Robberies
4 Aggravated Assaults
1 Arson
1 Forcible Rape
20 Motor Vehicle Thefts
35 Burglaries
149 Larceny-Thefts

One Index Crime Offense
Every 6.8 minutes

One violent crime every 2.6 hours

One property crime every 7.1 minutes

One murder every 9.2 days
One rape every 1.1 days
One robbery every 5.5 hours
One aggravated assault every 6.5 hours

One burglary every 41.2 minutes
One larceny-theft every 9.6 minutes
One motor vehicle theft every 1.2 hours
One arson every 1.0 day

Source: State of Hawaii Dept. of Attorney General "Crime In Hawaii," 1997.
See website for most recently updated statistics: http://www.maui.com/~hpd

CRIME

Youth gangs tend to be drawn along ethnic lines. On O'ahu, Kahuku School Principal Lea Albert identifies several groups, including Tongan Krip Gangsters, Hau'ula Boyz, La'ie Boys Incorporated and the North Shore Boyz.[7]

Meanwhile, some neighbor island students and educators insist the only gang activity comes from "wanna-bes" who take on gang colors and dress: a bandanna around the forehead or thigh, a tattoo or burn that signifies membership. Several schools forbid wearing headgear, a way to prevent gangs from displaying their colors.

A neighbor island high school freshman puts it this way: "There's wanna-be gangs, no real gangs. Sure, every place has gangs. I guess they think they're in gangs but anyone who lives on the mainland, like in Chicago or if you live in California, areas like that, you'll know what a real gang is."

Disorganized crime?

It is generally acknowledged that organized crime exists in Hawai'i. At times over the years it has seemed to be more *disorganized* crime, in part because Hawai'i is divided into so many ethnic factions. Beginning in the early 1960s, syndicated crime in the islands is believed to have been headed by Koreans, local-Asians, Samoan and Hawaiian bosses or sub-bosses. At least two murders — one in the victim's bed, another in a cane field — are believed linked to organized crime.

"The local syndicate was like a guerrilla force of unknown strength," write Gavan Daws and George Cooper in *Land and Power in Hawai'i*.[8] "It was known to be out there, a factor to be reckoned with in the equation of modern Hawai'i. But how big it really was, what territories it controlled, what high ground it might be seeking to occupy — these were things that few or none outside of organized crime knew."

Organized crime got a slow start here in part because until the mid-1940s prostitution and gambling were either legal or tolerated. Ironically, lotteries and other forms of legalized gambling have been voted down in recent years for fear of tarnishing Hawai'i's clean, wholesome image.

Weeding it out

On O'ahu and some of the sister islands, civilians and police working together have had success in cutting down on crime. The Honolulu police sponsor numerous programs such as Seniors Against Crime and The Community Policing Team which has volunteers walking "beats" to report crimes. The Waikīkī By Night program takes concerned citizens on walks spotting potential crime. Volunteer parking lot patrols have also contributed to a drop in auto break-ins on some islands, especially at beaches, where car robberies are frequent.

RESOURCES

- To call an ambulance, or report a crime, call **911** from any island
- **Any state office** toll free: 1-800-468-4644
- **Ho'ike Information line:** 1-800-529-3352 Information line provides public with a contact point to obtain answers or referrals for police-related questions. Call week days during business hours.
- **Honolulu Police Department annual report**: Available at Hawai'i libraries, includes crime statistics and reports for each O'ahu precinct or neighborhood. Valuable if you are choosing to live in a Honolulu neighborhood. **http://www. maui.com/~hpd**
- **The state Attorney General's crime report**: Includes crime statistics for the state, available at public and college libraries.

Creatures

Late one night, Margaret Norrie awoke to a nightmare. As she lay in her waterbed, she experienced a crawling sensation. Leaping up, she felt a fire-like pain singe her thighs. Norrie flipped on a light to see scores of tiny red fire ants attacking her flesh. Screaming, shivering in pain and horror, she ran to the shower to wash off the red menace.

Fire ants didn't get their name because they're red, but because their sting is like a second-degree burn. According to entomologist G. Nishida in *What Bit Me?*,[1] they "... grab the victim's skin with their mandibles while driving stingers into the victim. They tend to sting several times without letting go... blistering... and may eventually scar." The pain may be accompanied by a rash, faintness, blurring of vision, chest pains and abdominal cramps. If stung extensively, there may be nausea, vomiting, dizziness, perspiration and even shock. While Norrie did not experience those severe reactions, the red welts covering her thighs lasted for several days.

> "To live here is to learn to live with bugs."
>
> – Carlo Carbajal

For some reason, many years ago, a rumor passed across the world that Hawai'i had no pesky insects. That's only partially true; poisonous insects are relatively few here. There is only one kind of snake established here — a harmless tiny blind snake — and rabies is unknown in the Hawaiian islands, says Nishida, natural science collections manager at O'ahu's Bishop Museum. Nevertheless, an abundance of creeping, crawling, biting and otherwise scary critters make for interesting island conversation.

Like plants and people, insect transplants grow and thrive in Hawai'i's ideal climate. If you choose to live in a house or cottage, instead of a regularly sprayed condominium, you will come to have a grudging respect for huge cockroaches that look you in the eye, spiders that swath your yard in webs, swarming termites and tiny midges that find their way into the house despite your every attempt to block them.

Old-time Hawaiians often built their houses on stilts to discourage moisture and flooding, as well as to escape ground-dwelling bugs. It didn't always work.

Mosquitoes

Mosquitoes were once unknown on the islands. A legend says that whalers, angry because missionaries were discouraging island women from being friendly, loosed the first mosquitoes near a missionary house at Lahaina, Maui. Whatever their introduction, mosquitoes are *kama'āina* now, setting up nurseries in any stagnant water they can find, from rainforest mud puddles to *lānaʻi* flowerpots.

One of the problems with mosquitoes, Nishida said in an interview for this book, is that they transmit heartworm to pets, especially those left outdoors overnight. "If left untreated, your pet can die from heartworm" — not a very pretty way to go.

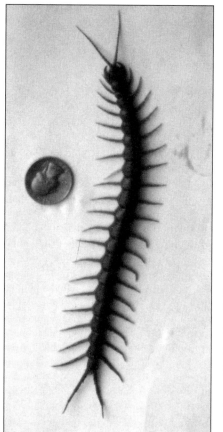

Centipedes

We residents like to exchange centipede horror stories. We'll swear we've encountered centipedes a foot long and measure off 14 inches with our hands as we talk about it. We are, of course, exaggerating. Centipedes are so ugly and move so quickly that they tend to appear larger than they actually are. Nine inches is about the largest Grant K. Uchida, an entomologist with the state department of agriculture, has seen. The ones hiding under leaves and wood in my backyard — and occasionally landing in my pool — are five to six inches. For the record, centipedes can't swim.

Maui school registrar Marty-Jean Bender, a former biology teacher, remembers waking on two nights to find a centipede hovering near her sleeping child's open mouth. Bender's first reaction was that of anyone seeing a centipede: swat it away. But that can be foolhardy — the centipede bites with two pincers, injecting a venom to which some are extremely allergic. The Chinese consider the centipede one of the five evils of the natural world, and anyone who's slipped his foot into a shoe and been bitten would agree.

Some of the nasty things said about centipedes are true, Uchida says. They tend to head for warm beds, occasionally biting unknowing sleepers who scare them. But centipedes aren't out for blood, they are just trying to stay warm.

There's a commonly held belief that if you find one centipede, its mate is lurking nearby; but that's not usually true, says Nishida. Centipedes don't travel with mates; if you see two or more at the same time it may be because their usual nesting places have been disturbed or because the humidity is not right for these "narrow comfort-range animals." Or they may just be out hunting for food — which does not include you.

One last thing. Superstition says it's bad luck to talk about centipede encounters, and if you talk about centipedes, you're sure to see one. So forget I mentioned it, okay?

Ants, ants, ants

There are over 40 species of ants in Hawai'i, Nishida says. Some prefer sugar; others prefer protein or fats. Answer the phone while you're making a meat sandwich and your food can be covered with the tiny creatures when you get back. In waving ribbon formation, they march *en masse* up walls, across bathroom tiles. Kill a few and their replacements appear, undaunted.

Ants can tunnel through concrete floors, into the grout between ceramic tiles, erect nests in tape recorders and telephones, and have been known to ruin computers. Kill a centipede or roach and leave it in your shower — ants will carry its body away to their nests within a few hours.

"To live here," says artist Carlo Carbajal, who woke in his cottage one night to find a centipede walking across his face, "is to learn to live with bugs. They are simply a part of your life here. You cannot escape them. But the worst is the ants. They or their scouts are everywhere!"

Geckos, the good guys

They frighten and fascinate tourists, who watch transfixed as geckos converge on a porch light or slither across a hotel wall. The little lizard with the round digits is Hawai'i's mascot and you'll learn to love, or at least tolerate, him.

Having a gecko take up residence in your home is considered lucky and the chances are you'll have at least two or three of various sizes "laughing" loudly and darting about at night. Fascinating as they are, geckos can grow to several inches in length, deposit egg sacs, and leave little ice-cream-cone droppings that are a nuisance, especially when they land in your toaster or computer. You'll want to keep tight screens on your windows.

Cane spiders

Like most Hawai'i spiders, cane spiders (also called banana spiders) are shy and relatively harmless. They don't bite unless cornered — they'll just scare you to death. Cane spiders commonly have three-inch leg spans, but islanders report spotting some as big as a man's hand. Brown and hairy, they are sometimes mistaken for deadly tarantulas, which do not live in these islands. Cane spiders are actually beneficial, eating other household insects, but their sinister appearance makes it hard to appreciate their timid nature.

Numerous other kinds of spiders live in the islands. The infamous Southern black widow shows up occasionally and the brown widow is common, often found hanging around outside homes. Brown and black widow spider bites are dangerous and require a doctor's attention. Nearly every spider will bite if cornered but most cannot penetrate your skin. Crab spiders spin enormous webs that drape backyard shrubs, hang from telephone wires or send shivers down the spines of unwary hikers. The bite of these spiders, a gardener says, causes aching welts. The violin spider is another one to watch out for; the bite is serious.

Daring jumping spider

Be on the lookout for this little fellow, very common inside most homes. He is so small and playful looking — usually a half inch or less — that when a "daring jumping spider" hops onto your desk or your countertop you'll be more startled than frightened, you may be tempted to either squash it with your finger or just watch it, fascinated. However, this spider's bite is "sharp and painful and produces pale, raised bumps surrounded by redness, accompanied by blistering and swelling," according to *What Bit Me?* "The swelling can be severe, extending beyond the immediate bitten area... A dull throbbing pain and itchiness may last several days." Best to leave this cute little spider alone.

Numerous other insects — hornets, fleas, mites — make our paradise less than perfect. The state department of agriculture makes valiant efforts to keep snakes, bugs and other pesky creatures away.

Fleas, ticks and their hosts

Fleas and ticks have been a problem on the islands for years. So have cats. Feral cats breed in colonies throughout the islands and many of the cats are flea and/or tick-infested. It is common, for example, to find litters of kittens at beaches and parks, begging for food yet frightened of people. Island humane societies work hard to combat feral dog and cat problems. Some societies loan cages for you to capture cats and a few veterinarians offer free or reduced-cost spaying and neutering for such animals. A new program tries a life-sustaining approach: cats are caught, vaccinated and neutered, then released back into the wild in monitored colonies. Some

It's dinner time behind a Hanalei, Kaua'i, restaurant.

Toni Polancy

homeowners and restaurant owners appreciate cats because they help to alleviate another island problem: rats.

Rat tales

Who came first? The rat or the mongoose? Actually, whalers and traders were the first to arrive here. Rats hitchhiked to the islands on their ships, went forth and multiplied. At some point, mongoose were imported in an ill-planned attempt to control the rats, but they are daytime creatures and rats are nocturnal, so their paths rarely crossed. Now the mongoose has become just another interesting island creature. You'll occasionally see them — blond flashes streaking across rural roads.

Today, most islands have rodent control programs. Those metal bands wrapped around palm tree trunks, glinting in the sun, prevent rats from running up the trees, a favorite nesting place.

In a true-life Pied Piper tale, the city of Honolulu once made a major assault on a rat-infested Waikīkī banyan tree after a rat ran up the mayor's leg, ironically, during a press conference to discuss the rat problem. Weapons included traps and heavy spray guns to scare the long-tailed creatures out of sewers.

"Ukus" (head lice)

Don't be upset if your school-age child comes home with head lice, known here as "ukus." Lice epidemics are common even in mainland schools; in Hawai'i's tropical weather, they are almost unavoidable. Teachers conduct regular checks for the sticky whitish-gray nits (eggs) or tiny lice that are almost invisible in hair. Children who have lice are sent home to parents for treatment. Over-the-counter shampoos are available, or ask your doctor to prescribe a stronger treatment.

Roaches

You'll also become accustomed to looking a three-inch long cockroach in the eye. Call it a water bug, if that lessens your aversion. You'll even learn to prefer large roaches, which visit in one and twos, to the smaller mainland varieties that invade by the hundreds. Hawai'i hosts many kinds of roaches, but most can be kept under control by cleanliness and chemicals. A small light-colored version, the German roach, is especially plentiful here.

No doubt you'll learn to live with and respect all these island creatures eventually and you will certainly overcome any fear you may have. If they become too great a nuisance, you can always spray. And spray. And spray again.

"I vowed I wouldn't use chemical sprays," says one newcomer. "But dealing with bugs here is like giving birth. You're in labor and all your good intentions are forgotten. It's like, 'Bring on the drugs.'"

➤ **TIP: New advances in flea and tick control** make it easy to keep domestic pets flea free. Monthly pills seem to work well, as do gels applied between the animals shoulder blades.

➤ **TIP: Eliminate any stagnant water**, virtual "nurseries" for mosquitoes. Trim palm trees often, keep yards free of litter, store grain and any food in rat-proof containers, and keep tight lids on trash cans. Most cats are too smart to attack a rat, but a rambunctious dog can discourage rats. Be careful. Rat bites are dangerous. If bitten, rush to an emergency room.

➤ **TIP: Chemical sprays,** applied around the exterior of homes and judiciously inside, help to avoid insect problems. Many residents, however, simply put up with the creatures or find ecologically-sound ways of dealing with them. Ground cinnamon is said to discourage ants. A solution of 3 cups water, 1 cup sugar and 1 teaspoon boric acid sprinkled near nests kills the colony

➤ **TIP: Ecologically-safe tricks**. Plantation camp residents had a few tricks to deal with insects. They put water-filled jars under each leg of the kitchen table, discouraging ants from crawling up. And the same system worked for keeping crawling creatures off beds. Bay leaves keep bugs (weevils) out of staples like flour and rice. It's also wise to avoid bed covers and dust ruffles that extend to the floor, easy ladders for crawling bugs.

➤ **TIP: Maintain a humorous outlook.** Have faith that eventually you will become accustomed to sharing paradise with a few of God's less welcome creatures.

Do tourists cause accidents?

It's the weekend and there's less traffic than usual along Kahekili Highway on windward Oʻahu. Although he's driven the road hundreds of times, Ted Sakai, administrative assistant to the state director of public safety, is enjoying the scenery, the deeply ridged Koʻolau Mountains.

Suddenly the car in front of him stops. Sakai slams on his brakes.

"At first I was mad," he says. "I couldn't understand why on earth someone would come to a complete stop on the highway. Then I realized it was a car with tourists.

"Then this guy sticks his head out the window and climbs up on top of the roof of the car and takes a picture. And I'm behind, stopped, watching."

Most longtime Hawaiʻi drivers have encountered similar situations: tourists jumping out of cars on busy roads to take a photo in front of a sugarcane field. Tourists watching for whales and almost driving over the *pali* (ocean cliffs). Tourists U-turning on a narrow road to go back to a waterfall.

So, do tourists cause accidents?

Bob Siarot, district engineer for state highways on Maui, says he often gets calls from local folks with complaints about visitors' driving habits. Some of the complainants must travel the notoriously wriggly road to remote Hana. Its speed limit is a grueling 10 to 20 miles an hour for much of the 50-mile trip and can take as long as three tortuous hours. There's even a souvenir tee-shirt: "I survived the road to Hana." Residents boast of making the trip in half that time.

"Hana people call and say tourists drive too slow and they get angry and call me. But usually tourists are going at the speed limit. It's actually the locals who are making the road unsafe for everybody by passing," he says.

Okay, so do tourists *contribute* to the accident rate?

"That's very difficult to surmise," Siarot insists. "Accidents are caused by both drivers. If a resident becomes impatient because a driver is slow, then the resident causes the accident. It's caused by bad judgment. People like to blame others for accidents, but really you've got to blame yourself."

So, relax, he says. This is Hawaiʻi. Hang loose. Slow down.

moku
'āina hea?

which island ?

An important decision

that will affect

your success or

failure here

Resident Population

by counties

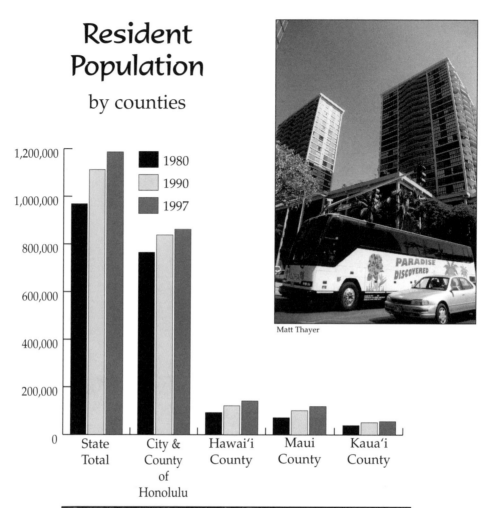

Matt Thayer

Legend:
- 1980
- 1990
- 1997

Y-axis:
- 1,200,000
- 1,000,000
- 800,000
- 600,000
- 400,000
- 200,000
- 0

Categories:
- State Total
- City & County of Honolulu
- Hawai'i County
- Maui County
- Kaua'i County

Matt Thayer

Abundant choices

Michael Miller, 40, came to the islands several years ago with friends, a family of four. They all shared a dream — a quiet bungalow by the ocean. They were sure they'd found it in a rented cottage in a quaint Polynesian community on the north shore of O'ahu, but within a few months the glow of paradise began to fade.

The father, a building contractor, could not find a job. Michael, a waiter, and the mother, a physical therapist, secured work, but it was in busy Honolulu — more than an hour's drive each way in rush-hour traffic.

Meanwhile, the two daughters, 10 and 14, had trouble adjusting to new schools, where they were among only a handful of Caucasians. They began to skip classes. Within a year, the family returned to California. Today, only Michael remains on the islands.

The family might have fared better if they had carefully chosen their location. Settling in an area closer to Honolulu, such as Kailua or Kāne'ohe, would have put the adults closer to work and the children in school districts with more *haole* children where they might have felt more comfortable.

People think of Hawai'i as all one place, but that is like saying all of the U.S. is Texas.

People elsewhere think of Hawai'i as one place, but that is like saying all of the United States is Texas or all of Europe is France. The six populated Hawaiian islands share certain advantages — and problems — discussed in other chapters of this book. Except for those similarities, the islands and towns vary greatly in climate, ambiance and lifestyle.

Choose your climate

Each Hawaiian island is, in effect, a small land mass with many geological variances: a sunny southern side where temperatures typically reach 90 degrees or more in the summer, but rarely drop below 60 degrees in the winter. Each island also has a rainy windward side. Some island neighborhoods are perched on mountains and temperatures can be much cooler, dropping into the 40s on winter evenings. If you don't like the climate in one locale — you can move to another.

Choose your ambiance

Hawai'i is a neoteric state, with similar people often settling in the same area thereby creating a distinctive ambiance. Many towns fall into easy categories which reflect the population. When visiting various towns, ask anyone: who lives here? You're sure to receive a simple, accurate answer. Typically, Hawai'i's towns fall into these designations: tourist; surfer/hippie; "local;" new/developing, or business.

Choose your decade

You have yet another lifestyle choice — one unique to the islands. You may, in effect, choose the era in which to live. The islands vary in the degree to which they have developed. Would you prefer to live on an island reminiscent of the 1970s or 80s (O'ahu); 1960s (Maui); 1950s (Kaua'i and the Big Island) or 1930s (Moloka'i and Lāna'i)? This is not a criticism. Most of us would prefer to live and raise families in a slower, more innocent time. Isn't that part of the island dream for which we search?

The following is an overview of each island and includes a list of resources for obtaining additional information. The number of McDonald's restaurants serves as a pop culture measurement of development. Population counts are given for two dates, 1980 and 1997 (the most current year they are available), to show the growth on each island.

➤ **TIP**: Unless you have a reason to choose a particular island — for example, friends or relatives or a job — you should visit at least two islands before finalizing your decision.

O'ahu

Size: 600 square miles
Population in 1980: 762,565
Population in 1997: 869,857
Predominant Occupations: Retail business (both local and tourist related); government, importing, exporting, health care, some agriculture
Unemployment: 5.3%
Number of McDonald's restaurants: 47
The best thing about O'ahu: Plenty to do
The worst thing about O'ahu: Traffic
What other islanders say about O'ahu: "Too noisy! Too crowded! Can't wait to get home."
What O'ahu says about itself: "We are the Hawaiian islands. We have three-quarters of the population."

Want to enjoy all the things you are moving to the islands for — perfect weather, sunshine, beauty — and still have a rich cosmopolitan life? In addition to swimming, surfing and soaking up sun, would you like to enjoy big-name concerts, well-stocked libraries, and Broadway-caliber plays?

Consider O'ahu.

About 75 percent of the state's 1,180,000-plus population is crammed on this third-largest Hawaiian island. More than 380,000 people live in Honolulu, the capital and largest city in the chain, and the nation's 11th-largest metropolis. Neighbor islanders deride busy, teeming O'ahu, vowing to learn from the island's over-development: too many skyscrapers, too much bustle.

True, in Honolulu, you will look out from your high-rise at houses spilling down mountains like sauce on giant ice cream sundaes. You may stare out the window of your condominium into the window of another apartment. You will gaze from your *lāna'i* down at lines of cars and hear, not the sound of conch shells serenading the sunset, but police and ambulance sirens.

O'ahu

Kawela
Kahuku Point
Lā'ie
Ka'ena Point
Nature Preserve
Dillingham
Airfield
Hale'iwa
Hau'ula
Punalu'u
Ka'a'awa
WAI'ANAE MTS.
Schofield
Barracks
Mākaha
Wheeler
Air Force
Base
Kapolei
Mililani Town
TO O'AHU MTS.
Waiāhole
Wai'anae
Kahalu'u
Kāne'ohe
Marine Corps
Air Station
Waipahu
Pearl City
'Aiea
Salt Lake
Kāne'ohe
Kailua
Barbers Point
Naval Station
Pearl Harbor
Naval Reservation
Makiki
Waimanalo
HONOLULU
Āina
Haina
Hawai'i
Kai
Makapu'u
Point
Waikīkī
Diamond Head
Koko Head

Still, as large cities go, Honolulu is lovely, clean and relatively safe. And all those high-rises allow you to live within easy walking distance of work, world-wide shopping, some very fine dining, the ocean and parks. A recent comparative study of the "quality of life" in 300 American metropolitan areas ranked Honolulu in the top third.

Here, you are residing in the very heart of the islands; stand still and you can feel it pulsating beneath your feet. During the day, downtown Honolulu is the center of power for the island chain. In tall glass business buildings and small historic palaces, decisions are made that will intimately affect the lives of all residents of every island.

After dark, the city lights up like a massive fireworks display stopped in mid-explosion, providing breathtaking scenes from balconies. On busy Kalākaua Avenue in Waikīkī, there's a carnival atmosphere. Mimes and musicians, hucksters and prostitutes ply their trades next to posh boutiques, open into the wee hours. O'ahu's 85,000 tourists (on any one day) can get anything they want nearly all night long.

O'ahu's economy

O'ahu has the highest employment rate of the islands and a wider variety of both blue and white collar positions. It is the shipping hub and the government center of the islands and the landing point for most tourists. Here are most of the islands' major television studios, banking centers, hospitals, advertising agencies, commercial and shopping centers. This is headquarters for the nation's Pacific military fleet, which provides $2.6 billion annually and provides jobs, directly and indirectly for an estimated 27,000 civilians.

However, even O'ahu's economy has suffered since the early 1990s, and except for the tourist/resort industry, jobs are more difficult to find than a few years ago. (See the chapter on Working.)

A tour of O'ahu

In addition to high-rises, Honolulu's neighborhoods contain an eclectic mix of old plantation-style houses and modern homes. Stand near the Ala Wai canal in Waikīkī. Look up at the mountains. These are mostly desirable, but costly older neighborhoods with sparkling views, just far enough away from town to offer respite from the busy highways, yet still close enough to

Characteristics of O'ahu Neighborhoods

Neighborhood	Resident population	House holds	Average size	% college grads	Median income
Oahu total	836,231	265,625	3.02	24.6	40,581
1. Hawaii Kai	27,432	8,835	3.08	41.7	65,901
2. Kuliouou-Kalani Iki	15,280	4,986	3.06	45.0	65,844
3. Waialae-Kahala	9,635	3,549	2.71	46.3	66,228
4. Kaimuki	18,425	6,216	2.90	26.8	45,397
5. Diamond Head/Kapahulu/ St. Louis Heights .	20,860	8,040	2.56	27.3	39,357
6. Palolo	13,034	4,097	3.16	20.7	40,844
7. Manoa	20,834	6,420	2.79	44.5	51,866
8. McCully/Moiliili	28,466	13,428	2.08	27.8	31,974
9. Waikiki	19,757	11,445	1.71	29.4	26,980
10. Makiki/Tantalus	29,989	14,681	2.03	36.0	33,623
11. Ala Moana/Kakaako	10,943	6,218	1.72	26.0	25,162
12. Nuuanu/Punchbowl	16,221	5,776	2.78	30.1	44,199
13. Downtown	11,752	5,814	1.89	26.6	25,436
14. Liliha/Kapalama	21,235	6,683	3.00	21.7	43,164
15. Kalihi/Palama	40,147	10,967	3.46	9.1	25,647
16. Kalihi Valley	17,798	4,079	4.33	9.5	39,794
17. Moanalua	12,260	3,576	3.30	24.9	43,706
18. Aliamanu/Salt Lake	37,442	12,029	3.11	23.3	38,078
19. Airport	26,734	5,877	3.40	19.3	29,989
20. Aiea	32,648	10,680	2.93	24.4	45,585
21. Pearl City	46,758	13,540	3.44	22.3	55,053
22. Waipahu	51,295	13,921	3.68	15.9	46,501
23. Ewa	42,967	11,449	3.65	15.9	40,679
24. Waianae Coast	37,411	9,429	3.93	8.9	32,392
25. Mililani/Waipio	34,681	10,630	3.26	30.9	51,807
26. Wahiawa	44,451	11,020	3.45	12.6	29,767
27. North Shore	15,749	4,764	3.23	18.9	37,209
28. Koolauloa	14,340	3,614	3.67	22.2	35,283
29. Kahaluu	14,397	4,258	3.37	26.4	50,454
30. Kaneohe	40,595	12,237	3.25	26.4	51,497
31. Kailua	41,886	13,283	3.13	34.5	56,788
32. Waimanalo	9,057	2,088	4.30	10.1	42,763
33. Mokapu/Kaneohe MCAS	11,662	1,996	3.85	13.3	26,927

Source: City and County of Honolulu Planning Department, tabulations from the 1990 U.S. Census as quoted in the Hawaii Data book For updated statistics see http://www.hawaii.gov/dbedt/index.html

avoid long, stressful commutes. If you can afford it, consider **Manoa Valley**, location of the University of Hawai'i; **Makiki, Nu'uanu, Kamehameha Heights** or **Pacific Heights**. Home prices start at about $350,000. Rentals abound. Your neighbors will be an interesting mix of longtime residents and newcomers.

Beginning at Waikīkī and heading south, Kalākaua Avenue becomes Diamond Head Road and proceeds through the cushy neighborhoods of **Diamond Head** and **Kāhala**. Though homes are expensive here — from $600,000 — rents can be comparatively reasonable, so don't discount these affluent neighborhoods, which include longtime residents and newcomers. Also consider **'Aina Haina**, just beyond, with its eclectic mix of architectural styles.

Houses pour down an O'ahu hillside

Matt Thayer

Diamond Head Road meets Kalaniana'ole Highway and leads to one of the most popular areas for newcomers, the carefully-planned community of Hawai'i Kai. **Hawai'i Kai** includes marina townhouses for water enthusiasts, as well as hillside homes and condos for view-lovers — all set around Koko Marina, a tasteful shopping center. As a rule the farther from Honolulu you travel, the less expensive housing becomes. Hawai'i Kai is Hawai'i's version of moderately expensive, in the $300,000 to $700,000 range.

Kalaniana'ole Highway clutches the *pali* (ocean cliffs), winding through beautiful, tranquil scenery to wide ocean vistas. Tucked around a corner and down a hill is Hanauma Bay, a popular marine preserve, and Halona Bay, where Burt Lancaster and Deborah Kerr rolled on the beach in *From Here To Eternity*.

Starting again at Waikīkī and heading northwest on Highway 1, homes are less expensive, but the area is crowded. **Pearl City, 'Aiea, Salt Lake** and **Waipahu** include military and government-subsidized housing, as well as the older homes of longtime residents and more shopping strips.

Condominiums here can be purchased for as low as under $100,000. If you have children, pay particular attention to the public schools here; some are overcrowded and have more than their share of problems. (See chapter 8: Children.)

Farther north off Highway 1 are several new planned communities like **Mililani Town** and **Kapolei,** with condos and single-family homes, mostly situated on small lots located around shopping centers. **Waikele**, an outlet center, has become the commercial hub of this area and more commercial developments are planned. This could be Anytown, U.S.A, plunked down in paradise between major highways. But these high-density developments are clean and neat close up, and provide a chance for young, middle-income families of all ethnic groups to own a brand-new house or attached "townhome" at prices that begin at just over $200,000. Life here appeals to many modern families: there are bike paths, community parks, a golf course with clubhouse and other amenities.

Returning to Honolulu, traverse the Pali or Likelike Highways and you are in for a treat. You'll pass through the deeply ridged and majestic Ko'olau Mountains to the town of **Kane'ohe**, overlooking Kane'ohe Bay. Just ahead, **Kailua** nestles near Kailua Beach, considered one of O'ahu's most beautiful. These two suburbs are *haole* enclaves, featuring newer developments as well as a few older homes (older, in Hawai'i, meaning 30 years or more) that tend to be medium priced for the islands, from $300,000 to $500,000. Although these towns have grown rapidly and haphazardly, with an overabundance of shopping strips and car dealerships, they retain much of their natural beauty and are a relatively easy commute to Honolulu. The public schools here are generally considered above average.

O'ahu's hidden treasures lie just beyond Kane'ohe: the Windward and North Shores. Kamehameha Highway winds away from the busy modern world to a quieter time. The rural Windward Shore is sheltered by the Ko'olau

Mountains, a fortress against modern madness. Here, cows graze in meadows against a curtain of verdant cliffs and children hawk bananas, pineapples, *leis* and farm produce from roadside stands. Old plantation houses huddle in tropical cul-de-sacs or perch on narrow beaches. In tiny beach towns like **Kahalu'u, Waiahole, Ka'a'awa, Hau'ula** and **La'ie**, *haoles* and locals live together in relative peace. Some newcomers can be uncomfortable, or at least lonesome, in the heavily local atmosphere, but others thrive.

Fifteen miles up the road, at the North Shore, **Hale'iwa** (population 2,442 and growing) is a quaint tourist town. Here, serious surfers tackle the waves of the famous Sunset Beach and Pipeline.

While the North Shore and the windward side of O'ahu remain somewhat pristine, several residents complain that these areas are too far from Honolulu (at least an hour's drive) for daily commuting. Excess speed along the narrow, tortuous Kamehameha Highway has contributed to many traffic accidents. More than 330 were reported in an 18-month period; crosses and flower-laden shrines mark the spots where people have lost their lives in auto crashes.

Across the Waianae and Ko'olau mountain ranges, the dry leeward side of the island is less lush. Here, a heavily "local" population deserves the right to call this area its own — if not by possessing the land, at least by living peacefully. **Mākaha, Wai'anae** and other small towns are tucked between the ocean and arid chunks of the Waianae Mountains. Most housing is older, smaller, and less expensive, from under $200,000.

You'll enjoy life on O'ahu if: You like beaches, warm weather, shopping, tourists, high-rises, traffic and don't mind a lot of other people and if you'd like life in a tropical New York City or Los Angeles as it was in the smog-free 1960s.

RESOURCES

- City job information line **(808) 523-4301**
- Business action line **(808) 586 2545**
- Rentals Illustrated magazine **(808) 949-3686**
- Chamber of Commerce of Hawai'i **(808) 545-4300** 1132 Bishop St., Ste. 200 Honolulu, HI 96813
- Kailua Chamber of Commerce **(808) 261-2727** P.O. Box 1469 Kailua, HI 96734
- For many other Hawai'i and Oahu sources of information, see the Resources section at the end of this book.

O'AHU

Kaua'i

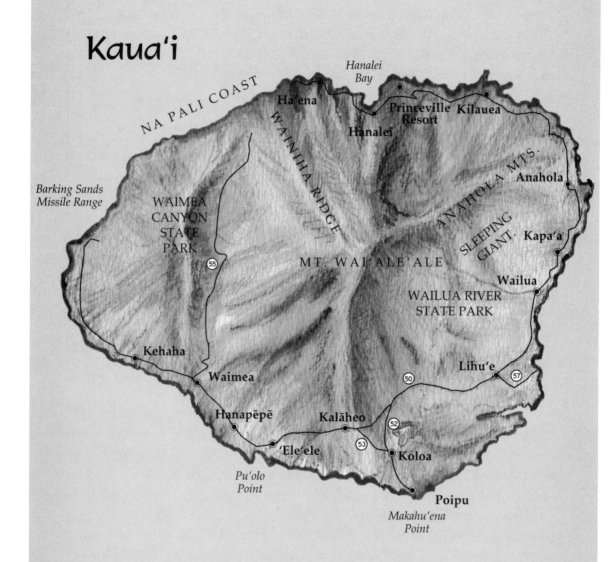

NA PALI COAST

WAINIHA RIDGE

Hanalei Bay

Ha'ena

Princeville
Resort
Hanalei

Kilauea

*Barking Sands
Missile Range*

WAIMEA
CANYON
STATE
PARK

ANAHOLA MTS.

Anahola

*SLEEPING
GIANT*

Kapa'a

(55)

MT. WAI'ALE'ALE

Wailua

WAILUA RIVER
STATE PARK

Kehaha

Lihu'e

(50)

(57)

Waimea

Hanapēpē

Kalāheo

(52)

'Ele'ele

(53)

Koloa

*Pu'olo
Point*

Poipu

*Makahu'ena
Point*

Kaua'i

Size: 552.3 square miles
Population in 1980: 39,082;
Population in 1997: 56,423
Predominant Occupations: Tourism; local business; some agriculture (including sugar plantations); military; health care and social programs
Unemployment: 11.3 %
Number of McDonald's restaurants: 5
The best thing about Kaua'i: Waterfalls and scenery
The worst thing about Kaua'i: Traffic through Kapa'a at 5 p.m.
What other islanders say about Kaua'i: "Beautiful, huh? Even more beautiful than here. But it rains too much."
What Kaua'i says about itself: "We survived (hurricanes) Eva and 'Iniki. We can do anything." (A popular T-shirt slogan reads: "Sharks. Centipedes. Hurricanes. Tsunamis. Kaua'i... it's not for wimps.")

Kaua'i is the seductive "Garden Isle" with which filmmakers have had a passionate affair for decades. The oldest Hawaiian island, it exudes a mystic charm: sharply peaked mountains and sheer cliffs, crashing waterfalls, mist-shrouded valleys and secluded swimming spots. Even a mini-Grand Canyon.

This little island flaunts itself like a maverick, jutting farther out into the Pacific than any of its sisters, vulnerable to hurricanes and Mother Nature's other whims. In 1982, Hurricane Iwa scoured Kaua'i; in 1992, Hurricane 'Iniki ravaged the island for five hours, destroying 14,000 houses, gutting more than 4,000 condominium and hotel units. Miraculously, it claimed only four lives. Destruction totaled about $2 billion.

Despite an exodus of residents after 'Iniki, Kauai's population has grown by about 10 percent over 6 years, to 57,000 people. Newborns and foreign-born people moving to the island make up most of the increase. About 1,387 foreigners came in the four years after 'Iniki, most from the Philippines.[1]

They persevered

Bob Fijal

When former Texas construction worker Larry Reisor and restaurateur Christine Ayers opened the Hanapēpē Café & Espresso Bar in the ramshackle southwestern Kaua'i plantation town, they were relying on tourists to appreciate their hearty meatless meals. And they knew that every new business needs heavy doses of optimism and perseverance. But they had no idea what fate had in store. On Sept. 11, 1992, just as they were becoming established, Hurricane 'Iniki hit. Determined not to be done in by the winds that damaged or destroyed nearly every home and business on the island, the partners made repairs and reopened their business within weeks. Despite difficulties in obtaining fresh vegetables (especially important in a vegetarian restaurant), by 1993 and through 1994 they were doing a brisk business, feeding the hundreds of construction workers who had flocked to Kaua'i to help with the rebuilding. But by 1995, their work finished, the construction workers left. Business was slow again, Reisor says, because few hotels had reopened and tourism was down. Reisor and Ayers hung in there, weathering the slow time. Eventually hotels reopened, tourists have slowly returned and business at the café has been steadily increasing, Reisor says.

The economy

Small businesses, mostly in the tourist industry, employ 19,000 people, just over 60 percent of Kauai's workforce. Farming and agriculture account for a few jobs. Like the other islands, Kaua'i hopes to nurture high technology to attract full-time residents and watches warily as tourism grows and dominates the economy.

The island is known for its excessive rainfall — Mount Wai'ale'ale is the wettest spot on earth with an average annual rainfall of 485 inches — and all that rainfall has a benefit: it keeps the island delightfully lush and green. Here is tropical Hawai'i as you and the film industry imagine it. Movies such as *South Pacific, Blue Hawai'i, Outbreak, Raiders of the Lost Ark, King Kong, Honeymoon in Vegas, Waterworld, Jurassic Park* and its sequels, among many others, have been filmed here. During a recent year, film producers spent $4.4 million in Kaua'i and some *kama'āina* enjoy auditioning as "extras." Kaua'i successfully pursues the film industry through its Kaua'i Institute for Communications Media and the Kaua'i Film Commission, a division of the county Office of Economic Development.

Today, Kaua'i strives to take advantage of its beauty to attract tourism, while still attempting to retain its old way of life. Towns were originally developed around sugar mills. Most of the mills are gone now and new crops attempt to pick up some of the slack: cane, coffee, corn and sunflower. Kaua'i has in recent years begun exporting coffee to the other Hawaiian islands and has long exported cookies and taro chips.

Two possible sources of employment are Wilcox Memorial Hospital in Lihu'e and the Hawai'i Department of Education. But be advised to buy a business or bring a job if you want to settle here — and your best bet would be a tourist-related business.

The good news: public schools on this island are generally considered better than average for Hawai'i.

An island tour

Strung along the ocean like shells on a *lei* are at least 20 towns, some so small you may miss them. **Līhu'e** (population 11,200), near Nawiliwili Harbor on the eastern coast, is the county capital and site of most business activity. It has the ambiance of a 1940s small town and closes early. To the southwest, **Kōloa**,

230

a quaint, historic town of plantation houses, is the site of one of Hawaii's first sugar mills. Days and evenings, Kōloa throbs with tourists. Small housing developments, old and new, are scattered throughout this part of the island, some half-hidden in overgrown cane and bush.

Up on Highway 50, **Kalāheo** is a "local" town, nearly devoid of tourists. Further west are **'Ele'ele, Hanapēpē**, the *paniolo* (cowboy) town of **Waimea**, and **Kekaha**, where newcomers and locals provide plenty of *aloha* to visitors on their way to misty Koke'e State Park and Waimea Canyon, a colorful 10-mile-long gorge called "the Grand Canyon of the Pacific." On the western shore of the island is Barking Sands, a civilian run U.S. naval facility, and the Pacific Missile Range Facility, an important, if not large (260 military and civilian personnel) employer on this small island.

To the north of Lihu'e is **Wailua**, a tourist area along Wailua River, Hawai'i's only river and site of the famous Coconut Palms Hotel, where the Elvis Presley movie *Blue Hawai'i* was filmed. **Kapa'a**, a modern center of commerce, hosts a 4 p.m. traffic jam every work day. A long stretch of Kūhiō Highway through pasture and valley takes you to the Anahola Mountains (where *King Kong* was filmed) and tiny **Anahola**, little more than a stopping place on the highway. Further along is **Kīlauea**, with its lighthouse, quaint stone churches and manager's houses, survivors from plantation days. *Haoles* and locals share a quiet, dreamy life here.

The northern tip of Kaua'i provides a visual treat: the posh **Princeville Resort** with its elegant Princeville Hotel overlooking Hanalei Bay. The resort is a major *haole* housing area, with a variety of

RESOURCES

- County of Kaua'i Office of Economic Development, 4380 B. Rice St. Lihu'e, HI 96766 **(808) 241-6390**

- University of Hawaii Small Business Development Center at Kaua'i Community College 3-1901 Kaumaualii Hwy Lihu'e, HI 96766 **(808) 246-1748**

- State Department of Labor and Industrial Relations, Lihu'e **(808) 214-3421** Fax **(808) 241-3518**

- State Department of Education **(808) 274-3507**

- County of Kaua'i Personnel Services **(808) 242-6595**

- Kauai Chamber of Commerce PO Box 1969 Lihue, HI 96766 **(808) 245-7363** **Fax (808) 245-8815**

Newspapers:
- *The Garden Island News* PO Box 231 Lihue, HI 96766 **(808) 245-3681**

- *The Kauai Times* PO Box 3272 Lihue, HI 96766 **(808) 245-8825**

condos and houses on wide green lawns overlooking ocean cliffs. Princeville also boasts a luxurious modern spa offering inexpensive membership.

Highway 56 winds spectacularly down to Hanalei Valley, ringed by waterfalls after heavy rains which feed the taro beds patching the valley floor. Bustling **Hanalei** town with ramshackle historic buildings is quaint and pleasantly touristy. The road climbs sea cliffs, passes a tempting variety of private and pristine homes in sheltered coves and bays tucked between mountain ridges, and finally comes to an abrupt halt just past **Ha'ena**, at the Na Pali cliffs and one of Kaua'i's many pristine beaches.

You'll like life on Kaua'i if: Your family is the center of your life and you don't yearn for a night life. If you enjoy scenery, hiking, snorkeling or surfing. And rainfall doesn't depress you.

Toni Polancy

The northwestern part of Kaua'i has a down-home, country feeling. Teens share cotton candy at a Waimea celebration.

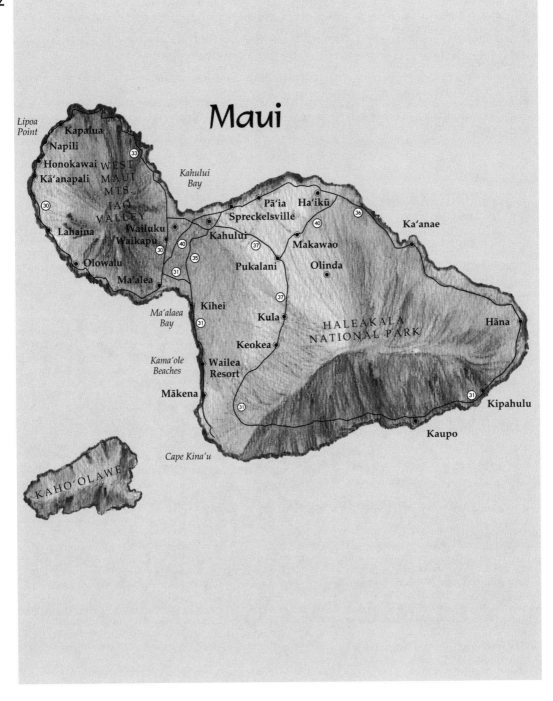

Maui

Lipoa Point

Kapalua

Napili

Honokawai

Kā'anapali

WEST MAUI MTS.

IAO VALLEY

Kahului Bay

33

30

Lahaina

Wailuku

Waikapu

Olowalu

30

40

35

31

Kahului

Ma'alea

Ma'alaea Bay

31

Kihei

Kama'ole Beaches

Wailea Resort

Mākena

Pā'ia

Ha'ikū

Spreckelsville

37

Makawao

Pukalani

Olinda

Kula

37

Keokea

Ka'anae

36

40

HALEAKALA NATIONAL PARK

Hāna

31

Kipahulu

Kaupo

31

Cape Kina'u

KAHO'OLAWE

Maui

Size: 728 square miles
Population in 1980: 70,991
Population in 1997: 118,864 (including Molokai and Lanai)
Predominant Occupations: Tourism; small and large agriculture; small businesss and business development; technology; arts
Unemployment: Approximately 7%
Number of McDonald's restaurants: 9
The best thing about Maui: A good blend of small rural island community and modern sophistication
The worst thing about Maui: Cane smoke
What other islands say about Maui: "Too developed. It's going to be the next Waikīkī."
What Maui says about itself: "We've learned from O'ahu—we'll avoid over-development."

Maui is called "the Valley Isle" — but it might better be called the "lucky island." Maui blends, so far successfully, some of the best of busy Honolulu and the more placid life of the other islands.

Chosen "Best Island in the World" by Condé Nast *Traveller* magazine for three consecutive years and drawing over 2 million tourists annually, Maui is also blessed with what seems to be a more stable economy than some of her sister islands. Her population is also growing faster, by 16.6 percent between 1990 and 1996; the state's population grew only six percent in that period.

Projections say that by the year 2005, approximately 41 percent of Maui's jobs will be in the service industry, but it is fortunate in also having a somewhat diversified economic base. Whereas the sugar and pineapple industries have nearly deserted the other islands, they continue here, often to the chagrin of environmentalists who decry the effects of sugar cane smoke and pineapple runoff. In the bustling town of Kīhei, the Maui High Performance Computing Center includes one of the world's most powerful parallel-processing computers and the Maui Research and Technology Park is a business incubator, supporting innovative new businesses during their early development.

Steve Brinkman

From the air, The Maui Research Park, including the Maui High Performance Computing Center, seems isolated amid kiawe trees and desert; it's actually near the center of Kīhei.

And looking down from its perch atop the summit of Haleakalā Volcano is Science City, a research facility that draws some of the world's top astronomers to the world's most advanced telescopes — including the Air Force Phillips Laboratory. Several Pacific Rim institutions are expected to build telescopes at Science City in the next several years.

Maui has a downside. Its hotel room occupancy rate has dropped slightly due to tough competition for Asian tourists who can fly directly to the Big Island. And from 1991 to 1996, the number of Chapter 7 personal bankruptcies rose faster on Maui than in any other county in the state, quadrupling in those years. Several factors account for this increase, including the state's rigorous business climate, its soft real estate market and its low-cost, do-it-yourself bankruptcy proceedings.

Jobs. Development. Growth. Lucky island. But perhaps more than any other island, Maui faces the Hawai'i Catch 22: managing enormous growth while maintaining the natural beauty that spawns that growth.

Already resort developments blot out some of the island's spectacular ocean views. Houses creep up the jagged West Maui mountains and towns dot Mount Haleakalā's slopes.

Tourists arriving at Kahului airport will eventually be enchanted by eerily beautiful 'Iao Valley, by Haleakalā's immense crater, by Honolua Marine Preserve's mesmerizing underwater world, by Kā'anapali's posh hotels and by Wailea's tropical beaches. But first those tourists must drive through a version of mainland U.S.A.: used car lots, shopping strips, fast food restaurants.

As for living on Maui? If you are coming from a large city, you'll find the atmosphere still quiet and polite. About 75 percent of the island remains wilderness, with breath-taking vistas and plenty of hiking trails. And Maui has a rich cultural life that enhances its sophisticated image. **Hui No'eau Visual Arts Center** in upcountry Maui is a rambling Mediterranean-style mansion of a former missionary. **The Lahaina Art Society**, located in a former jail under the state's largest banyan tree, has a lovely gallery for local artists' work. Several artists' co-operative galleries also dot the island. **The Maui Arts and Cultural Center**, between urban Kahului and Wailuku, is a striking mini-cathedral to both the visual and entertainment arts. It draws international performers who relish their time in Maui's sun-denched elegance.

An island tour

West Maui is a tourist area unabashedly devoted to fun — sensuous and languid. Golden sunsets reflect on store windows along Front Street in the quaint old whaling port of **Lahaina**, once the center of island government. The entire town of 16,000 residents is on the national historic record. West Maui sometimes seems to be an island unto itself — people who live on the west side travel the 27 miles to Kahului reluctantly. Single family homes, starting at about $300,000, are relatively scarce here and tend to be more costly than on some other areas of the island.

A strip of condominium hotels (built in the last 30 years) extends up the western shoreline from the lush green golf courses of **Kaanapali Resort** to the town of **Napili,** with homes tucked cozily along the shoreline. Carefully planned and lushly landscaped **Kapalua Resort** sits majestically atop West Maui. The total west side population (including visitors) is about 40,000.

In South Maui, **Kīhei** (population 20,000), sandwiched between busy Pi'ilani Highway and South Kihei Road, has the nasty reputation of being a hectic community of tourist condos. But those who live in its residential neighborhoods find it family-oriented, friendly and convenient. The Kama'ole beaches, three lovely open vistas along busy South Kihei Road, offer views of breathtaking sunsets — standing in awe of them is a nightly tradition for tourists and *kamaʻāina*. Kīhei post office, the busiest rural post office in the state, is a neighborhood meeting place — patrons in business dress and bathing suits stand in long lines, relax, trade gossip and listen to friendly clerks explain postal regulations to tourists who speak no English.

There's a saying in this part of Maui: You can measure a person's income by how far south he lives. There is a graduating scale of *malahini* (newcomer) lifestyles, from Kihei Villages, a high-density condominium complex (prices in the low $100,000) in north Kihei through a variety of residential areas and condominiums of increasingly higher cost to **Wailea Resort**. Exclusive and lushly landscaped, Wailea is composed of upscale townhouses (from $250,000) and small mansions (from $600,000) set amid golf courses and tennis complexes, most with ocean views. Prices continue to climb as you head south from Wailea to **Makena**, with its gated ocean-front estates.

On Maui's northern shore, **Spreckelsville**, named after a sugar baron, includes pricey newer homes (from $500,000) near a golf club and a sheltered beach. Up the road, **Paʻia** is an old sugar town turned hippie enclave and now gone touristy. With crayon-colored plantation houses, it retains vestiges of each era.

Farther north, **Haʻiku** — rural, wet, jungle green and lovely — appeals to people who want privacy and space. Prices tend to be a bargain here (from about $300,000 for a house with an acre or two), a bonus to those willing to put up with the rain and occasional bouts of mildew.

At the southern-most tip of Maui, forty-five corkscrew miles away, is rustic **Hana**, small, tropical, and isolated. A few entertainers who cherish their privacy live peaceably here among the many longtimers.

"Real Mauians," *kamaʻāina* will tell you, eventually move to the area known as Upcountry, halfway up Haleakalā mountain, to areas like **Pukalani, Makawao** and **Kula** with a wide variety of home prices and almost no condos. This is *paniolo* (cowboy) country. Horses graze on broad pastures, an occasional cow crosses Haleakalā Highway, school buses carry kids to better-than-average schools and smoke curls from chimneys on cool winter nights. Ball games, polo and rodeos are the talk of the town. Jobs include big-scale ranching, small agricultural enterprises, home businesses. And all this occurs against a panorama of the isthmus and ocean below. Artists and writers are also drawn to cool, serene, beautiful Upcountry Maui.

The central valley includes two towns, **Wailuku** and **Kahului**, so close they seem to embrace. Wailuku, the county capital, is a picturesque historic

Maui

"The Valley Isle" is famous for its beautiful beaches, like Wailea's Elua Beach. Longtime residents are likely to live in towns, like Wailuku, tucked into mountains.

Steve Strand

Steve Brinkman

The Big Island

Climates vary on The Big Island of Hawai'i. A horse grazes in the Waipi'o Valley; a snow-mobiler takes advantage of snow atop Mauna Kea

Photo courtesy of Big Island Visitor's Bureau

G Brad Lewis

"The Garden Island" deserves its nickname; at left, the overlook at Kalalau Valley; below, taro patches at Hanalei.

G Brad Lewis

G Brad Lewis

Moloka'i

The "Friendly Isle,"
more than any other
Hawaiian island,
eyes tourism warily.
Concerned
volunteers carefully
conduct treks
across Kamakou
Preserve, the highest
point on Moloka'i
at 4,970 feet.

Toni Polancy

Lāna'i

The bright lights
of Maui beckon
just a few miles
away, but most
residents of
"Privacy Island"
prefer a simple life,
including fishing
at Kaumalapau
Harbor.

Steve Brinkman

community tucked against the West Maui Mountains. Unfortunately, its downtown has been nearly abandoned as car dealerships moved to more commercialized Kahului and local stores closed in deference to incoming national chains. But housing and commercial developments are replacing pineapple fields outside of town, creating a new Wailuku. And Old Wailuku may eventually find a niche as an attractive locale for boutiques, galleries and antique stores.

Kahului, the center of commerce, is a busy port. The population is primarily local — families of longtime *haoles*, Filipinos, Chinese, Japanese and other ethnic groups who originally came to work the sugar fields. In the mid 1960s, plantation workers began an exodus from camp housing to a development just outside the Pu'unēnē plantation. Nicknamed "Dream City", the development comprises much of the residential area of Kahului. Originally costing about $20,000, these cement block homes surrounded by gardens and fruit trees now sell for $200,000 or more. Nearby is the Saturday morning swap-meet where *kama'āina* pick up inexpensive flowers and produce and tourists select souvenirs and clothing at half of boutique prices.

• Small Business Development Center 590 Lipoa Parkway, Kihei, HI 96753 **(808) 875-2402.** E-mail dfisher@maui. com

• The Business Information Center 590 Lipoa Parkway, Kihei, HI 96753 **(808) 875-2400.** E-mail corn@maui.com or sonia @maui.com

• County of Maui **800-272-0026**

Newspapers
• *The Maui News* **(808) 244-6363**

• *The Haleakala Times* **(808) 572-9289 fax** **(808) 572-0168**

• *The Lahaina News* **(808) 667-7866 fax** **(808) 667-2726**

Also see the Resource section at the back of this book.

Longtime Mauians complain about the island's rapid development, even as they shop in Kahului's new stores. A local *tutu* (grandma), pushing two toddlers in a cart at Kmart remembers calmer times thirty years ago, before investors from around the world began to build hotels and condominiums.

"You could go Kīhei, go to beaches and not hear nothing, no one there. Private," she says. "Not like now. Noise. Cars. People." She pushes the cart up the Little Caesar's pizza aisle and places her order.

You'll like Maui if: You're the kind of person who keeps snorkel gear or a surfboard in your car. (Maui has 120 miles of coastline... more of it easily accessible and swimmable than any other island.) If you like a touch of sophistication along with peace and natural beauty.

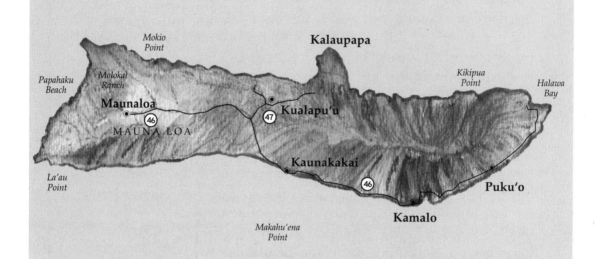

Moloka'i

Moloka'i is shaped somewhat like a shark. The back fin is Kalaupapa Peninsula, a Hansen's Disease colony. Modern drugs have controlled leprosy and patients are no longer incarcerated. Fewer than 60 patients remain at Kalaupapa, which is now a national park and a memorial to the disease that was once the scourge of these islands.

Moloka'i

Size: 260 square miles
Population in 1980: 6,049;
Population in 1997: about 7,000
Predominant Occupations: Teaching; health care; social work; farming; fishing; tourism
Unemployment: Approximately 14%
Number of McDonald's restaurants: 0
The best thing about Moloka'i: Deer running across a dewy meadow
The worst thing about Moloka'i: The threat of change
What other islanders say about Moloka'i: "Beautiful. Beautiful. Quiet. But so poor, no?"
What Moloka'i says about itself: "Leave us be. We are old Hawai'i and we like it that way."

Moloka'i has many nicknames: "The Lonely Island," "The Most Hawaiian Island," "The Friendly Isle" and "Hawai'i As It Used to Be." It is all of these.

Half of Moloka'i's residents are of Hawaiian extraction. And here is Hawaiian life as you picture it: secluded, bucolic. On Moloka'i, many Hawaiians and *hapa* (half) Hawaiians live off the land as their ancestors did — harvesting the ocean, gathering fruits and plants, hunting deer, pigs and goats.

It's a simple life, yes — but, not necessarily ideal. Moloka'i's struggling economy and high jobless rate means some residents *must* live off the land and sea; 18.9 percent receive some form of public assistance.[1] A few jobs are available on Moloka'i, but, in the words of one longtime resident, "They don't pay enough to make it worthwhile for people to get off welfare." Adding to economic hardships was cancellation of twice daily ferry service that carried residents to work at Maui's westside resorts.

The 52,000-acre **Moloka'i Ranch** comprises roughly one-third of the island. From the 1920s until the 1980s, the ranch employed many islanders in the pineapple industry. Today, a major issue divides residents: development. Longtimers fight gently but firmly to slow development, which could mar island tranquility and change the lifestyle. Other factions encourage the growth and change that could mean jobs. Meanwhile, its New Zealand owners are promoting Moloka'i Ranch for hiking and trail adventures.

A Moloka'i tour

Moloka'i is shaped somewhat like a shark. The back fin is Kalaupapa Peninsula, a Hansen's Disease colony. Modern drugs have controlled leprosy and patients are no longer incarcerated. Fewer than 60 patients have chosen to remain at Kalaupapa, which is now a national park and a memorial to the disease that was once the scourge of these islands.

The center of Moloka'i contains two towns and the only airport. Neat little **Kualapu'u** (Population 1,661) is the center of the budding agricultural community experimenting with coffee and exotic fruits. **Kaunakakai** (population 2,658) is the island's commercial center, boasting a dock, small hospital, library, three markets, one bakery, two gas stations, two banks, and a sizeable liquor store that stays open late, as well as several small churches queued along Kamehameha Highway.

Tiny Moloka'i has something many major cities do not: two newspapers. Both are weeklies, very down-home, personal and strongly opinioned.

This island also has several sandy beaches, the state's highest waterfall, mountains, a few small condo developments and a resort, **Kaluako'i**, on its western shore. Nearby is **Pāpōhaku Ranchlands**, a planned community with roads and underground utilities in place, but few houses as yet. Five-acre tracts start at about $135,000, reasonable for Hawai'i.

Pāpōhaku's white sand beach — three miles long and 100 yards wide — is deserted, devoid of footprints. A few small estates lounge on a rise above the far end of the beach. At one home, a gracious resident says, "Yes, it's peaceful here, but this very quiet life is not for everyone." She and her husband have trouble keeping household help. Several mainland couples have come to work and stay in a cottage on the premises, but they soon get bored and leave. She has now hired a local couple, who are accustomed to this quiet life. She praises the standards and efforts at Maunaloa Elementary, the public school her sons attend.

A few miles up the road, the tiny town of **Maunaloa**, on Moloka'i Ranchlands, is being renovated. A few shops are sprinkled along the main street sporting kites, dolls, souvenirs. Maunaloa also boasts a small new housing complex and an apartment complex — government subsidized. The school is set on a hill surrounded by trees and broad lawns and also serves as the town library. Perhaps a sign of things to come: a Kentucky Fried Chicken outlet has opened at the once sleepy pineapple town.

You'll like life on Moloka'i if: You like to hunt, hike or hide out. If you love nature, silence. And if you have a way to support yourself. If you long to go back to rural small town life as it was in the 1930s. (Remember, that was the decade of a major depression.)

RESOURCES

- Moloka'i is part of Maui County. See Maui
- Federal Job Information Center, O'ahu: **(808) 541-2791**
- Hawai'i State Workforce Development Division, Kaunakakai: **(808) 53-3281**

Newspapers

- *Moloka'i Advertiser-News:* **(808) 558-8253**
- *The Moloka'i Dispatch:* **(808) 552-2781**

G. Brad Lewis

A swimmer walks Moloka'i's deserted Pāpōhaku Beach, largest in the state.

Lāna'i

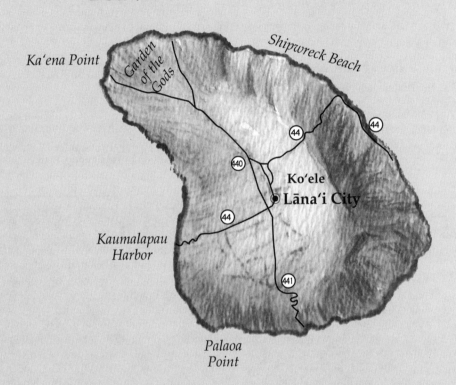

Ka'ena Point

Garden of the Gods

Shipwreck Beach

44

44

440

Ko'ele

● Lāna'i City

44

Kaumalapau
Harbor

441

Palaoa
Point

Lāna'i

Size: 140 square miles
Population in 1980: 2,426
Population in 1997: about 2,800
Predominant Occupations: Resort hotel and restaurant; teaching; nursing; some small business; airport; civil service
Unemployment: Approximately 6%
Shopping: Three grocery stores, three restaurants, a hardware store, one movie theater (recently reopened).
Number of McDonald's restaurants: 0
The best thing about Lāna'i: Community spirit
The worst thing about Lāna'i: Very confining
What other islanders say about Lāna'i: "Too quiet, but... The Lodge at Ko'ele is really something, huh?"
What Lāna'i says about itself: "Peaceful. A great place to raise kids."

It's afternoon. Except for a few birds chattering, all is quiet in **Lāna'i City**, a grassy oasis atop this round, desert-like island. Small shops and old plantation houses with bright tin roofs circle the town square; it is so quiet you could hear a needle drop from one of the many Cook pines. Then school lets out down at one end of the square and children scamper through the park, sunlight dancing on their faces. Their tinkling laughter hangs in the air. Lāna'i City seems a town suspended in time, an Andy Hardy movie.

But is this a place where you'd want to live? In one of the Hawaiian islands' most remote villages, on a "company-owned" island? Surprisingly the answer may be "yes."

For nearly seventy years, Lāna'i was the world's largest pineapple plantation — 18,000 acres owned and operated by Dole Food Co. In 1985 Los Angeles entrepreneur David Murdock, CEO and chairman of Castle and Cooke, Inc., bought Dole's share of the land with an eye to exclusive tourism and rechristened Lāna'i "The Private Island."

Today, the tiny island is on its way to achieving Murdock's goal. Built in the early 1990s, its two resorts, The Mānele Bay Hotel and The Lodge at Kō'ele, are so grand *kama'āina* go there for second honeymoons — most can't afford it for first ones. Its golf course is already world-renowned. In addition to resorts, The Lāna'i Co. is developing chic condominiums and townhouses for those who want the kind of seclusion the island offers. Buyers usually have primary residences elsewhere, says Kay Okamoto, who runs the island's only real estate office.

When Microsoft magnate Bill Gates wed on the island in the early 1990s, a reporter covering the event was "escorted" from the "private island," causing a national uproar. In truth, Okamoto says, "People are free to come and go. We have the same state and county services other islands have. Roads, beaches, harbors open to the public; it's just most of the land (98 percent) is owned by Castle and Cooke." Almost half of Lāna'i's 2,800 people work for The Lāna'i Co.

Life on a tiny island

Because much of it is company-owned, the island retains a plantation ambiance. A Lāna'i Co. employee, raised in the rural northeastern U.S., has been on the island for six years. She says she loves life here, where everyone knows each other and families gather for Friday evening *pau hana* (done working) barbecues at the beach. She also volunteers a few hours each month at an art co-op, selling her ceramic ornaments to tourists and earning several hundred dollars a month in addition to her generous wages.

"Still, it's a company town," she points out, "so if an employer becomes unhappy with you, you're screwed. And if you quit or lose your job you have two weeks to vacate your home. That gives the bosses a lot of power." Most often, she amends, bosses are fair and island life is ideal.

There are a couple of inconveniences. Lāna'i has no air tower; when skies are very overcast, planes can't fly for a few hours and travellers can be delayed. Also, new mothers must travel off island to give birth. Lāna'i Community Hospital director John Schaumburg explains the hospital does not have the advanced technology to handle emergencies. And because airlines don't like to carry mothers-to-be during the last month of pregnancy, women usually leave a month before their due date.

As a rule, the perks to living on this 10-mile-wide island far outweigh the inconveniences. Most resort employees belong to unions, and their wages are on a par with other Hawai'i workers, yet rent in company-owned housing is half the cost of that on other islands. Over the years, Dole had occasionally sold plantation houses and land to workers. Lāna'i may be the island of the rich and famous, but a few older plantation houses on small lots are still available for as low as $135,000, reasonable for Hawai'i. Most need renovation, Kay Okamoto warns. Posh condominiums and homesites are also sold "fee simple." Buyers own the land.

Entertainment includes hunting Mouflon sheep, deer and game birds in the desert-like scrub that surrounds Lāna'i City, and snorkeling off a couple of pristine beaches. A four-wheel drive vehicle is the best way to get around the island's many unpaved roads and paths.

> **RESOURCES**
>
> Lāna'i is part of Maui County. See also Maui.
> - The Lāna'i Co.
>   Main number
>   **(808) 565-3000**
>
>   Housing
>   **(808) 565-3977**
>
>   Employment
>   **(808) 565-3876**
> - Lāna'i Community Hospital
>   **(808) 565-6411**
> - Lāna'i Schools
>   **(808) 565-7224**

Cultural activities consist of a guest artists series at The Lodge at Kō'ele. Internationally known musicians, writers, lecturers (like humor writer Dave Barry) and chefs come to The Lodge to perform and to talk about their work. All events in the guest lecture series are free to residents as well as visitors.

Jobs available

Sound like an ideal life? The good news: you may be able to find a job here. "Jobs are pretty basic and are often available," says one resident. "You either work for the state, as a teacher, or a nurse at the hospital. Other than that, you work for the hotels — that's The Lāna'i Company."

A spokesperson for the company said eighteen positions, from management to staff, were available the June day we called and that was an unusually low number. Food service jobs are easy to come by, but promotions are usually made from within the current staff.

The world is just learning about Lāna'i and it is a fascinating place to watch.

You'll enjoy life on Lāna'i if: You are a recluse, perhaps an artist or writer or if you are healthy, and wealthy enough not to have to earn a living, and can just fly in and out for a spell. Or, if you are looking for an interesting job assignment in a friendly place. (Be careful; you may fall in love and stay.)

'Upolu Point

25

27

24

Parker Ranch

19

Waimea

KOHALA

26

HĀMĀKUA COAST

MAUNA KEA

19

19

HILO

Pōhakuloa Military Camp

Saddle Road

Hilo

19

KAILUA-KONA

11

Ha'ena

KONA

11

MAUNA LOA

PUNA

13 **Pāhoa**

11

KONA COAST

Captain Cook

Kalapana

Ka'u Desert

Ka'ena Point

The Big Island
of Hawai'i

Punalu'u

Ka Lae
South Point

The Big Island
of Hawai'i

Size: 4,028 square miles
Population in 1980: 92,053;
Population in 1997: 141,458
Predominant Occupations: Resorts, tourist-related business; cattle ranching; coffee production and exporting; small flower and produce cultivation and exporting; real estate; arts and crafts; astronomy; geophysical endeavors; health care.
Unemployment: 10.2%
Number of McDonald's Restaurants: 9
The best thing about the Big Island: Economic diversification.
The worst thing about the Big Island: Vog.
What other islanders say about the Big Island: "It's nice to have space to get in the car and drive. You can't do that on the other islands."
What the Big Island residents say: "We are environmental pioneers! It's exciting, invigorating to live on an island that is still forming."

Want to settle in the Hawaiian islands as inexpensively as possible?

Consider the island named Hawai'i, called simply the Big Island.

The Big Island lolls at the southern tip of the island chain like a handsome, angry giant — growling, churning, and flexing his muscles. It's almost twice the size of the rest of the islands combined and still growing. Kīlauea, an active volcano in Hawai'i Volcanoes National Park, has been continuously spewing lava since 1983. The lava flows toward the ocean, mostly through natural underground tubes, spurts into the sea in a hissing cloud of steam, cools and hardens, constantly increasing the Big Island's size and creating the famous black sand beaches. Since 1983 it has coughed up more than 500 acres of new land, mostly black hardened lava at the southern and eastern edges of the island — crunchy, "rocky" land, almost impossible to build on or use for agriculture.

Concerned with the high cost of living, neighbor islanders sometimes consider moving to the Big Island, where land and houses in some areas can cost much less than on other islands. There are two reasons this is so: first, the Big Island is so big there is more land available, and second, some of the land is either covered by recent lava flow and is very difficult to live on or is in the probable path of lava.

The volcano's lava production also releases gases that mix with moisture in the air to form vog, a smog-like condition that is blamed for decreased crop yields and increased breathing problems for people with conditions like asthma and bronchitis.

Small, usually harmless, earthquakes also occur often on the Big

Now a desolate lava landscape, this was once the junction of Gardenia and Royal streets in Royal Gardens subdivision.

Island. They sometimes include swarms of "microearthquakes" such as those recorded near camp-grounds in the Hawai'i Volcanoes National Park in 1997. In the first four hours of that episode, 60 earthquakes were recorded, along with many additional quakes too small to record. No injuries or damage occurred.

All that geological activity is not as unpleasant as it sounds. The Big Island is so vast, and its two major commercial centers so far apart (about 100 miles) that volcanic activity on the **Hilo** side is hardly noticeable on the **Kona** side, except for the influx of a million curious tourists each year. Direct flights from Japan to the Kona coast began in the mid-1990s, bringing 60,000 Japanese visitors and an additional $45 million annually. Meanwhile, to the North, far from the tourist hoopla, **Waimea** — cattle country — sleeps peacefully amid misty ranch lands.

The Kona side

Along the dry, sunny western Kona Coast the population has doubled since 1980 and new housing developments, with prices almost equal to those on other Hawaiian islands, overlook the ocean. Life in **Kailua-Kona** is focused on **Kailua Bay**, laced with tourist shops. The bay is prized for its abundant fishing. Meanwhile, Kona's 2,500 acres of coffee orchards are world famous. Kona coffee, coveted for its intense flavor, contributes about $15 million annually to the Big Island economy.

Along Queen Ka'ahumanu Road in Kona, KMart, Costco, WalMart, Ross, Safeway and other stores compete for *kama'āina* attention. A few miles south, brand new Keauhou Shopping Center sits as though waiting for the boom to catch up with it. Farther south, a few small quaint towns like **Captain Cook** greet those who venture this far.

North of Kona, the **Kohala Coast** includes a galaxy of fancy resorts — oases carved in a black lava desert — hoping the new influx of Japanese tourists will wipe out deficits from past lean years. The resorts are spectacular, but the South Kohala coast is a desolate moonscape of lava — miles of it as far as eye can see. Using white coral stones gathered from beaches, enterprising residents have written messages on the black crust, a unique Big Island graffiti: *"Welcome Rick"*; *"Aloha, Laurie"*; and a simple ode to one of Hawai'i's favorite foods: *"SPAM."*

Strange passage

It's a three-hour ride from Kona to Hilo on **Saddle Road**, which winds between two dormant volcanoes, Mauna Kea and Mauna Loa. This road is an adventure. **Waimea** (population 6,000 plus), a beautiful, historic ranch town set amid graceful mountains and sloping green valleys, is dotted with art galleries and craft shops. **Waikoloa Village** (population 2,248) is a brand new town of modern houses and condominiums built to house workers for Kohala's hotels.

Along Saddle Road, the verdant pastures of Waimea's beautiful **Parker Ranch**, the largest privately owned ranch in the U.S., give way to the barren desert of **Pohakuloa Military Training Area**, marked on one map as a "High Danger Area." The road then winds through years of lava accumulation, finally passing swampy areas where spindly young trees loom like gray ghosts in the mist. No wonder numerous UFO sightings have been reported here. No wonder people whisper of seeing the Night Marchers, ancient Hawaiian ghost troops in full regal attire. Some people still believe the Hawaiian Goddess Pele dwells in these mountains and the volcanic eruptions are evidence of her wrath.

The Hilo side

Come at last to **Hilo**, the state's fourth largest city. This charming old town on **Hilo Bay** is the island's major seaport and commercial center. We're in volcano country now; gray-brown vog hangs in the air.

With about 140 inches of rain a year, this part of the island has ideal growing conditions, relatively inexpensive land, and is one of the world's foremost exporters of macadamia nuts as well as exotic flowers: orchids, anthurium, ginger and bird-of-paradise. Should you decide to join the new growers in the **Puna District**, you'll find plenty of support and advice from a mix of big ranchers; longtime small farmers who sell their wares at Hilo's popular Saturday morning open-air farmer's market; local crafters trying to make a living; entrepreneurial businessmen; and another kind of grower who has settled here, where privacy abounds. Historically there has long been a popular crop grown in the Puna district: marijuana. In the 1970s, it was estimated to be the Big Island's third largest source of revenue.

Perhaps Big Islanders are fatalistic, but **Hilo**, on the quiet eastern shore, seems to be calmly poised for disaster. In 1946 a large tidal wave

G. Brad Lewis

The morning bartering at Suisan Fish market in Hilo is conducted in a melange of languages. Over-fishing by international trawlers has affected the catch, fishermen say, but fishing continues to be an important source of employment — and food — on the island.

swallowed much of the downtown area. The town rebuilt but was again inundated by a tsunami in 1960 that killed 61 people. Some islanders believe that tidal waves are cyclical and time is ripe for another big one.

Still, in *The Best of Hawai'i,*[1] writer Jocelyn K. Fujii advises: "Watch this town. It's a sleeper that has much more going for it than meets the eye: new restaurants, from Thai to Italian; a restoration effort that is reviving downtown businesses and attracting new ones; and the abiding charm of one of Hawaii's last genuine old towns."

The Big Island has many small towns too — mostly dotting its coastline and sprinkled through the interior. Each has unique characteristics. **Pāhoa** (population just over 1,000) looks like a set for a spooky old western movie — one part *High Noon*, two parts *Psycho* — and attracts a mix of entrepreneurial locals, aging hippies, recluses, and a few curious tourists who come to see where the lava wiped out **Kalapana** and flowed over the highway nine miles away, down Route 130.

The economy: growing

You'll read mostly gloom and doom about the Big Island's economy. Like the rest of the islands, the Big Island suffers from the demise of the 175-year-old sugar industry but this island has space and diversification on its side. Employment is up from a recent low of 88 percent to about 91 percent. New businesses and housing developments abound in the Kailua-Kona area. And the island's population has been growing consistently in the past 18 years, from 92,000 in 1980 to over 139,000 today.

Big Island growers account for much of the state's produce; half of the state's 10,000 farms and ranches are located here.[2] Almost two-thirds of the beef raised in the state comes from Big Island ranches. It is also the only major coffee producer in the U.S. (some of the other islands are beginning to produce coffee on a limited scale) and the world's largest orchid grower. Most of the world's macadamia nuts are also harvested here.

Looking toward a time when the bulk of the state's fruits and vegetables can be homegrown, Big Island farmers produce everything from coffee and cacao (chocolate) to bananas, papayas, guavas, passion fruit, avocados and cabbages. And they are on the cutting edge of growing new kinds of produce, experimenting with exotic fruits like rambutan (similar to lychee).

Usually, nature provides the water necessary to keep the Big Island fertile, but droughts occasionally occur. The island is served by about two dozen municipal water systems, plus a half-dozen private ones. Thousands of residents rely on rainfall for their water, using catchment systems. People in some less accessible areas rely on generators for power.

The Big Island's notorious volcanoes add to its economy. Several countries from around the world have perched telescopes atop the 13,796-foot summit of sleepy Mauna Kea. In the East Rift Zone of Kilauea Volcano, experimental geothermal energy supplies some of the island's electricity.

On the South Kohala coast, the Natural Energy Laboratory of Hawai'i conducts research using warm and cold ocean water temperatures to generate electrical power. And aquaculture has enjoyed some success in producing fish, lobsters, seaweed and microalgae food supplements. In some of the more remote areas, commercial forestry and eucalyptus tree planting are being attempted.

Alternative medicine, combining tourism with health as a business venture, is seeing some success on the Big Island.[3] The 50-bed North Hawai'i Community Hospital in north-central Waimea offers a combination of Western medicine and alternative therapies.

You'll like the Big Island if:

Kona side: You like tourists, people, fishing — and if big beaches are not necessary to your island dreams. (There are a few nice small beaches, including black sand beaches.)

Hilo side: If you like solitude, plants, lava, and seek relatively cheap land for farming. And don't mind rain and cloudy skies.

RESOURCES

- Hawai'i State Employment Service, Kailua-Kona **(808) 326-2855**
- Hawai'i Island Economic Development **(808) 966-5416**
- Research and Development **(808) 961-8366**
- Kailua-Kona Chamber of Commerce **(808) 329-1758**
- Hawai'i Island Chamber of Commerce **(808) 935-7178** (For $20, either Chamber will send you a directory with specific information.)
- For Information about volcanoes, use these Internet URLs: **http://hvo.wr.usgs.gov./** http://volcano.und.nodak.edu/

Newspapers:
- *Hawai'i Tribune Herald* 355 Kino'ole Street Hilo, HI 96720 **(808) 935-6621**
- *West Hawai'i Today* 75-5560 Kiawe Street Kona, HI 96740 **(808) 329-9311**

Also see Resources at the back of this book

THE RIDDLE OF KALAPANA:

The state of Hawai'i wants to attract the movie industry — and here's the perfect horror story. When man and nature conspire to create a psychological/geological disaster like Kalapana, who needs fiction?

I am driving Route 130 in the Puna District on the Big Island. This is the heart of volcano country and Kīlauea has been spouting continuously all week, yet there is no sign of mountain or lava — just a hot sun glinting through a veil of grey-brown vog.

The highway sways left, passing a quaint old church, and the ocean glimmers, bright and cool, on the horizon. The road then curves gracefully right and comes to a dead stop. A fence bars further travel; a sign warns visitors to stay away. And there is the lava — frozen thick, black twisted coils crawling across the highway, over a beach, and into the sea.

G. Brad Lewis

Once this was the town of Kalapana and the housing development called Royal Gardens. And this is its story:

In the late 1950s, shortly after Hawai'i became a state, a subdividing free-for-all took place in Puna. Authors George Cooper and Gavan Daws in *Land and Power in Hawai'i*[1] describe the land boom. It began when two Colorado businessmen bought 12,000 acres of land between Kurtistown and Mountain View from a local politician and businessman and formed a *hui*, a corporation of investors. The land was divided into 4,000 lots, named Hawaiian Acres. Costing just $500 to $1,000, they were heavily advertised on the mainland for as low as $150 down and $8 a month.

Interest in the exotic new state of Hawai'i was high. The project sold out and more developments followed.

According to *Land and Power*:

"... the developments unique to the Big Island were in the mold of the one in Puna that set off the boom: sizable acreage in remote areas, of little or no real economic use value, subdivided into house lots on which practically no one ever actually built homes..."

For many years, ignored, or even encouraged by government legislators and officials, there was virtually unrestricted development.

"By the time the Big Island boom came to a halt in the mid-1970s, something like 80,000 lots of this kind had been created — on an island whose population at the time was somewhat less than 80,000."

Sales brochures had painted glorious pictures of paradise:

"Along the southern shores of the Big Island, Hawai'i, largest of the Hawaiian chain lies the historic and legendary land of Kalapana. This is the setting for Royal Gardens. A fertile area directly adjacent to the Hawai'i Volcano National Park with its spectacular attractions, yet only walking distance away from lovely beach and shore areas. Royal Garden lots are all one acre in size, making it possible for the owners to have a small orchard or truck garden or a magnificent garden, as well as a home and a haven for retirement."[2]

Land and Power continues: "...To have a truck garden or magnificent home garden of the kind the brochures talked about, a lot owner would have to catch his own water, possibly haul in his own soil, and anyway use chemical fertilizer."

In truth, Royal Gardens was on volcanic land, a variety of types of recent lava flow. Water was scarce. The brochure was correct in one respect: Royal Gardens was close to Volcano Park — dangerously close. In was near Kilauea's east rift zone. In 1974 a U.S. Geological Survey wrote, Kilauea and its rift zones "must be expected to erupt repeatedly in the future" and "all areas downslope from volcanic vents should be considered vulnerable to eventual burial by lava flows." Royal Gardens was also within a fault zone, making it at risk for earthquakes.

Several state legislators and public employees, including future governor George Ariyoski, invested in Royal Gardens.

For their book, Cooper and Daws sampled Royal Gardens owners. About 72 percent said at the time of purchase they believed their lots had fertile soil, and 69 percent did not know it was in a zone of serious volcanic hazard.

More than 60 people *did* settle in Royal Gardens, optimistic people who worked hard to develop their cheap land and build their homes.

In 1977 a lava flow nearly wiped out the village of Kalapana, about three miles northeast along the coast from Royal Gardens. Then, in 1985 a total of seven lava flows entered Royal Gardens, destroying altogether 22 homes, about one in three of all residences.

By 1996, the village of Kalapana was entirely destroyed. So was a nearby beach. And much of Royal Gardens. At Royal Gardens, one by one, homeowners watched their work go up in flames as lava slowly flowed this way and that, sparing a few houses while torching others.

"You watch and wait and that's the worst," said G. Brad Lewis, a photographer who lives near Kalapana and specializes in photos of volcanos. "Maybe it will destroy your home; maybe it will turn and destroy your neighbor's instead. When your house finally does go up in flames, it's a relief. After waiting weeks, you are just glad the waiting is over."

There are numerous other such developments in the Puna districts. Some never went beyond the subdividing and selling stage; others became full-fledged neighborhoods, dangerously close to rift zones and fault lines. Today, Volcano Park visitors see signs designating areas in the likely path of flows. Rated 1, 2 or 3, they indicate the chances of various neighborhoods being inundated.

The lava's flow is usually slow and, although homes and dreams are destroyed, there is seldom loss of life. And people who value privacy do build and survive on this vast, exotic land. Some generate their own electricity and catch rain water for household use.

A young man building a house on a field of a black crust puts it this way: "It's like a gamble, a big roulette wheel. You always think the lava will flow somewhere else. That you'll be the lucky one who doesn't lose everything."

➤ **TIP**: **Some of the Big Island's cheap land** — as low as $2,500 for a one- to three-acre plot — lies in the most isolated areas with no utilities and may be three or four miles on a gravel road, difficult to navigate, warns a Hilo realtor. "You have to remember you are living in a high rainfall area, very primitive. It's tropical rain forest but not like you think of it, it's isolated and not much vegetation."

➤ **TIP**: **Never buy property sight unseen**. If you are considering buying property you *have* seen, talk first to farmers or homeowners in the area, stop at county agricultural offices and the courthouse. Confer with people in the nearest town. Before you buy, find out all you can from independent sources — those who do not stand to make a profit from your purchase.

Kapu: Two forbidden islands

The small islands of Kaho'olawe and Ni'ihau loom softly just offshore the main island chain — shadowy seductresses. But forget living on either of these islands. They are kapu: forbidden.

Kaho'olawe

Poor Kaho'olawe. This small, shy island, hunching red and barren just offshore of Kihei, Maui, has a sad past. Archeological evidence suggests the island — barren, windy and dry and just 45 square miles in size — once supported a small Hawaiian community, decimated in the 1700s by disease or island wars. In the mid-1800s the island became a penal colony, then served as a place for Maui ranchers to graze cattle and sheep. The cattle devoured the vegetation, allowing high winds to blow off much of the topsoil.

Adding injury to insult, the United States military then used the island as a practice bombing site during World War II and for many years after. In 1990, bowing to protesters, the U.S. government returned "Target Island" to Hawaiians and committed $400 million to clearing away unexploded bombs and debris. The cleanup is expected to take generations, if it can be achieved at all.

Today, a handful of Hawaiians travel to Kaho'olawe to engage in rituals and Kaho'olawe is destined to become a spiritual and cultural preserve. Those who have visited say the island has something special going for it: dramatic views. On a clear day, you can allegedly see four of its more fortunate sisters: Maui, Moloka'i, Lāna'i and O'ahu.

Ni'ihau

Ni'ihau, the "The Forbidden Island" has been more fortunate, but could face a future as dreary as Kaho'olawe's past. A cattle and sheep ranch, owned by the Robinson family since 1864, Ni'ihau is private property. Visiting its 230 residents, mostly Ni'ihau natives, is by invitation only.

Eliza Sinclair, 63, widow of a Scottish sea captain, brought her family to Kaua'i from New Zealand in the 1860s and purchased Ni'ihau from King Kamehameha IV for $10,000. Later, she bought the *ahupua'a* of Makaweli on Kaua'i. (Hawaiian kings divided the islands into *ahupua'a*, a pie-shaped tract of land that runs from the ocean to the top of a mountain.)

Sinclair's heirs, the Robinson family, have so far scorned development of Ni'ihau and have strived to protect its residents. For over a century, they kept the island off-limits to visitors. At this writing, despite the protests of islanders and some Kaua'i residents, the U.S. Navy is considering Ni'ihau as a site for missile launchings. As part of a $50 million upgrade to the Pacific Missile Range Facility on Kaua'i's west side, the Navy would build several test launch sites and a 6,000 foot-runway on Ni'ihau.

Steve Strand

Like a mother whale nurturing her young, the island of Kaho'olawe shelters little Molokini.

Making your decision: Tips from a counselor

So, you've read all the chapters in this book — and reread the ones on costs and working. You've used a computer and the URLs in the resources to find as much information as you can about life here. You have a realistic idea of what it is like to live in Hawai'i. And you've probably at least a good idea about what you will do to earn a living here. A counselor, who has himself twice moved back and forth from the mainland, suggests you now hone in on the personal and emotional side of your decision. It's time to ask yourself and your loved ones some hard questions. Like:

- **Why are you moving?** Are you escaping California's traffic? Washington state's rain? Pennsylvania's snow? Family problems? Or do you just want a fresh start? Are you attracted by the ocean? Hawai'i's natural beauty? Write down your reasons for wanting to come. Review them in a week, in a month, in a few months, as you make one of the most important decisions of your life.

- **Who wants to move?** In any relationship, it's usually one person who most wants to make the move. Others — children, a spouse or lover — go along. Schedule a meeting at which every person involved in the move will talk about his or her feelings. Ask someone to jot down notes on the conversation or tape record it. Everyone will have a maximum of five minutes to speak without being interrupted. The person who most wants to move should begin speaking and he or she should express exactly why the move means so much. Listen carefully as others, including children, discuss any feelings or fears they have about the move. Make no decisions during that meeting. Schedule another a few days later, after everyone has had time to ponder each other's responses. If your spouse or teenage children really don't want to come, you should probably delay or reconsider the move. Starting a new life here will be difficult enough without negative feelings.

- **Remember the people you are leaving behind.** You are euphoric, excited about your move. But your parents, your children, your siblings and friends do not have that happy anticipation to bolster their spirits now. Most likely, all they can see is that you are leaving. It's helpful to set definite dates when mom or dad or children from a former marriage, for example, can look forward to coming to visit. Make it a holiday — Christmas or a birthday — a time when they are apt to miss you most.

- **What are your goals and how will you achieve them?** You've decided why you are coming... now decide what you hope to achieve in paradise. The goals don't have to be monetary. You may be seeking a more peaceful lifestyle, more time to spend with your family. List the goals in that notebook and refer to them in the hectic days and months to come. Setting your sights on those goals will help you keep your perspective.

    Refer to the list again in five years. Have you achieved what you set out to do?

The One-Week Experiment

Many people who move here make the same mistake: they are so smitten and sure they will never want to leave that they burn all their bridges behind them, perhaps giving up a lucrative job and saying a final farewell to friends and neighbors. It is wiser to come to the islands for a time and try out life here. If you can't arrange an extended "living period" here, come to Hawai'i for at least one full week. Use this time, not to enjoy Hawai'i as a tourist, but to live as a *kama'āina*, a resident. In a visit as short as one week, you can learn a lot about life here. Yes, it will be costly... but not nearly as costly as a mistake might be. The information you gain will be well worth the cost.

- **Two months before your trip**, order a week's subscription to the newspaper from the island you are considering. Newspapers are listed in the Resources section at the back of this book and most are accessible on the Internet.
- **Rent a place to live.** From the classified ads, find houses, cottages, condominiums or studios for rent and call those that seem to offer what you desire as a long-term rental. Chances are, the owner or rental manager will be trying to rent it for six months or a year. Discuss what you are doing — trying out Hawaiian life — and offer an extra 50 percent above the rental price for just one or two weeks occupancy. If the first few owners reject your offer, keep trying. You'll instigate some lively discussion about life in Hawai'i... and chances are you'll find a willing landlord within four or five calls.
- **As soon as you arrive, begin to live** your life just as you would if you had moved here. Maintain a daily schedule. Drive or take TheBus to wherever you expect to work every day at about the time you would leave for work. Spend a minimum of six hours each day looking for work in your field and

finding out all you can about jobs here. This is extremely valuable time. Visit the state employment office, private employment firms and businesses, offices or resorts at which you can realistically expect to work. Talk to human relations directors. Talk to the people in jobs similar to yours. Are they adequately paid? What are the chances of finding a job in your field? You will learn a great deal and you may even find a job, as one person who tried this approach did. "The best time to find a job is when you don't really need it. When you aren't desperate," he commented.

- **If you expect to be self-employed**, use these six hours a day to pursue information. Talk to economic development directors, business and tourism officials, rental agents, suppliers, and people in businesses related to the one you are considering.

- **If you have a spouse and family**, make sure they are spending at least part of their days in ways they would if they lived here. Will you need child care? Visit child care centers. Visit schools, talk to students and teachers. Encourage your teenage children to interact with peers at youth centers.

- **Food shop to fill the larder for your stay.** Plan to prepare food and dine as you do in your current life. No restaurants — unless you dine out often in your current life. You're not on vacation now: your goal is to sample real life here.

- **Spend your leisure time** as you would spend it if you lived here. If you are into sports like softball, find a diamond. Tennis? Most islands have plenty of public courts. Golf? The links are great places to pick up job leads and information. Interested in community service? Check out the newspapers' events calendars and get in touch with people with interests similar to yours.

- **Finally, each evening**, spend 10 or 15 minutes writing down your impressions of the day. Take time to assess the information you've gained and your feelings about what you've learned. Talk over the day's experiences with your spouse or family.

- **On the seventh day, rest**. Review your impressions. You've sampled a little of real life in paradise. Do you still want to move here? If you do, you will have developed some good contacts, advice and firsthand knowledge.

ka neʻe
ʻana

moving

Lighten

your

load

The Esbensens did it right

There are two ways to move to Hawai'i. The first is on impulse. You fall in love with the islands on vacation and simply never leave, or you return home, pack up or dispose of your worldly possessions, and return on the next available flight.

The second, wiser, way is to plan for your move, conducting thorough research, visiting the islands, and choosing the best possible location. That's a luxury not all of us can afford, but Dan and Bonney Esbensen were fortunate — they had the time and resources to plan their move carefully.

Nick, Bonney, Este and Dan

Dan is a partner in a successful San Diego-based computer software research and development firm. His profession lets him work wherever he can plug his high-speed, memory-packed computer into the Internet. Dan's company would pay for his family to move anywhere in the United States, so one day he and Bonney sat down with a map and chose Hawai'i, a place neither had ever visited.

Dan's computer knowledge allowed him to take the next step — finding out all they could about the islands — by pushing a few keys. He looked up everything he could find about Hawai'i on the Internet and communicated with prospective landlords via e-mail. He also subscribed to Honolulu and neighbor island newspapers.

Dan and Bonney were concerned about how such a drastic move would affect her two children, ages 12 and 10, in their crucial pre-teen years, so they discussed the move and most decisions with the children.

"The children were enthusiastic," Bonney says. "If they had not wanted to come here, that would have ended the idea."

By a process of elimination (O'ahu? Too crowded; the Big Island? Too rural.) Bonney and Dan decided to visit Maui first. That visit, lasting four days, was spent exploring. They cruised the island in a rented car and, "We tried to visualize ourselves in the community. We asked each other questions. 'How would it feel to live here? What did you think of the schools? How are the people?'"

More importantly, they visited the intermediate school in each community.

"They were all very hospitable, very open," Bonney recalls. "We asked for documentation including any papers that they might have with discipline policies and codes.

"At Lahaina, the children came up to us and asked, 'What are you doing here?' When we told them they teased us, 'Oh, your kids are not going to like it here!' but they were very sweet, very charming. Even though we didn't see a lot of *haole* kids, we thought 'Well, the attitude here is very open.'"

On their third day on Maui, the couple stopped at a beachfront festival in Kihei and Bonney won a medal in a swim meet. That clinched it; they felt part of the community and decided to live in Kīhei, a rapidly growing town that includes many *haole* newcomers.

"The truth is, Bonney felt connected as soon as we got off the plane and each day on Maui she felt more so," Dan says.

Once they had decided on a town, the Esbensens scheduled a second trip, this time for seven days, to find a home. They planned to rent a three-bedroom house for a year or two and become acquainted with neighborhoods before buying, but were very disappointed in the rental market. Prices were high and many rental properties contained several units, offering little privacy or requiring families to share a yard. Building quality was poor compared to mainland houses and some of the rental homes were dirty or in need of repairs.

"Most of the rentals were from $900 to $1200 which was pretty much what we were paying in New Hampshire," Bonney remembers. "For $1,400 things started to look better. For $1,600 they were still better and, of course, you can just keep climbing.

"So we found a house in Kīhei that was very nice and very clean. It was $1,600 (plus all utilities) which was more than we really felt we could comfortably pay, but we decided we could stretch our budget because the others were just totally unacceptable. We learned a lot in that year."

After one year at the house, the Esbensens moved to another in Kīhei, which they expect to someday buy for about $350,000. The four bedroom, three-bath stucco, in a neighborhood of new homes, overlooks roof tops to the ocean

So far, the Esbensens are happy — perhaps because they excel at an important aspect of adapting to Hawai'i: becoming involved in the community. Bonney paddles in a canoe club; Dan is active in the Chamber of Commerce and teaches at the community college, donating his earnings back to charity.

"I'm very impressed with the high level of problem solving in this community," Bonney says. "For example, kids skateboarding through the business area were destroying concrete, so the community started a fund to build a skateboarding facility in the park.

"At my canoe club, anyone who wants to come and paddle is welcome — tourists, visitors, it doesn't matter. We say 'Experience the ocean! Look at the whales! Look at the turtles! That's what it is all about.'

"I have heard people say you are drawn [to Hawai'i]. I think that's true. There was a greater influence guiding us here."

➤ **TIP**: **Use all available resources to get information**, including subscribing to several newspapers, communicating via e-mail and studying the Internet. Then, visit several islands if possible, before you choose one on which to settle.

➤ **TIP**: **Once you've moved, don't look back** for six months to a year. It takes that long to get even a little accustomed to life here, advised several people.

➤ **TIP**: **Temporary housing** — a place to reside for a few days or a few weeks while you search for permanent housing — is difficult to come by on all islands. Most people arrange with a travel agent to remain in a vacation condominium for a week or two while they search for a more permanent home. A rental agent can be useful, or check the newspaper classified ads. Good news: many long-term rentals are furnished and immediately available, so you may be able to move in within days.

Packing

Less is best

Dan and Bonnie Esbensen, whose story begins this chapter, said they walked through their mainland home and tried to decide which furniture to ship, which to dispose of. Then they considered the weight of each piece, whether it could be replaced, and how expensive that would be. "And we still brought a lot more furniture than we should have," Dan said.

Almost everyone moves to these islands with more than they need. Until you've lived here for a few months, it's difficult to envision how truly simple your day-to-day needs will be.

Malihini and transplanted *kama'āina* we talked to for this book all had the same advice:

1. Don't bring anything you can buy here — and with the advent of Kmart, Sam's Club and Price Costco, almost anything can be bought here.

2. Do bring small, cherished items that can't be replaced — mementos, family photos, keepsakes.

➤ TIP: **You may be tempted to bring** family antiques or favorite pieces of large furniture. You should consider that Hawai'i's climate (very damp in some places; very dry in others) and insects (termites) can be damaging to some furniture. Kona and trade winds tend to blow dust and dirt, making upholstered furniture difficult to clean.

Bringing a little

On the plane

Much of the small stuff can travel with you. Airlines will usually let you carry on two small bags and check through two additional large suitcases. For a minimal amount, usually about $20 per suitcase, you can check through at least two more large suitcases. Those four large suitcases and two bags will probably hold all you really need: a few items of clothing, sandals and sneakers or loafers; a few towels and toiletries, perhaps a small stereo or electronics such as cameras. Most apartments are geared to tourists and include eating utensils, pots and pans and all appliances, even a coffee pot.

Via the post office

If you decide to bring more than a few suitcases of belongings, a friend or contact on the island to which you are moving is a valuable resource — someplace to send boxes so they'll be on island when you arrive. The least expensive way to ship is via **parcel post** from your U.S. post office. Pack your valuables in cardboard boxes and make sure none weighs more than 70 pounds. Seal well with a strong plastic tape, wrapped both vertically and horizontally. Currently, you can ship a 70-pound box from Pennsylvania to the island of O'ahu for $39.03, a postal representative says. It should take seven to ten days. (Longer for the neighbor islands.) You can buy additional insurance for valuable items.

Or you may decide to have a friend send those boxes later, after you have an address. Once you've lived here for a few months, you'll also have a better idea of which items you really want.

➤ **TIP: Pack your boxes to store for shipment later.** Mark the boxes 1, 2, 3, etc. and make a corresponding list of what is in each box. Take the list with you to Hawai'i. Have the cartons shipped as you need them, referring to the list and asking for the boxes by number. Why not just mark the contents of the box on the outside? Because "Grandma's antique silver" might prove a little tempting for thieves.

➤ **TIP: Compare costs.** Unless you are shipping heavy items, first class postage via the U.S. Mail may be only a few dollars more than third class. At this writing, United Parcel Service (UPS) has a bulk rate as low as 57¢ a pound from the West Coast. Visit Mailboxes, Etc. or similar packing outlets for current rates.

➤ **TIP: Keep a list of boxes and contents** so you can track which have arrived. If you are sending many boxes, it can be extremely confusing.

➤ **TIP: Books may be shipped "book rate"** which is considerably less expensive. They may take up to a month to appear at your doorstep, but when you first move here you'll be too busy to read anyway.

Bringing a lot

Using a mover

If you cannot bear to part with your furniture, have a moving company store it to ship later, after you've chosen a residence. Honolulu moving company owner Jim Yarbrough says you can figure about $1 a pound to have the items packed and shipped by a moving company. That may not sound like much, but furniture is heavy.

A moving company will pack your items in special "vanpacks" and ship them to Honolulu with many other people's possessions in an oceanic shipping container. If you live on a neighbor island, your items will then be shipped on a separate barge to your island.

Doing it yourself

You can do some of the work, packing and arranging shipment from Los Angeles, Oakland, Seattle or Portland. At least three "freight forwarders" ocean-haul to Hawai'i, including Sea Land Service, Inc. and Aloha Cargo Transport. The name you'll hear most often here is Matson Navigation Co., which has been around for a long time. It is owned by one of Hawai'i's Big Five companies, Alexander & Baldwin.

The Matson brochure says you can put about three rooms of furniture in a 24-foot container (1,426 cubic feet), which costs $2,200 or $2,400 to ship, depending on which port you are shipping from. If you have a full container, the goods go by "space" — not by weight. In other words, you can put a certain amount in the container, no matter how heavy it is. (Grandma's baby grand!) Packing according to Matson's regulations may require a professional packer or mover. If you have a large household, you can opt for the 40-foot container (2,397 cubic feet) at just less than twice the cost.

➤ **TIP: Get full details and reservations well in advance.** In fact, consider the information before you make decisions about whether to ship your furniture.

➤ **TIP: Contract to ship a full, not a partial container.** If you ship just a few large items (a partial container), your items will be mixed with others on

Get the children involved

Long-distant moves are especially traumatic for young children. Here's a way to make the move easier. Let your child choose four or five favorite toys, dolls or stuffed friends and help pack the toys in a separate box. Let him (or her) decorate the outside of the box with colorful magic markers and help address the box. Take your child with you to the post office when you mail it and let him wave goodbye to his "friends." Tell him they are traveling to Hawai'i first and will be waiting for him to come too. Once your child arrives on the islands, opening his special box and seeing familiar faces—Bert or Ernie or Barbie—will soothe the transition.

their voyage across the sea. That can lead to mishandling or loss as other people's goods are added and removed, Dan and Bonney Esbensen were advised by former Hawai'i residents. The Esbensen's full container was packed at their New Hampshire home, sealed by the moving company, and arrived in Maui looking much as it had when it left New Hampshire. The cost for 6,000 pounds of goods packed, shipped, and unpacked on Maui was $10,000, Dan says.

Shipping a car

Matson Navigation also moves cars from the west coast of the United States to the Hawaiian islands. Cost at this writing is about $816 one way for a passenger auto from the West Coast to Honolulu; $857 to the outer islands. Vehicles shipped from the West Coast (Seattle, Oakland, Long Beach or San Diego) take three to four weeks. Phone numbers under resources, at the end of this chapter, will give you current costs. The car must be empty during shipping; the gas tank should be very low.

➤ TIP: **Should you bring your car?** The cost of shipping your auto versus buying here is a calculation only you can make. If your car is relatively new, if you are tied to a lease, if you are still making payments on a car you have purchased and owe more than you would net selling it, you may want to ship it. New cars are expensive here; used ones are quite reasonable. (See Autos, chapter 4: Necessities, pages 95 - 97)

Bringing plants

Plants must go through a cumbersome quarantine and inspection before being allowed into Hawai'i, so household plants are best left behind. Those that go through inspection must be free from insects, disease and sand, soil or earth or deteriorated peat. If you are determined to do this, contact the address below for details. They will explain applications for permits.

U.S. Department of Agriculture

Animal and Plant Health Inspection Service

Terminal Box 57

Honolulu International Airport

Honolulu, HI 96819

Keep Important documents at your side

Having all personal papers and documents within easy reach will ease your transition to Hawai'i. These should travel with you at all times, in your carry-on. The best way to transport them is in an expanding file with compartments, available at office supply stores. Make sure you have the following documents:

PERSONAL RECORDS
- Birth certificates of all
  family members
- Citizenship papers
- Children's report cards
- Passports
- Shot records
- Marriage license
- Child custody documents

- Medical records
- Adoption papers
- Death certificates
- Military: Armed Forces
  identification cards
- Wills
- Annulments of any
  previous marriages
- Divorce papers

FINANCIAL RECORDS
- Motor vehicle ownership papers
- Insurance cards and insurance documents
- Stock certificates and other investments
- Household goods shipping information

- Property deeds
- Savings account books
- Checkbooks
- Credit cards

274

- Names and addresses of companies where you recently opened or closed accounts
- Bills due during the time you move as well as record of any you have paid in past three months (in case questions or problems arise).
- Military: Copy of application for allotment (if any).

➤ TIP: **If you take prescription drugs**, be sure to ask your current doctor to provide enough medication for at least two or three months while you settle in and find a new doctor. Be sure to bring all information relating to the prescription, as well as your current doctors' phone numbers and addresses.

➤ TIP: **Bring all your family's health records** and shot records, including records of any mammograms that were taken so that future x-rays can be compared.

Cargo containers are unloaded from ships at the Honolulu harbor. About 95 percent of Hawai'i's goods are imported. Some malihini *bring households of furniture and belongings.*

RESOURCES

TRANS-OCEAN SHIPPING COMPANIES

- Matson Navigation Co. **(800) 462-8766** moves goods from mainland to islands.
- Sea Land Service, Inc. **(800) SEA-LAND** from anywhere in U.S. This company ships 20, 40 and 45-foot containers from the Far East and mainland at prices comparable to Matson's, a spokesperson says.
- Aloha Cargo Transport **(800) 327-7739** Pacific Northwest freight forwarder to the Hawaiian islands.

Inter-island shippers

- Young Brothers Limited **(808) 543-9447**
- Postal Service **(800) 275-8777** Information on shipping boxes weighing under 70 pounds.

MOVING COMPANIES

(Among many listed in the Honolulu phone book)

- Island Movers **(808) 848-5200**
- American Movers **(808) 676-6683**
- The Moore Group **(808) 483-7447**

Also see the Resources section of this book

Should your pet come along?*

Because of its isolated location, Hawai'i has a unique, fragile ecosystem. To prevent the introduction of diseases like rabies and crop-destroying pests, incoming produce and creatures (except man, and rodents who can sneak in on cargo ships) are subject to inspection and/or quarantine.

Pets moving to the islands must undergo a several-months-long regimen that includes at least two trips to the veterinarian before they even set paw on an island-bound plane — and they are subjected to a 30-day quarantine and additional pricking and prodding after they arrive. Total cost is usually from $500 to $1,000 per animal.

Contact the Department of Agriculture's Animal Quarantine Station six months in advance of your move. Make sure you follow the procedures exactly. The vaccination and testing time is crucial, there's a lot of paperwork and the regulations are a bit complicated.

According to the Department of Agriculture's State of Hawai'i Quarantine Law, you must pre-qualify within 90 days before the animal's arrival. The following may help you decide whether or not to bring Fluffy and Fido.

Pre-qualification requirements

1. **Vaccinations.** A minimum of two rabies vaccinations, not less than 60 days apart, with particulars recorded on a veterinarian-approved health certificate. The certificate must be issued not more than 14 days prior to arrival and must also include proof that the animal was dipped, sponged or dusted for external parasites and has been inspected for any infectious or contagious diseases. You must provide the results of a heartworm test and all other vaccinations (for distemper, parvovirus, etc.) must be current. Costs vary, but expect to pay about $25 for a general examination, plus $15 to $20 for each vaccination, plus the cost of the vet visit.

2. **Microchip implant**. The Department of Agriculture will issue an official electronic microchip identification disc that must be implanted at the nape of your pet's neck (between its shoulder blades) by a qualified vet before it

travels. Even if your animal already has an identification microchip, it must have an official State of Hawai'i-issued microchip. Cost of the chip: $17 including shipping and handling to the mainland; $27 to a foreign country. Cost of implantation, approximately $30 plus an office visit.

3. **OIE-FAVN test**. The OIE-Fluorescent Antibody Virus Neutralization Test is a rabies blood test and must be conducted not less than 90 days prior to arrival. A sample of whole blood cells is also required. Cost: $20 to $40.

Methods of traveling

Once a pet is pre-qualified for quarantine, it can be shipped to Hawai'i. If you are traveling by air with your pet, it will be considered baggage and will cost about $50 on most trans-Pacific flights and $20 between islands. It must be shipped in a waterproof pet carrier. You should get specific instructions from your airline. Be warned: your pet is considered freight and may be shipped on a "space available" basis on some airlines. Shipping a pet by air freight (instead of with you) costs from $300 to $500. Some airlines will not ship animals as freight during hot summer months.

From the airport, the pet must be transported to the quarantine station on O'ahu. A few outer island veterinarians maintain satellite quarantine stations, but they are usually reserved for animals with medical conditions and the cost can be up to 50 percent greater than the main station.

At the quarantine station

1. A post-arrival rabies blood test. Owners must submit a signed consent form allowing the state to collect a blood sample and to sedate the animal for the test if necessary. If test results indicate antibody levels that fall outside the established parameters, the animal must be quarantined 120 days instead of 30 days. Cost is $45.
2. Registration fee: $25
3. Health record fee: $10
4. Daily fee for dogs: $7 (Add a $1 per day if the dog requires mediation such as insulin.)
5. Daily fee for cats: $6.50 (Plus $1 medication cost if necessary).
   Additional costs may be incurred during the quarantine period if more

tests are deemed necessary, if your pet requires veterinary services or if copies of records are needed for any reason.

You should also know

The Oʻahu quarantine facility is clean and well-managed, but its purpose is to keep incoming animals in isolation. Quarantined pets are held in cages with little interaction with humans and no socialization with other animals. You can also hire a caretaker who will visit your pet to play with it daily.

Free brochure

A free brochure is available from the

Animal Quarantine Station
99-951 Halawa Valley Street
ʻAiea, HI 96701-3246

You may also call **(808) 483-7151**, but lines are usually busy. Writing or faxing **(808) 483-7161** may be more effective.

*Meg Skellenger, who produces the Maui Humane Society's newsletter, researched and wrote this information

A faithful friend awaits his master's return at Kapaʻa, Kauaʻi.

MOVING

Your moving budget

Here's a list for calculating your moving costs to Hawai'i, including some items you may have forgotten.

Cost

1. Flight from home to Hawai'i for yourself . . . . ·＿＿＿＿＿＿

for each family member . . . . ·＿＿＿＿＿＿

2. Shipping car

travel to coastal city (L.A. or San Francisco) . . . . ·＿＿＿＿＿＿

over-night stays enroute . . . . ·＿＿＿＿＿＿

stays in coastal city as you wait to ship the auto . . . . ·＿＿＿＿＿＿

food during trip and stay . . . . ·＿＿＿＿＿＿

auto rental while you wait for your car to arrive

in Honolulu or outer island (cost per day times number of days) . . ·＿＿＿＿＿＿

additional shipping to outer islands . . . . ·＿＿＿＿＿＿

3. Purchase or lease car (if you have not sent yours)

lease deposit . . . . ·＿＿＿＿＿＿

to buy new ($13,000 up) . . . . ·＿＿＿＿＿＿

to buy used late model ($6,000 up) . . . . ·＿＿＿＿＿＿

to buy used "cruiser" ($2,000 up) . . . . ·＿＿＿＿＿＿

4. Shipping furniture

cost to move furniture to coastal city for shipping . . . . ·＿＿＿＿＿＿

cost to pack and ship to Hawai'i . . . . ·＿＿＿＿＿＿

additional costs to outer island . . . . ·＿＿＿＿＿＿

storage while you house hunt . . . . ·＿＿＿＿＿＿

5. Housing

hotel or short term apartment . . . . _____

permanent housing . . . . _____

rental deposit - usually one month's rent . . . . _____

first month's rent . . . . _____

utility deposits and turn-on cost: phone . . . . _____

electricity . . . . _____

6. Bringing a pet

pre-shots (estimates) . . . . _____

microchip implant (estimate) . . . . _____

boarding (dog) at $7.00 a day for 30 days . . . . _____

boarding (cat) at $6.50 a day for 30 days . . . . _____

if you live on outer island, round-trip to visit pet . . . . _____

if you live on outer island, cost of caretaker to visit pet . . . . _____

if you live on outer island, round-trip to pick up pet . . . . _____

Total moving costs _____

7. Living cost while you search for job (three-to-six months)

food costs . . . . _____

estimate $80 per person per week for adults . . . . _____

estimate $50 per person per week for child . . . . _____

total living Costs _____

Total
living costs _____ **+** Total
moving costs _____ **=** Total cost of
your move _____

You know you are kama'āina...

- when Hawaiian and Japanese words begin to dot your conversation. "Did you enjoy your *musubi*? Has anyone taken the dog *shi shi*? Are you *pau*?"

- when you automatically remove your shoes before you enter a home — even while you're visiting relatives in Boulder and it's 10 below.

- when you put Spam and *shoyu* on your grocery list under "staples."

- when you slide into pidgin during everyday conversations.

- the day you give all your winter clothes to the Salvation Army.

- when you never take your bathing suit off entirely.

- when you automatically walk out of the ocean facing it.

- when a two-inch long cockroach flies at you and you don't duck.

- when you know the difference between shave ice and *guri guri*.

- when you know what an *okole* is.

- when you find yourself smiling unexpectedly, for no good reason except that it's great to be alive.

resources

Resources

All islands

Housing

- *Landlord Tenant Code*
  For a booklet on state rental laws, send $2 to:
  Cashiers Office
  P.O. Box 541
  Honolulu, HI 96809
  or call **(808) 586-2630**

- *Homes & Land* real estate magazines
  Free full-color magazines with photos and prices of homes, condos and land for sale throughout the islands and the nation, including all Hawaiian islands. Call **(800) 277-7800** or via the Internet at **http://www.homes.com**

- National realtor network
  http://www.realtor.com

- *Rentals Illustrated*
  Free twice monthly pictorial of apartments and homes
  (808) 949-3686
  1240 Ala Moana Blvd.
  Honolulu, HI 96814

Business

- For a free workbook *Starting a Business in Hawaii* call:
  The Business Action Center
  (808) 586-2545
  This branch of the Hawaii Dept. of Business, Economic Development and Tourism provides entrepreneurs with information, business forms, licenses and permits. Access via the Internet:
  www.hawaii.gov/dbedt/

- Professional and Vocational Licensing Division, Department of Commerce and Consumer Affairs **(808) 586-3000**

- High Technology Development Corporation **(808) 625-5293**

- Small Business Information Service
  (808) 586-2600

- Retail Merchants of Hawai'i
  (808) 592-4200

- Small Business Hawai'i
  (808)396-1724

Living

- Newcomers Club **(808) 528-6986**

Crime

- The Honolulu Police Department's annual report lists crimes reported in every area of O'ahu. Helpful for choosing neighborhoods. Available at Hawai'i's main library or at the main police station, 801 Beretania Street, Honolulu.

General

- The *Hawai'i State Data Book* published through the Hawaii State Department of Business, Economic Development & Tourism is available at libraries or by writing the Department of Business, Economic Development & Tourism
  P.O. Box 2359
  Honolulu, HI 96804
  or via the Internet at
  http://www.hawaii.gov/dbedt/index.html

- For further information about data and sources, call the Research and Economic Analysis Division's Business Resource Center Library
  (808) 586-2424

Newspapers and periodicals

- *Honolulu Advertiser*
  (morning and Sunday)

- *Star-Bulletin* (afternoon and Saturday)
  For either paper call,
  (808) 538-6397 or write
  Hawai'i Newspaper Agency
  Attention: Circulation
  Post Office Box 3350
  Honolulu, HI 96801

- *The Honolulu Weekly*
  Contains a comprehensive arts and entertainment guide **(808) 528-1475**
  1200 College Walk, Suite 214
  Honolulu, HI 96817

- *Honolulu* magazine. An upscale monthly chronicle of lifestyle **(808) 524-7400** fax **(808) 531-2306**
  36 Merchant Street
  Honolulu, HI 96813

- *Island Family.* A free monthly newspaper includes a calendar of family events **(808) 689-0000**
  P.O. Box 2429
  Ewa Beach, HI 96706-0429

- *Hawaii Jewish News*
  A bimonthly publication of the Jewish Federation of Hawaii **(808) 595-5218**
  2550 Pali Highway
  Honolulu, HI 96817

- *Filipino Chronicle*
  A free twice-monthly newspaper **(808) 874-6701**
  1449 North King Street
  Honolulu, HI 96817

- *Island Lifestyle*
  A monthly alternative newspaper (gay and lesbian) **(808)737-6400**
  Lifestyle Publishing Co. Inc.
  P.O. Box 11840
  Honolulu, HI 96828

Politics and taxation

- Send for *Government in Hawaii* a booklet by the Tax Foundation of Hawai'i. Call **(808) 536-4587** or **fax (808) 536-4588**
  126 Queen Street, Suite 304
  Honolulu, HI 96813

O'ahu

Business and jobs

- The Chamber of Commerce of Hawai'i **(808) 545-4300**

1132 Bishop Street, Suite 200
Honolulu, HI 96813

- Kailua Chamber of Commerce **(808) 261-2727**
  P.O. Box 1469
  Kailua, HI 96734

- City job information line: **(808) 523-4301**

- Business action line: **(808) 586-2545**
  See also the working section of this book

Big Island

Business

- Hawaii Island Economic Development **(808) 966-5416**

- Research and Development **(808) 961-8366**

- Kailua-Kona Chamber of Commerce **(808) 329-1758**

- Hawai'i Island Chamber of Commerce **(808) 935-7178**
  For $20, either Chamber will send you a directory with specific information

Information about volcanoes:

- Use these Internet URLs
  http://hvo.wr.usgs.gov./
  http://volcano.und.nodak.edu/

Newspapers:

- *Hawaii Tribune Herald*
  355 Kinoole Street
  Hilo, HI 96720
  (808) 935-6621

- *West Hawaii Today*
  75-5560 Kaiwe Street
  Kona, HI 96740
  (808) 329-9311

Maui

Business

- Small Business Development Center
590 Lipoa Parkway
Kihei, HI 96753
(808) 875-2402
E-mail **dfisher@maui.com**

- The Business Information Center
590 Lipoa Parkway
Kīhei, HI 96753
(808) 875-2400
E-mail **corn@maui.com** or
sonia @maui.com

- County of Maui **(800) 272-0026**

Newspapers

- *The Maui News* **(808) 244-6363**

- *The Haleakala Times* **(808) 572-9289 fax**
(808) 572-0168

- *The Lahaina News* **(808) 667-7866**
fax (808) 667-2726

Moloka'i

Moloka'i is part of Maui County.
Also see Maui.

Business, working

- Federal Job Information Center,
O'ahu: **(808) 541-2791**

- Hawai'i State Workforce
Development Division,
Kaunakakai: **(808) 553-3281**

Newspapers

- *Moloka'i Advertiser-News*
(808) 558-8253

- *The Moloka'i Dispatch* **(808) 552-2781**

Lana'i

Lanai is part of Maui County.
Also see Maui.

- The Lāna'i Co.
Main number **(808) 565-3000**
Housing **(808) 565-3977**
Employment **(808) 565-3876**

- Lāna'i Community Hospital
(808) 565-6411

- Lāna'i Schools **(808) 565-7224**

Kaua'i

Working

- County of Kaua'i Office of Economic
Development,
4280 B. Rice Street
Lihue, Hawaii, 96766
(808) 241-6390

- University of Hawai'i
Small Business Development Center
at Kaua'i Community College
3-1901 Kaumauali'i Highway
Līhue, Hawaii 96766
(808) 246-1748

- State Department of
Labor and Industrial Relations,
Līhue: **(808) 214-3421**
Fax: (808) 241-3518

- State Department of Education
(808) 274-3507

- County of Kaua'i Personnel Services
Office **(808) 421-6595**

- Kaua'i Business Guide and
Membership Referral Directory,
Kaua'i Chamber of Commerce,
P.O. Box 1969
Līhue, Kaua'i, HI 96766
(808) 245-7363
Fax (808) 245-8815

Newspapers

- *The Garden Island*
P.O. Box 231
Līhue, HI 96766
(808) 245-3681

- *The Kauai Times*
P.O. Box 3272
Līhue, HI 96766
(808) 245-8825

Additional Reading

Religion

- *Hawai'i's Religions* by John F. Mulholland © 1970 by Charles E. Tuttle Company, Rutland, Vt., and Tokyo, Japan.
- *Hawai'i's Missionary Saga* © 1992 by Piercy LaRue. Mutual Publishing.

Living

- *What Bit Me?* By Gordon M. Nishida and Joann M. Tenorio 1993 University of Hawai'i Press, Honolulu.

Business

- *Mason on Management* - 65 columns on business management from *Pacific Business News* magazine's former editor and publisher George Mason. Down to earth and helpful advice. Crossroads Press, Inc. P.O. Box 833, Honolulu, HI 96808 or phone (808) 596-2021.
- *Business Basics in Hawaii* by Dennis Kondo 1988 University of Hawai'i Press. General business knowledge.

Politics, history and costs

- *Land and Power In Hawaii* by George Cooper and Gavan Daws. Paperback edition published by University of Hawai'i Press 1990; Originally published 1985 by Benchmark Books, Inc. The deals and doings that forever changed Hawai'i during the Democratic years of government.
- *Hawaii State and Local Politics*, James C. F. Wang, University of Hawai'i at Hilo, 1982

- *Hawaii: The Sugar-Coated Fortress* by Francine du Plessix Gray. 1972. Haddon Crofsmen, Scranton, Pa. This beautifully written essay sensitively probes the military and business influence in the Hawaiian islands. Available in libraries.
- *Hawaii, Compass American Guides,* by Moana Tregaskis. 1996. Fodor's Travel Publications, Inc. This ultimate tourist guide book includes concise history of each island, details about many towns and cities and contains spectacular photos.
- *Notable Women of Hawaii* edited by Barbara Bennett Peterson, @1984 University of Hawaii Press
- *The Best of Hawaii*, by Jocelyn K. Fujii, 1994, Random House, New York.
- *The Peopling of Hawaii*, Eleanor C. Nordyke, the University Press of Hawaii, 1977
- *The Price of Paradise, Volume I,* Randall W. Roth, editor. 1992. Mutual Publishing Honolulu. A must-read collection of editorials, articles, written by a variety of specialists in their fields. Great cartoons. Good overview of some of the more controversial aspects of island life from politics to taxes to government efficiency.
- *The Price of Paradise, Volume II* 1993. See above. This volume less diverse than first volume. But still important reading. Heavy government.
- *The Islands of Aloha* by Carl Giamplo, editor. 1983. Paradise Books. Good maps and overview of each island. Excellent articles on Hawaiian history and the advent of each ethnic group to the islands.

Pamphlets, other publications

Available at most libraries or by calling directly

- *A Practical Guide to Divorce in Hawaii.* by Peter J. Herman, University of Hawaii Press, 1991

- **Crime in Hawai'i**. State of Hawai'i, department of the attorney general annual report.

- **Government in Hawai'i**. A handbook of financial statistics by the Tax Foundaton of Hawai'i. Write Tax Foundaton of Hawai'i, 126 Queen Street, Suite 304, Honolulu, HI, 96813 or call **(808) 536-4587.**

- **Handbook for Employers on Unemployment Insurance**. Hawai'i Department of Labor and Industrial Relations, employer services **(808) 586-8926**.

- **Hui 'Imi Task force for Hawaiian services**. Report of the state of Hawai'i Office of Hawaiian Affairs, 1991

- **Job Hunter's Guide to Hawai'i**. A labor market information publication of the Hawai'i Department of Labor and Industrial Relations.

- **How To Find A Job**. The Research and Statistics Office, Department of Labor and Industrial Relations.

- **Population growth, policies and strategies; a public opinion**. Commission on Population and the Hawaiian Future, 1977.

- **Sex Discrimination and the Law in Hawai.** A guide to your legal rights by Judith R. Gething (The University of Hawaii Press 1979)

- **People at Work, the City's Heartbeat, City Civil Service opportunities**, City and County of Honolulu, **(808) 523-4301.** http://www.cohonolulu.hi.us/depts/per

Useful Internet sites

Use the Internet and the world wide web to learn about Hawaii and its individual islands. Here are a few helpful Net locations:

http://www.mauigateway.com/msgs.html
To "Ask a Local" questions about Hawai'i life

http://www.ivv.nasa.gov/
Take a virtual trip to Hawai'i

http.://www.mapquest.com/
See maps, including street maps, for anywhere in the nation. The Esbensens used this to locate possible rentals on the islands.

http://www.homes.com
http://www.realtor.com
To see homes and their prices around the nation, including Hawaii.

http://www.starbulletin.com
To read portions of a Honolulu afternoon newspaper.

http://www.mauinews.com
To read portions of the Maui newspaper.

http://www.ttinet.com/hawaiiantravel
Fare and accommodation bargains.

http://www.hawaii.gov/dbedt/index.html
Access the *Hawaii Data Book.*

http://www.maui.com/~hpd
Honolulu Police Dept. Annual Crime report.

http://www.bookshawaii.com
Books about Hawai'i

⟨⟩Chambers of Commerce⟨⟩

Hawai'i has at least 19 Chambers of Commerce, including several ethnic groups. A complete list:

Chamber of Commerce of Hawai'i
(808) 545-4300

Junior Chamber of Commerce
(aka Honolulu Junior Jaycees)
(808) 537-6686

Hawai'i Island Chamber of Commerce
(808) 935-7178 fax (808) 961-4435

Kona Kohala Chamber of Commerce
O'ahu **(808) 329-1758**
fax (808) 329-8564

Kauai Chamber of Commerce
(808) 245-7363 fax (808) 245-8815

Maui Chamber of Commerce
(808) 871-771 fax (808) 877-6646

Molokai Chamber of Commerce
(808) 553-3070

African American Chamber of Commerce, Honolulu
(808) 947-7493

Australian American Chamber of Commerce, Honolulu
(808) 526-2242

Chinese Chamber of Commerce, Honolulu **(808) 533-3181**

Filipino Chamber of Commerce, Kalihi, O'ahu **(808) 843-0322 (808) 847-6089**

Hawai'i Hispanic Chamber of Commerce, Honolulu
(808) 545-4344 fax (808) 682-5101

Hawai'i Korean Chamber of Commerce, Honolulu **(808) 536-1539**

Honolulu Japanese Chamber of Commerce **(808) 949-5531**

Kailua (O'ahu) Chamber of Commerce **(808) 261-2727**

Native Hawaiian Chamber of Commerce, Honolulu **(808) 531-3744**

Portuguese Chamber of Commerce, Honolulu **(808) 523-5030**

Vietnamese-American Chamber of Commerce, Honolulu
(808) 523-5866 fax: (808) 228-2969

Japanese Chamber of Commerce of Hawai'i, Hilo, Big Island **(808) 934-0177**

Tourist Bureaus

Hawai'i Visitors Bureau-Big Island **(808) 961-5795**

Kaua'i Vistors Bureau **(808) 262-1400**

Maui Visitors Bureau **(808) 244-3580**

Moloka'i Visitors Bureau **(808) 553-3876**

O'ahu Visitors Bureau **(808) 524-0722**

footnotes

Introduction

[1] Name changed for privacy.

People

[1] *Hawai'i State Data Book*, 1996 figures

[2] *The Price of Paradise*, Volume II, Mutual Publishing (Honolulu , HI) 1993

[3]. "Hate crimes hard to track," *The Honolulu Advertiser*, Sept. 10, 1997

Politics

[1] Information for this section comes from various sources, including four primary ones: *Land and Power in Hawai'i*, *The Price of Paradise*, volumes 1 and 2, and the *Honolulu Advertiser* of Oct. 29, 1997.

[2] *Hawai'i's Religions* by John F. Mulholland. Copyright in Japan, 1970, by Charles E. Tuttle Company, Inc.

[3] *The Honolulu Advertiser*, Oct. 29, 1997

[4] *Honolulu Advertiser*, February 16, 1997

General Information

Bali Hai story
[1] The Bali Hai site appears to be an island. It is actually Mt. Makana, a promontory of the island of Kaua'i.

Health
[1] *Star-Bulletin*, June 16, 1997

[2] *Hawaii State Data Book*

[3] A study by the Centers for Disease Control and Prevention as quoted in an AP story in the *Maui News* February, 1997

[4] Ibid.

Establish Residency
[1] *Hawai'i Drivers' Manual*, Tongg Publishing Co., Ltd. (Honolulu, HI), 1991.

Andrea's Farewell
[1] From The Cremation Association of North America, The Maui News, June 3, 1997.

Necessities

Housing
[1] *Pacific Business News*, March 3, 1997.

Transportation
[1] *Pacific Business News*

[2] "Few drivers will find big cuts in insurance reform," *The Honolulu Advertiser*, Feb. 9, 1998.

Taxes
[1] From *Government in Hawai'i*, 1995 published by the Tax Foundation of Hawai'i.

[2] 6,633,840 visitor arrivals in 1995. From the state of *Hawai'i Data Book*, 1995.

[3] *Maui News*, May 28, 1997

[4] *Maui News*, August 25, 1997

Work

Working
[1] "Slumming Your Way to the Top" by Alex Salkever, *Honolulu* magazine.

Business
[1] *Maui News*, July 22, 1997

[2] *Maui News*, January. 20, 1997

[3] *Honolulu Star-Bulletin*, Oct. 4, 1997

Military

The Perks
[1] *Your Military in Hawai'i*, Hart Publishers Inc, Honolulu. 1996.

[2] Ibid

Retirement

Cover
[1] Richard Kalolo'okalani Keaulana quoted in *The Wai'anae Book of Hawaiian Health*, by the Wai'ainae Coast Comprehensive Health Center (Wai'anae, HI), 1993.

Sampling of Island Residences
[1] "Housing ready for Kauai elderly," the *Honolulu Advertiser*, Oct. 2, 1997.

Children

Pay your child support
[1] *Pacific Business News*, Nov. 10, 1997

Cradle to college
[1] From an Associated Press report in *Maui News* Feb. 18, 1997

[2] *Honolulu* magazine

[3] Associated Press report in *The Maui News*, July 17, 1997

[4] *The Maui News*, July 21, 1997

[5] *The Maui News*, June 13, 1997

[6] Associated Press, *The Maui News*, April 9, 1997

Romance

[1] University of Hawai'i Press, 1991

[2] *Sex Discrimination and the Law in Hawaii*, University of Hawai'i Press, 1979.

Trouble

Civil rights
[1] Associated Press, Maui News, Oct. 31, 1997

DUI Laws
[1] "One Drink Less," *Honolulu* magazine, July 1995

Crime
[1] "Crime rate in Hawai'i tumbling," the *Honolulu Advertiser*, Sept. 26, 1997

[2] "Crime in Hawai'i, 1996." Hawai'i Department of the Attorney General report.

[3] *The Stress of Paradise*, John Heckathorn,

Honolulu magazine, April 1994

[4] Associated Press

[5] Honolulu Police Department 1996 annual report.

[6] *Kaleo o Ko`olauloa* (a Windward Oahu newspaper), September 25, 1997

[7] Ibid.

[8] *Land and Power in Hawaii, The Democratic Years* @ 1985 by George Copper and Gavan Daws. Paperback edition published by University of Hawaii Press 1990.

Bugs
[1] *What Bit Me?* by Gordon M. Nishida and Joann M. Tenorio, University of Hawaii Press

Which Island

Kauai
[1] *The Garden Island*, March 23, 1997

Molokai
[1] State Department of Human Services calculation, not including those who receive SSI, food stamps only or Medicare only.

Big Island
[1] Crown Publishers 1988, 1994 by Jocelyn K. Fujii

[2] "Big Island drought getting worse," *The Honolulu Advertiser*, Feb. 12, 1998

[3] *Island Business*, May, 1997

The Riddle of Kalapana
[1] *Land and Power in Hawai'i* paperback by University of Hawai'i Press 1990; originally published by Benchmark Books, Inc. @ by George Cooper and Gavan Daws.

[2] *Land and Power in Hawai'i*

Forbidden Islands
[1] "Town meeting one-sided; many don't attend," *Star-Bulletin*, Dec. 31, 1997.

Index

AARP 153
activists, Hawaiian 47, 48
additional reading 285-286
advertising, employment 123
agriculture 23
ahupua'a 41, 260
'Aiea 223
'Aina Haina 223
Air Force Phillips Laboratory 234
air quality 78
airlines 96, 103, 269-270
airports 234, 248, 252
Akaka, Senator Daniel K. 44
alcohol
   fatalities 202
   youth use 192-193
Alexander & Baldwin 43, 44, 271
Alexander & Baldwin Sugar Museum 58
ali'i 39, 40, 41
alternative medicine 76, 256
aloha 25, 26, 46
Aloha Friday 101
Aloha Stadium 105
ambiance, islands 218
American Factors (Amfac) 43, 44, 101

Anahola 230
Anahola Mountains 230
animals 207-213, 275-277
'Anini beach 20
annexation 44
ants 209, 213
apartments 86-88, 370, 282
Apology Bill 47
Ariyoski, Governor George 258
arts & culture 26, 50, 53-73, 150, 159, 187, 282
   employment 115-130, 221, 249
   Hawai'i 53-73, 54, 58, 59
   Kaua'i 52, 53, 55-60, 229
   Lāna'i 56, 248-249
   Maui 55, 59-60, 73
   Moloka'i 126, 244-245
   O'ahu 53-54, 57, 59-60, 219
automobiles 22, 95-100
   insurance 97, 99, 145
   shipping from mainland 99, 272
   theft & crime 96, 200, 205
   used 96

Baby lū'au 162
Baldwin House 58

Bali Hai 52
bankruptcy 136, 234
banyan tree (Lahaina) 56
bars, hostess 203
Barbers' Point 143
Barking Sands 231
"Bayonet Constitution" 43
Big Five 43, 101, 271
Big Island see Hawai'i
Bingham, Rev. Hiram 63
Bishop, Bernice Pauahi 42, 55, 168
Bishop Estate 42, 104
Bishop Museum 50, 56-58, 207
Blue Cross/Blue Shield 75
Brigham Young University 178
budget, relocation 278-279
bus service 95, 145, 149, 150, 151
business
    new 131-138, 282
    resources 138, 282-284, 285-286

C. Brewer Company 43
Campbell Estate 44, 92
camping 68, 73
cane fields 78
cane spiders 210
Captain Cook (Hawai'i) 253
cars see automobiles
Castle & Cooke 43, 44, 92, 247-248
centipedes 208-209
Chamber of Commerce 137, 255, 264, 279, 283 (list)
    Hawai'i 138, 256, 283
    Kaua'i 230
    Maui 287
    O'ahu 225, 283
Chaminade University 63, 178
children 161-177
    child care 142, 163-164
    college 178-180
    drugs & alcohol 192-193
    health statistics 163

racial incidents 171, 173
    schools 165-177
Chinatown (Honolulu) 203
churches 43, 57, 63-65
civil rights 201
Cleveland, President Grover 43-44, 47
climate 217-218
Clinton, President Bill 47
clothing 101
cockroaches 207, 212-213
coffee industry 229, 244, 251, 253, 255
college 178-180, 284
common law marriage 191
computers, employment 125
condominiums 85 (photo), 89, 91, 92
conservation issues 49-50
    Moloka'i 243-244
Contemporary Museum 55
Cook, Captain James 39, 40, 43
Cooper, George 206, 257-259, 285
cost of living 21, 80-104, 143-145 (military)
creatures 207-213, 275
crime 200-206, 286
culture see arts & culture

Dating 183-191
Daws, Gavan 206, 257-259
Democratic party 45, 50
Department of Agriculture 273, 275
development 49-50, 243-244
Diamond Head 223
dining 61
    Hawai'i 61, 255
    Kaua'i 61, 228
    Maui 61, 235
    O'ahu 61, 221
discrimination 282 see also racism
disease 39, 42
divorce 188-189, 192
Dole, Sanford 43, 44
Dole Food Company 247
domestic violence 188, 203

driving 58
drugs
    crime 201-203, 286
    youth use 174-175
drunk driving 262

E Kanikapila Kakou 53
earthquakes 252
economy 12, 23, 45-47, 91, 111-112, 115-116, 141
    Hawai'i 251-252, 255
    Kaua'i 227, 229
    Lāna'i 247-249
    Maui 233-234
    Moloka'i 243
    O'ahu 219, 221
education see schools
'Ele'ele 230
employment 23, 30, 111, 113-138, 145, 286
    "casual employees" 121
    government 46, 124
    future employment needs (chart) 122
    Hawai'i 251, 254-255, 256, 283
    job opportunities 123-129
    Kaua'i 227, 229, 230
    Lāna'i 135, 247-249, 284
    Maui 233, 234, 236
    Moloka'i 243-245, 284
    new business opportunities 131-138
    O'ahu 119, 219, 220, 225, 283
    resources 124-125, 127, 129, 130
    statistics 115, 131
    wages 116, 118, 120-121, 124
    white-collar 115-116
entertainment 52-63
environmental concerns 49-50
emergencies 78
ethnicity 13, 25-28, 32, 43, 162, 163-164

F ilm industry 52, 223, 227, 229, 230
fire ants 207

fishing 68
fleas 211, 213
food shopping 80-86
Fort DeRussy 142
funeral services 74
furniture 102, 269, 271

G ambling 206
gangs 204-205
Garden Island, The 198, 230, 284
gardening 94, 231
gasoline, cost of 99-100, 145
Gates, Bill 248
gay community 29-30, 189, 283
geckos 210
golf 66, 68, 189
government, Hawai'i 45-47, 124
Great Mahele 42
Green Party 50
grocery stores 80-85
    employment 109
Guam 130
Gulf War 46
guns 70

H a'ena 231
Ha'iku 197, 240
Haleakalā 17, 71 (photo), 119, 234, 239
Haleakalā Times, The 241, 284
Hale'iwa 225
Halona Bay 223
Hana 68, 104, 136, 240
Hanalei 56, 70 (photo), 134, 231
Hanalei Bay 52, 199, 230
Hanalei Valley 231, photo
Hanapepe 56, 228, 230
Hanauma Bay 223
Hansen's Disease 242, 244
hate crimes 28-30 see also racism
Hawai'i (Big Island) 218, 250 (map), 251-259, 283

Hawai'i (Big Island) continued
   arts & culture 53-55
   dining 229
   earthquakes 252
   economy 251-252, 255
   employment 251, 254-255, 256, 283
   Hawai'i Volcanoes National Park 251, 252, 254, 256, 257-259, 283
   housing 152-153, 255, 257-259
   hospitals 77, 256, 260
   map 250
   neighborhoods 251-259
   newspapers 256
   population 251, 253, 255
   shopping 253, 254
   tourism 256, 287
   transportation 95
   unemployment 251
   vog 251, 252
Hawai'i International Film Festival 60
Hawai'i Pacific University 178
Hawai'i Tribune Herald 256
Hawai'i Volcanoes National Park 251, 256, 258
Hawaiian Acres (Kalapana) 257
Hawaiian Credit Counseling Service 88, 98
Hawaiian Homelands 47, 98
Hawaiian music 43, 54
Hawaiian renaissance 54
health benefits 21, 124, 132-133
health care 75-78, 274
   employment 125-126
   senior citizens 151
health insurance 75, 117
Hickam Air Force Base 141, 143
high technology 63-64, 125, 138, 233-234, 282
higher education see college
hiking 68,69
Hilo 195, 196 (photo), 250, 252, 254
Hilo Bay 88
HMSA 75
Hoe, Allen K. 38, 48,49

holidays 55
home schooling 172
homeless shelters 21-22
homicides 188
homosexual relationships 29-30, 189, 283
Honolua Marine Preserve 239
Honolulu 33 (photo), 36 (photos), 105 (photo), 108 (photos), 149
   arts & culture 53, 56, 60, 62
   life in 17, 149, 219, 221
   newspapers 54, 135,186, 282
   population 219
   transportation 22, 95
Honolulu Advertiser 282
Honolulu Library 57
Honolulu magazine 112, 200
Honolulu Star-Bulletin 135, 282
Honolulu Weekly 54, 186, 282
Honolulu Zoo 186
Ho'okipa Beach 70 (photo)
ho'oponopono 76
hospitals 77, 78, 112
   employment125
   Hawai'i 256
   Kaua'i 78, 229
   Lāna'i 248-249, 284
   O'ahu 75, 77-78, 125, 142
housing 22, 85-92, 116
   Hawai'i 152-153
   Kaua'i 152-153, 230-231
   Lāna'i 248-249
   Maui 234
   military 143, 146
   Moloka'i 152-153, 244-245
   O'ahu 85-86, 221-225
   senior citizens' 150-151, 152-158
hula 53-54
hunting 68-69
hurricanes 90, 195-197, 227-228

'Iao Valley 239
immigrants 25-26, 43
industries, Hawai'i 42-43
  agriculture (sugar, pineapple) 23, 25, 42, 45, 49, 183, 241, 243, 244, 247, 255
  construction 49, 90-91, 118, 133
  military 141, 285
  real estate 23
  tourism 23, 45, 111, 119
  whaling 41, 208, 212
'Iniki, hurricane 90, 93, 227-228,
Inouye, Senator Dan 48, 50
insects 207-213
insurance
  automobile 97-99, 145
  health 75, 117
  home 93, 197
Internet resources 138, 175, 206, 241, 256, 282-286
'Iolani Palace 43, 57

Jobs see employment

Ka'a'awa 225
Ka'ahumanu, Queen 40
Ka'anapali 239
Ka'ena Point Nature Preserve 186
Kāhala 20, 223
Kahalui 234, 239-241
Kahalu'u 225
Kaho'olawe 112, 260, 261 (photo)
Kahuku High School 174, 175
Kailua (O'ahu) 149, 186, 219, 224, 225
Kailua Bay (Hawai'i) 253
Kailua Beach (O'ahu) 186, 224
Kailua-Kona (Hawai'i) 253, 255
Kalāheo 230
Kalākaua Avenue 223
Kalākaua, King David 43, 57
Kalalau Valley 239 (photo)

Kalapana 255, 257-259
Kalaupapa 242, 244
Kaluako'i 244
Kamakou Preserve 17, 240 (photo)
Kamali'i Elementary (Maui) 168-169
Kama'ole 239
Kamehameha I, King 40
Kamehameha II, King 40
Kamehameha III, King 42
Kamehameha IV, King 261
Kamehameha Day 55
Kamehameha Heights 223
Kamehameha Highway (O'ahu) 225
Kamehameha Highway (Moloka'i) 244
Kamehameha Schools 42, 168
Kanemitzu Bakery 127
Kāne'ohe 217, 224
Kāne'ohe Bay 224
Kapa'a 230
Kapalua 239
Kapalua Bay Hotel 56
Kapena Falls 186
Kapi'olani Park 54, 123
Kapolei 224
kapu 39, 40, 210, 260-261
Kaua'i 18, 52, 218, 227-231, 284
  arts & culture 56
  dining 61, 228
  economy 227, 229
  education 230. 284
  employment 134, 227, 229, 230, 284
  hospitals 229, 260
  housing 90-91, 157, 230-231
  Hurricane 'Iniki 90, 93, 196-197, 227, 228
  map 226
  neighborhoods 229-231
  newspapers 230, 284
  ocean dangers 198-199
  population 227
  schools 229
  tourism 87
  transportation 95

INDEX

unemployment 227
Kaua'i Times, The 230, 284
Kaumalapau Harbor 240 (photo)
Kaunakakai 127, 136, 244
Keahou Estate 20
Keahou Hotel 55
Keawekapu Beach 237 (photo)
Kekaha 230
Keopuolani 40
Kīhei 233, 239
Kīlauea (Kaua'i) 78, 94, 134, 230
Kīlauea Volcano 256
Kohala 253
Koke'e State Park 58, 231
Kona 71 (photo), 252-253, 256
Ko'olau Mountains 33 (photo), 224-225
Kualapu'u 244
Kūhiō Highway (Kaua'i) 230
Kula 240
Kurtistown 18, 257

Labor unions 25, 45, 111, 119, 124, 125, 248
LaCroix, Sumner J. 179-180
Lahaina 55, 58, 74, 235
Lahaina News, The 241
La'ie 186, 225
Lāna'i 35, 136, 218, 240 (photo), 246 (map), 246-249
  airport 248
  arts & culture 56, 249
  beaches 248-249
  economy 247-249
  education 284
  employment 135, 247-249, 284
  hospitals 248, 249, 284
  housing 249, 284
  map 246
  neighborhoods 247-249
  population 247-248
  schools 249
  tourism 247
  transportation 95

unemployment 247
Lāna'i Company, The 248, 249, 284
land ownership 42, 44
  ahupua'a 41
  Great Mahele 42
  Kalapana 257-259
Land and Power in Hawai'i 206, 257-259
landscaping 94
language, Hawaiian 13, 41
Lanikai 186
Lassen, Christian Riese 123
Lei Day 55
leprosy see Hansen's Disease
lice 212
life expectancy 76
Liholiho 40
Līhu'e 56-57, 239
Lili'uokalani, Queen 40, 43 (photo), 46, 57
Lodge at Kō'ele, The 56, 248
Lyman House 58

Makaha 225
Makahiki 54, 55
Makapu'u 186
Makiki 186, 223
Makiki Heights 56
Makawao 17, 56, 104, 236
Makawele 261
Makena 20, 236
Manele Bay Hotel 248
Manoa Valley 223
marijuana (pakalolo) 174, 201, 254
marriage 182-184, 191
Matson Navigation Co. 267, 268, 270
Maui 17-20, 35 (map), 50, 69-71 (photos) 106 (photo), 105 (photo), 107 (photo), 108 (photo), 218, 239-244
  arts & culture 53-54, 55-62, 109, 123, 237 (photo), 239
  bankruptcy 234
  beaches 239, 241
  dining 61, 239

economy 233-234
employment 233-234, 240
housing 154-155, 239-241
map 232
neighborhoods 20, 64, 239-241
newspapers 241
population 233
tourism 233-235, 287
transportation 95-97
unemployment 233
Maui News, The 132, 173, 241
Mauna Kea 238 (photo), 253, 256
Mauna Loa (Hawai'i) 253
Maunaloa (Moloka'i) 56, 127, 245
Maunaloa Elementary (Moloka'i)
169 (photo), 244
McKinley, President William 44
Meals on Wheels 151
Medicaid 149
medical benefits 21, 132
medical care 274
middle class, Hawai'i 22
Mililani Town 224
military 112, 139-146
   Hawai'i 253
   Hickam AFB 141, 143
   Kaho'olawe 112, 260
   Kaua'i 230
   Ni'ihau 260-261
   O'ahu 51, 53
missionaries 41-43, 58, 63-64, 208, 285
Moloka'i 17, 50, 56, 127, 218, 242-245, 260,
284
   airport 244
   arts & culture 127, 244
   beaches 244-245
   economy 243
   employment 243-245, 284
   housing 243
   Kalaupapa (Hansen's disease colony) 242,
   244
   map 242

Moloka'i Ranch 56, 243-244
   neighborhoods 244-245
   newspapers 245, 284
   population 127, 244-245
   schools 127, 169 (photo), 244
   shopping 245
   tourism 287
   transportation 95
   unemployment 243
Moloka'i Advertiser-News 245, 284
Moloka'i Dispatch, The 245, 284
Molokini 119, 261
Momilani Elementary 171
mongoose 212
mosquitoes 208, 213
Mountain View 257
movie theaters 60
moving 265-280
   resources 274
murder 188, 202-203, 205
Murdock, David 247
museums 56
music 56, 62, 230
   Hawaiian 43, 54, 57

Na Pali (Kaua'i) 231
Napili 20, 239
Narcotics Anonymous 78
National Archives 57
natural resources 49
Nature Conservancy 186
Nawiliwili Harbor 229
newspapers 230, 256, 282-284
night marchers 254
Ni'ihau 58, 260-261
North Shore (Kaua'i) 134
North Shore (O'ahu) 119, 224
Nu'uanu 223

O'ahu photos: 33, 36, 69, 105, 106, 108, 274
   arts & culture 53-54, 56-60, 62

dining 61, 221
economy 219, 221
employment 119, 219, 221, 283
hospitals 75, 77, 78, 125, 142
housing 155-156, 221-225
maps 34, 220
neighborhoods 221-225
newspapers 54, 135, 186, 282
population 219, 222 (chart)
shopping 101-102, 221
tourism 221
transportation 95
unemployment 219
ocean dangers 198-199
'Ohe'o Gulch 70 (photo)
organ donors 77-78
Organic Act 44

*P*acific Business News 136, 285
Pacific Missile Range Facility 112, 230, 26,
Pacific Heights 186, 223, 230
Pāhoa 62 (photo)
Pa'ia 240
paniolo 240
Pāpōhaku beach 244-245
Pāpōhaku Ranchlands 244
parenting, resources 165
Hawai'i State PTA 175
Parker Ranch 58, 253
Pearl City 223
Pearl Harbor 141
Pele 254
periodicals 282-283
pets 211, 213, 275
"picture brides" 183
Pipeline (O'ahu) 225
people 16-32
pidgin 24
plants 273
Pohakuloa Military Training Area 253
police
    crime resources 206, 282

employment 124
politics 37-50, 283, 285
Polynesian Cultural Center 64
population, statistics 27, 43, 187
    Hawai'i 251, 253, 255
    Kaua'i 227
    Lāna'i 247-248
    Maui 233
    Moloka'i 127, 244-245
    O'ahu 219, 222
Portlock 20
post office 270, 274
poverty 19, 21-22
Practical Guide to Divorce in Hawai'i, A
192
precipitation 217, 229, 254, 256
pregnancy
    Lāna'i 248
    teen 77
prejudice 25-30, 286
Price of Paradise, The 179-180, 285
Prince Kuhio Day 55
Princeville 52, 78, 94, 134, 230
priorities 22, 117-118
prostitution 203, 206
public housing 22
Pukalani 240
Puna 41, 254-255
Punahou School 42, 166
Pu'unēnē 58, 241

Quarantine 273, 271-272
Queen's Bath 85
Queen Emma Summer Palace 57

Rabies 207, 275-276
racism 25-30, 286
radio 59-60
rainfall *see precipitation*
rats 212
real estate 23, 85-92, 110, 126

religion 11, 41, 57, 63-74, 285
rental housing 225, 86-87, 267-268, 270, 282
Rentals Illustrated 86, 282
Republican party 44, 45, 47, 50
residency 58
resorts
    general employment 121, 128
    Hawai'i 20 (photo)
    Kaua'i 134
    Maui 18, 104
    O'ahu 119, 121, 142
retail 120, 128, 282
retirement 147-159
Robinson family 260-261
"rock fever" 115
romance 21, 181-192
Royal Gardens (Kalapana) 257-259

Saddle Road 253
Sacred Falls 71 (photo)
sales, employment 129
sales, retail 120 (chart), 128, 150
Salt Lake 223
schools 42, 45, 111, 164-180
    A-Plus program 175
    colleges 178-180, 284
    employment, turnover 128, 165, 169-170
    employment, wages 128
    Hawai'i 167-168
    Hawai'i State Teacher's Association 128-129, 175
    home schooling 172
    Kamehameha Schools 42, 168
    Moloka'i 200, 244
    O'ahu 168, 224
    private 165-167
    Punahou School 42, 166
    resources 175
scuba diving 70, 129
Sea Land Service Inc. 271, 274
senior citizens, resources 153-154

sex offenders 203
shipping 269-274
    automobiles 96-97
    furniture 102
    pets 275
shopping 11, 80, 84, 101-102
    Hawai'i 55, 253
    Kaua'i 56
    Maui 55-56, 239
    Moloka'i 56, 245
    O'ahu 56, 101-102, 221, 223-224
Sinclair, Elizabeth 261
Sleeping Giant 18
Slom, Sam 132
smoking 76
snakes 207, 211
social security 149, 191
sovereignty 38, 47-49
spiders 210-211
sports 22, 50, 66-70, 100, 129, 225, 237 (photo), 238 (photos), 240 (photo)
Spreckelsville 240
statehood 45
Stevenson, Robert Louis 40 (photo)
sugar cane fields 78
sumo wrestling 67
Sunset Beach 225
supermarkets 80-85
    employment 125
surfing 22, 66, 225

Tantalus 186
"Target Island" 260
taxes 45-47, 81-82, 84, 109-111, 119, 133, 284
teaching 127, 128-129, 170, 175
temperature 217-218
termites 93 (photo), 207
theaters 56, 59, 60 (movie), 62
TheBus 57, 149-150, 151
Theo H. Davies 43
tidal waves *see tsunamis*

ticks 211, 213
tourism 23, 110-111, 119, 128, 129, 132, 150, 214
   Hawai'i 284
   Kaua'i 287
   Lāna'i 247, 248
   Maui 233, 234
   Moloka'i 244, 245
   O'ahu 221
traffic 33, 99, 100, 102, 214
   laws 204
transportation 145, 158-159
   neighbor islands 95-100
   O'ahu 95-100, 167-168
tsunamis 194-197 (194, 196 photos)

UFOs 253
ukupau 117
unemployment 286
   Hawai'i 251
   Kaua'i 227
   Lāna'i 247
   Maui 233
   Moloka'i 243
   O'ahu 219
unions see labor unions
Upcountry (Maui) 235, 236
universities 59, 66, 142, 178-180, 223
University of Hawai'i at Mānoa (O'ahu) 59, 66, 142, 178-180, 223
unwritten rules 23, 24
utilities 144

Vanpool Hawai'i 100
violent crime 200
vog 254, 257
Volcanoes National Park 256

Wages 116, 118-120, 124, 128, 129, 170, 248, 249
Waiahole 225

Wai'ale'ale, Mt. 229
Wailua 70 (photo), 230
Wailua River 230
Wai'anae 225
Wai'anae Army Recreation Center 142
Wai'anae Mountains 225
Wai'anpanapa State Park 68
Waikele Center 102, 224
Waikīkī 95, 123, 142, 150, 203, 221, 223
Waikoloa Village 253
Wailea (Big Island) 20
Wailea (Maui) 235, 236
Wailuku 235, 237 (photo), 241
Waimea (Big Island) 58, 59, 252, 253, 256
Waimea Bay (Kaua'i) 39
Waimea Canyon (Kaua'i) 230
Waimea Falls Park (O'ahu) 186
Waimea Fire Station (Hawai'i) 55
Waipahu 223
Waipi'o Valley 238 (photo)
Washington Place 57
water quality 77
wealth 19-21, 189
welfare (state aid) 21-22, 243
West Hawai'i Today 256
whaling 41
work see employment
worker's compensation 116, 133, 135
working class 22
World War II 45

Young Brothers Shipping 96-97, 102, 274
Your Military in Hawai'i 141, 146

There are actually two original "languages" spoken in Hawai'i. The first is Hawaiian. Brought by early Polynesians who settled the islands, it was much changed by outside influences. The second language is pidgin, a blend of words and colorful phrases that originated in plantation days as a way for the mix of nationalities to communicate with each other. Pidgin, which can be as difficult to understand as a foreign language, is still so commonly spoken today it is the bane of the public school system. Here are some common words:

aikane (aye-KAH-NEH) - friend

akamai (AH-kah-my) - wise or smart

ali'i (Ah-LEE-ee) - chief, nobility

hana hou (hah-nah-HO-oo) - do it again, encore!

hale (HA-lee) - house

hanai (ha-NY-ee) - adopted

haole (ha-O-le) - see page 13

hapa (HAH-pa) - half or part as in hapa-haole, half or part Caucasian

heiau (HEH-ee-ah) - ancient Hawaiian burial ground or place of worship

holoholo (ho-lo-HO-lo) - to travel around visiting, as in "go holoholo"

hui (HOO-ee) - club or association, especially to do business

hula (HOO-lah) - Hawaiian dance

imu (ee-MOO) - pit for roasting

kahuna (kah-HOO-nah) - priest or teacher

kai (KY-EE) - sea or toward the sea

kama'āina (ka-MAH-eye-nah) - see page 13

kanaka (ka-NAH-kah) - a native Hawaiian

kane (KAH-neh) - boy or man

kapu (KAH-POO) - keep out, forbidden, taboo

kaukau (KAH-oo-kah-oo) - food

keiki (KAY-kee) - child

kiawe (Kee-AH-vay) - mesquite tree, prolific "weed" tree

lanai (lah-NY-ee) - porch or balcony

lei (LAY-ee) - necklace of flowers, feathers or shells

lu'au (LOO-ah) - traditional feast

mahalo - (ma HA lo) thank you

mahu - (MA-hoo) homosexual or gay

makai - (MA-kay-ee) toward the sea

make (MA-kay) - dead

malihini (mah-lay-HEE-nay) , see page 13

mauka (MAH-oo-ka) - toward the mountain

mauna (MAH-oo-nah) - mountain

Mele Kalikimaka (me-leh kah-lee-kee-MAH-ka) - Merry Christmas

menehune (meh-nee-HOO-neh) - legendary dwarfs, nocturnal workers

niu (NOO-ee) - big

'ohana (oh-HAH-nah) - family or adopted family

'okole (oh-oh-KO-lay) - rear, buttocks

'ono (OH-no) - delicious

pali (PAH-lee) - ocean cliff

paniolo (pah-nee-OH-lo) - cowboy

pau (PA-aw) - finished, done as in *pau hana*, done working

poi (POY) - soft food from pounded taro root

puka (POO-kah) - hole, opening, cubicle

pupu (POO-poo) - hors d'oeuvres or appetizers

shishi (shee-shee) - to urinate, childs phrase

tutu (TOO-too) - grandmother, term of endearment for old person

wahine (wa-HEE-neh) - girl or woman

wikiwiki (wee-kee-WEE-kee) - quick, fast

Mahalo

Thank you...

Friends and strangers who, over the seven years of gathering material for this book, answered endless questions, sharing lifestyle details and financial information;

Government, business and university researchers, most of whom went an extra step to provide information. Very few said, "I don't know." Most said, "I'll find out;"

Especially to G. Nishida at the University of Hawai'i, and Grant K. Uchida at the state Department of Agriculture; Allen Hoe, attorney and activist; Sam Slom, state senator and small business reformer, and Marcia Sakai, attorney at the Hawai'i state tax department.

Author Gavan Daws for permission to quote abundantly from *Land and Power in Hawai'i*;

The editors: Christine Flanagan in New Jersey and Honolulu, who knows so much about Hawai'i; Bob DiNicola in Indianapolis, encouraging when I needed it most; and Francine Godzwa in Erie, Pa., a tough taskmistress;

Talented writers Meg Skellenger, Mary Chase, Barbara Santos, for sharing;

Graphic designer Ann Greenwood for her endless patience; Edith Bagley for proofreading;

Literary agent Roger Jellinek for steering me in the right directions;

Photographers Matt Thayer of the *Maui News*, a fine photo journalist, and, Brad Lewis on the Big Island who so abundantly shared his excellent work;

To food shoppers around the nation: Bonnie Fijal in Cleveland, Peggy Lawyer in Malibu, Lisa Hill in Lake Tahoe, Gretchen Balsley in Tallahassee, Jane Sutton on the Big Island and Bob Fijal in Phoenix;

Family, friends and clients who tolerated my reclusiveness and offered their resources.